RAF
FIGHTER
COMMAND
1936-1968

Patrick Stephens Limited, a member of the Haynes Publishing Group, has published authoritative, quality books for enthusiasts for a quarter of a century. During that time the company has established a reputation as one of the world's leading publishers of books on aviation, maritime, military, model-making, motor cycling, motoring, motor racing, railway and railway modelling subjects. Readers or authors with suggestions for books they would like to see published are invited to write to: The Editorial Director, Patrick Stephens Limited, Sparkford, Nr Yeovil, Somerset, BA22 7JJ.

RAF FIGHTER COMMAND
1936-1968

NORMAN FRANKS

Patrick Stephens Limited

First published in 1992

British Library Cataloguing in Publication Data
A catalogue record for this book is available from the British Library

ISBN 1 85260 344 5

Patrick Stephens Limited is part of the Haynes Publishing Group P.L.C., Sparkford, Nr Yeovil, Somerset BA22 7JJ.

Typeset and printed by J.H. Haynes & Co. Ltd.

Contents

Acknowledgements

THE DIFFICULTY OF writing a history of RAF Fighter Command is that it can so easily be bogged down by facts, figures and non-essential trivia that readers begin to lose their way. From the outset it was not my intention to record an in-depth study, but rather to present an interesting view of the Command looking at it with, I hope, a different eye. This book is therefore aimed at those who would like to know less of the bureaucracy and political intrigue, and more of the 'what was it like' aspect.

To achieve this, I have tried to provide a balanced view covering a number of specific areas. Luckily over the years a number of former fighter pilots have been pleased to help me in various projects all more or less concerned with fighter operations, and many of these were delighted to help yet again. Others I met or corresponded with for the first time, but each were chosen for a specific reason and I am glad to say that all were only too willing to help.

The result of all this is, I hope, a readable account of how the fighter pilots of Fighter Command fought their war during World War Two, how Hugh Dowding helped to build the Command in the late 1930s, and to record, briefly, what happened in the years following the end of the war. Some will think this latter part all too brief but, by its very nature, Fighter Command achieved its greatness in wartime.

For their help and kindness, I wish to thank the following gentlemen who delved into their memories to answer the questions I put to them. In the final analysis, however, the conclusions and emphases are mine.

Air Vice Marshal J. E. Johnson CBE, DSO**, DFC*, DFC(US), Legion of Merit, AM, Order of Leopold, CdeG
Air Commodore J. A. Leathart CB, DSO
Air Commodore G. A. Mason DFC, DFC(US), FBIM
Group Captain F. W. M. Jensen CBE, DFC*, AFC, AE, FBIM
Group Captain G. C. Unwin DSO, DFM*
Group Captain J. A. Wray CBE, DFC
Group Captain A. R. Wright DFC, AFC
The late Wing Commander R. M. B. Duke-Woolley DSO, DFC*, DFC(US)
Wing Commander R. W. F. Sampson OBE, DFC*, TEM, DL, CdeG
Wing Commander J. G. Sanders DFC
Squadron Leader A. C. Bartley DFC*
Squadron Leader C. Haw DFC, DFM, Order of Lenin
Squadron Leader M. A. Liskutin DFC, AFC
Squadron Leader H. N. Sweetman DFC
Squadron Leader J. A. Stephen
Squadron Leader J. G. West DFM
Flight Lieutenant M. S. Allen DFC**, AMCT, FIPM
Flight Lieutenant W. T. Clark DFM
Flight Lieutenant F. W. T. Davis
Flight Lieutenant W. A. Goold DFC
Flight Lieutenant F. B. Lawless DFC
Flying Officer F. Mares DFM
Warrant Officer J. A. R. Pope

In addition I wish to thank my friends Chaz Bowyer, Martyn Ford-Jones, Flight Lieutenant Andy Thomas RAF, the Keeper and staff of the Public Record Office, Kew. And my wife Heather – she knows why!

CHAPTER 1

Origins

RAF FIGHTER COMMAND was officially born on 14 July 1936, but its ancestry stretched back to the Great War of 1914-18. When the guns fell into an eerie silence shortly after 11 am on Sunday, 11 November 1918, the Royal Air Force had the most powerful air force in the world.

From the early faltering steps to the skies in the first dozen years of the twentieth century, which saw man's first heavier than air flights and the momentous event in 1909 as a Frenchman named Blériot crossed the English Channel, events had snow-balled. The aeroplane had stamped its dominance on military thinking, a complete air corps and then an air force had been formed and built, and by the end of that terrible war the aeroplane was part of the new century's future.

That November of 1918, the Royal Air Force could count some 3,500 aeroplanes of all types and of many varied shapes and sizes. It had over 290,000 men and women within its ranks, the majority serving in 188 first-line squadrons plus virtually the same number of reserve and training units. Along the Western Front in battle-torn France, 100 front-line squadrons had battled to the bitter finish, having steadily grown in number since the embryonic Royal Flying Corps had sent just a handful of men and machines to France in August 1914.

That Royal Flying Corps (Naval and Military Wings) had been formed, being almost reluctantly accepted by the army generals, in 1912. During the succeeding years, the RFC had grown, gone to war and developed tremendously owing to the expedience of the war. The Royal Naval Air Service too had expanded, flying not only at sea but in support of the RFC in France. Both services had seen overseas duty too, in Italy, Greece, the Middle East and even India. They were joined together to become the Royal Air Force on the first day of April 1918, to become the most powerful air weapon in the world.

In the early days of the First World War, the aeroplane was used almost exclusively for reconnaissance work, observing what the other side was up to, once the mammoth trench systems appeared across the French landscape in the winter of 1914-15. With the coming of trench warfare, with its barbed wire entanglements and machine-guns, the hitherto traditional 'eyes' of the army, the cavalry patrols, became ineffective. Suddenly the generals, needing to know what the enemy on the other side of the trenches was doing, became totally reliant on what the men in their flying services could see, or photograph.

This in turn began to change the nature of war flying. Cavalry actions to attack a supply column or a rear area arms dump were also at an end, so these, and other targets, had to be attacked from the air with aeroplanes carrying bombs. But, whether carrying bombs or cameras, both sides quickly realised that they needed to stop, hinder or curtail these intrusions. With those objects in mind, and with aeroplanes now a little stronger, so they could carry the extra weight of a machine-gun and ammunition, the fighting pilots began to emerge.

Many air-minded youngsters of the 1920s and '30s, grew up on the stories of the great air fighters of the First World War – the first air war. Mannock, McCudden, Ball, Fonck, Guynemer, Rickenbacker, Luke, Baron von Richthofen, Boelcke, Immelmann and Voss – all were names to conjure with. These had been the successful air fighters who had daily pitched their wits and skill in the dog-fights above the trenches, in the clean blue sky, high above the mud of Flanders or Verdun. They became the popular heroes of the pulp-aviation and fiction writers too, who equally made up stories of would-be heroes like Biggles or Arnold Adair.

By the end of the Great War, there were almost 60 fighter squadrons in France – or to use the correct terminology, scout squadrons. Daily these scouts had patrolled, battled and shot down the enemy bombers and reconnaissance machines of their opposite numbers, or fought in scout versus scout actions. But the Great War had also seen, for the first time in any war, the belligerent countries attacking each other's towns far behind the battle lines. The advent of the aeroplane made that possible. Germany could bomb England or France, the British and French could bomb Germany, the Austrians could bomb Italy, the Italians could bomb Austria. This called for another form of fighting machine, a scout that would be merely for home defence.

The Germans had used the aeroplane against England and France since the early days of the war, albeit in limited fashion at first. Later, with the use of huge airships, designed by Count von Zeppelin or the Schutte-Lanz Company, they had brought terror and death to the civilians of both countries. The Allies did not develop an attacking airship, but both sides did build larger aeroplanes with which to bomb each other's towns and cities. For the British it was the Handley-Page 0/100 and 0/400s, for Germany it was the Gothas, Friedrichshafens or the Staaken Giants.

To combat these, the RFC/RAF eventually had 16 Home Defence squadrons by the war's end, while training units might also send up pilots to help. From time to time too, front-line scout squadrons had to be brought back from France. It was this latter phase of the new air war, the attacks on British towns and civilians, men, women and children, that caught the imagination of the mass of population and the men of government. A war being waged across the Channel, even with the loss of a loved one, a father, a son, a husband, a friend, a man who had lived down the street, was still a war at a distance. Bombing from the air brought total war to one's doorstep. It threatened one's children, the old and infirm, the recuperating wounded. Britain had not had its homeland civilians touched directly by war since the Norman Invasion 850 years earlier. Rape and pillage happened to countries who bordered others. Since 1066 the Channel and North Sea had been a protective barrier, British seamen the defenders. Blériot and now the Great War had changed all that. It would be these lessons that would dominate much of the political thinking in Britain in the peaceful years following November 1918. Great Britain had to be defended from the air as well as the sea.

From Great Oaks to Acorns

No sooner had the armies of the Great War gone home than each of the victorious countries depleted its armed forces, almost as if by scrapping the war machines, war as a disease would go away. For the vanquished, their armies could only return home and wonder why.

For a while the RAF kept a small force with the Army of Occupation in Germany, but nevertheless, within 15 months of the signing of the Armistice, nearly 90% of the RAF's strength had been cut away, its personnel demobilised, most of its aeroplanes scrapped, many of its airfields closed down and returned to the farmers. Just one year after the war's end, only one squadron remained in Germany, No.12, based at Bickendorf, where it was eventually disbanded in 1922.

By early 1920, the RAF comprised just 25 squadrons, with a further eight in the process of reformation. However, most of these were not in Britain but overseas, some serving in various trouble spots in the Empire. India, the North-West Frontier, Egypt, and so on. From the massive wartime numbers, the peacetime air force was planned around just 3,280 officers and 25,000 other ranks. During the war something to the tune of £1m per day had been spent on the flying services, now the Government budgeted at £15m – per year – for the next five years.

Behind this figure was the Government's estimation that Britain would not be involved in any major conflict for at least the next ten years, which was sound thinking. The German and Austro-Hungarian Empires had been defeated and bowed, Russia seemed poor and uncoordinated, and perhaps a little behind the times if not downright feudal despite the rising Bolshevik regimes. Of the other great powers, Britain was hardly likely to go to war with her erstwhile allies, America, Italy, Japan or any of her Empire countries. All the air force really had to do was keep a few hostile natives and rebels under some sort of control, assisting the army in these tasks. And they were all far from British shores.

This thinking became known as the 'Ten Year Rule', but sadly, this was stretched by succeeding governments until 1932. Meanwhile, the RAF in England became a truly peacetime air force, known by many as the Greatest Flying Club in the World. And why not? The stories of the air fighters in the recent war bathed the peacetime pilots and aircrew (the latter mostly air gunners of NCO rank) in the aura of latter-day knights. They flew silver-doped biplanes, each squadron having its coloured markings emblazoned on their wings and fuselages. They flew in beautiful formations, swooping and diving in air shows, such as the prestigious annual Hendon Air Display. Later still there were the High Speed Flights to read about, Schneider Trophy Races, and so on. While there might have been nothing for the RAF to defend against, they could carry that demeanour of being Britain's defenders of the air, just in case some tin-pot little country might turn aggressor.

The problem, of course, was that this all helped Britain into thinking that all was well in the world and in any event, there were more urgent economical problems other than building up an air force which was hardly used, or in developing new engines or aeroplane designs which would equally be unused. Unused maybe, but development was essential for the future in all things. That Britain was fast becoming air-minded was a fact, but it was all the peaceful pursuits of speed records, long distance flights, solo journeys by both men and women flyers. Lindbergh, Wiley Post, Cobham, Mollison, Amy Johnson, Amelia Earhart – these were the current heroes of aviation.

Fortunately there were some men of vision and drive who saw things very differently and actively pursued developments in aviation. Mostly civil aviation, of course, but with faster and more reliable aeroplanes, better and more powerful engines, came the thought that in the event of any future conflict, these could be turned to a military use.

However, there were still people who thought it important to build and keep a strong aerial defence force. One of the foremost was Sir Hugh Trenchard, the Chief of the Air Staff. It had been he who had created the RAF's Independent Air Force in WW1, formed and built to bomb Germany's factories and storage depots. In 1922 the Government allowed him the concession to provide a metropolitan air force of just 14 bomber and 9 fighter squadrons, purely for home defence. The reason for more bomber than fighter units might seem odd, but it reflected the view that the best form of defence might still be offence! However, despite the peacetime euphoria, the next year alarm was felt when it was realised that Britain's disparity with our recent major ally, France (with whom and for whom Britain had fought so long and hard) in size of comparable air strengths needed redressing. Was France, therefore, thought to be a possible aggressor? She had been Britain's traditional enemy for centuries but could people really think that France's air might was a menace?

Whatever the reasons, the British Cabinet decided to expand the metropolitan air force to a total of 52 squadrons (35 bomber and 17 fighter), with a first-line establishment of 394 bomber aircraft and 204 fighters. The Secretary of State for Air quickly advised the Prime Minister, Stanley Baldwin, that with the monetary and practical problems they faced, these numbers would take at least five years to produce, but Baldwin merely said that the new establishment was to be achieved with as little delay as possible!

At first the planned expansion made good headway, and within two years, 25 of the planned 52 squadrons were in existence. However, to 'help' in the planning and cost of the new force, 13 of the new squadrons were to be what was classed as 'non-regular' units. Six were to be Auxiliary Air Force squadrons, raised and maintained by local County Associations, with a further seven classed as Special Reserve units. The AAF was created in 1925, its members initially coming from Territorial Associations. The men, both pilots and ground personnel, were locals, who, because they usually had week-day jobs and occupations, were dubbed by the media and their Service contemporaries as the weekend airmen. Four squadrons were formed at first, a total of 13 were in being by 1930.

Air Defence of Great Britain

With the increase of squadrons and aircraft, other matters became important. With the speed of the modern aeroplanes, part of the defence plan would be to know where the enemy was. Radar was still in the future, but the visual sighting of approaching bombers by men on the ground, with sound locators, especially on the coasts, led to the creation of the Observer Corps. There was also a new command title, Air Defence of Great Britain (ADGB), which would eventually be responsible for all control and direction of the bomber and fighter forces, as well as anti-aircraft guns, searchlights, observers, etc. The ADGB started life in 1925, its first Commander-in-Chief being Air Marshal Sir John Salmond CMG CVO DSO, following a command in Iraq. Sir John was in his mid-40s and had learnt to fly before the war. By 1918 he was a major-general of the RAF, and GOC of the RAF in the Field. However, soon after his arrival at his temporary HQ at the Air Ministry in London, a committee chaired by Lord Birkenhead recommended that as it appeared that relations between Britain and France were secure on a political front, the scheme for 52 squadrons might now be revised or even suspended! With the coming of the new Conservative Government, and with economic problems still besetting the country, the Cabinet thankfully decided that the scheme could be slowed down again; the target date was set tentatively for 1936.

Resulting from this, only six further squadrons were added to the home defence plan over the next three years, bringing the total to 31. Between 1928 and 1932 only ten squadrons came into being, which was still short by ten of the expected 52. Forced to accept this delay, Sir John spent a good deal of his time building up his command to the best effect, moving his HQ to RAF Uxbridge, and reorganising the command into two zones. One was called the Wessex Bombing Area, for regular bomber squadrons, the other a Fighting Area, for regular fighter units. Meanwhile, the AAF and SR squadrons that were in being were known as No.1 Air Defence Group.

As 1930 began, Sir Hugh Trenchard (to many the Father of the RAF) retired as CAS, his place taken not unnaturally by John Salmond, who, despite the economies forced on him, had set up ADGB faithfully. The world at large were still idealistically pursuing peace and disarmament which made any increase in money to the military an unpopular move for any government. Any government, that is, except for Germany. As the 1930s progressed and Adolf Hitler came to power, all the conferences for world peace seemed suddenly to be in danger of achieving nothing. By 1934 the signs seemed clear to those who could see and read them, although there was a strong body of opinion that had faith in German good intentions.

However, in late 1933 a committee under Sir Maurice Hankey concluded that Nazi Germany would be the next potential enemy of both Britain and Europe, if not the whole of the free world. This thinking was supported by the British General Staff, who had already estimated that Germany might well be in a position to wage a war by 1938. Despite official restrictions on Germany following the Great War, by the end of 1934, training mostly in secret, the Luftwaffe could count 22 squadrons of both bombers and fighters, with nearly 600 aircraft, both figures being actively increased. This and the efforts of men such as Winston Churchill finally roused the Government to recognise the dangers. Thus in July 1934,

a motion was passed in the House of Commons to increase the RAF by 41 squadrons. Subsequently, the Government began to question the size of the Luftwaffe, quoted by RAF Intelligence, believing instead figures supplied to them by Adolf Hitler himself!

Nevertheless, expansion did begin, although slowly at first. Money became available, airfields began to be built or extended, equipment was purchased and new aeroplane designs encouraged and called for. Because of the increases in men and aircraft, it was deemed necessary to reorganise the operational command, the Bombing and Fighting Areas being found too limited. Almost overnight, in a sweeping and far-reaching decision, the ADGB and its Wessex and Fighting Areas were cancelled, replaced by five separate Commands. Bomber and Coastal, for attack and sea defence/reconnaissance, Training Command to support and provide men for the front line units, with Maintenance Command to back up the whole service. And for the defence of Great Britain: Fighter Command.

CHAPTER 2

Birth

THE EXPANSION PLAN of 1935 called for the provision of 70 bomber and 35 fighter squadrons for the British mainland force. It was hoped that this number could be achieved by 1942 – at the latest! The emphasis was still on a large bombing force for the view, strongly held, that any future air war would be mainly a bomber contest, with fighters defending against the other country's bombers, or giving limited escort to its own bombers in the immediate battle areas.

With the creation of the new Fighter Command, its first commander as Air Officer Commander-in-Chief, was Air Marshal Sir Hugh Dowding KCB CMG, who had commanded the RAF Inland (fighter) Area in its early days of ADGB but had then become Air Member for Supply and Research. In retrospect, this gave him the insight into development and the knowledge of what might or certainly what could be achieved by various branches of scientific research.

Hugh Caswell Tremenheere Dowding was 54 years of age. He had joined the army in 1900, a graduate of the Royal Military Academy at Woolwich, serving with the Royal Artillery until 1914. He learned to fly in 1913 and when war came he was attached to the RFC. During WW1 he held several command posts and in 1919 commanded both 1 and 16 Groups. Between the wars he held commands in England, Iraq, Transjordan and Palestine, before becoming AOC of the Fighting Area.

A dour man with an austere outward appearance, he was known to both friend and critic alike as 'Stuffy', for that is how he came across to those he met. Nevertheless he had a brilliant mind and was always very keen and interested in talking, and more importantly, in listening to anyone who could put forward a good idea. He gave time to any military or scientific advisor who felt he could improve something or add something

The creator of Fighter Command: Air Marshal Sir Hugh Dowding – Man of Vision.

Command HQ, Bentley Priory, Stanmore, just to the north of London.

to the country's defence system, but just as easily could dismiss someone, if he thought his ideas of no value. And it was not just a case of his not understanding. His analytical brain could follow a train of thought to a logical conclusion, and if merited, he would give any idea his full support. Indeed, he would pursue the point until the item proved useless or was achieved.

He took up his appointment at Bentley Priory, Stanmore, just to the north of London, and immediately threw himself into the task of organising his Command. He, more than most, could see the potential danger of a rearming Germany, and knew that the present limitations of not only the RAF but of his meagre fighter force, would be no match for the emerging Luftwaffe. In hindsight, it had to be a fascinating time to be in command of such a task as defending one's country with all the new technology and aeroplanes he was about to see. However, he had no comforting hindsight in 1936, or a blueprint, only a task ahead and only his own drive and dedication to achieve what he believed was needed. He proved totally honest, totally fair, extremely professional and a gentleman, the last the 'weakness' that others were later to exploit.

Dowding's Command consisted of just two Fighter Groups, numbered No.11 and No.12, plus No.22 Army Co-Operation Group – for admin purposes only – together with the civilian-manned Observer Corps. No.11 Group was formed in June 1936, primarily for the defence of London, while 12 Group was formed the following May to defend the eastern approaches across the North Sea. Dowding's immediate target was to achieve the 'Ideal Air Defence' system. It was something that was new – it had to be, it had not been done before.

In the First War, attacks by airship or aeroplane upon Britain came with almost no warning. There were no detection methods save for men guarding the coasts who might hear or see the raiders. Just to hear them was insufficient, for they could have been friendly aeroplanes on patrol or just flying about. Only when it was certain that the 'planes were hostile could the defence units be sent up and that took time to organise as well as time for the somewhat fragile biplanes to gain height over a blacked-out countryside at night or a sun and cloud filled day. There was no radio to guide them to the raiders, just their own eyesight.

Things had not improved all that much in twenty years. Ground to air radio had not advanced greatly. Detection of incoming aircraft was still visual, with perhaps the help of sound detectors, or a lucky sighting by a ship at sea. There had to be a way of knowing when a potential attacker might come and where he was. There had to be a way of sending one's fighters to intercept, and to know at what height the 'enemy' was flying. Dowding had lots of questions. What he needed was answers.

Dowding's Needs

The aeroplanes in Fighter Command comprised biplanes such as the Hawker Fury and Bristol Bulldog, but these were being replaced by the Gloster Gauntlet and the two-seat Hawker Demon. All had twin ·303 Vickers machine guns in the forward fuselage, firing through the propeller, and the Demon had an additional single gun in its rear cockpit. Each had limited range and endurance, and unless they could be put in touch with raiders quickly, they would soon have to land and refuel. There was the prospect of a new fighter, the Gloster Gladiator (another biplane, but with an enclosed cockpit) for the new year of 1937, yet none of these types had the hitting power that would be required against what surely must be the target of the future, the heavily armed and armoured fast bomber.

The exciting prospect was for two promised fighters which had only recently made their maiden test flights. What was exciting and different about them was that they were monoplanes, not only with enclosed cockpits but retractable undercarriages. More important still, they were designed to carry eight ·303 machine guns – in the wings! The range wasn't so different from the biplanes but the new fighters would carry radio and would therefore be guided to their targets, provided Dowding could come up with a way of locating them for his pilots.

In fact both types of fighter had come about as a direct result of Dowding's insistence that rather than their following a course of trying to achieve further high speeds and collecting trophies for so doing, Hawkers and Supermarines should be asked to tender plans for high-speed fighters for the RAF. The results of his proposals had been the acceptance and advent of the two new fighter types, named now as the Hawker Hurricane and the Supermarine Spitfire.

The answer to the problem of locating hostile aircraft seemed to be the new radio direction finding (RDF). Robert Watson-Watt, a civilian scientist at the National Physical Laboratory, had demonstrated in early 1935 the possibility of detecting an approaching aircraft by means of transmitting a wave pulse by radio and receiving back an echo pulse. This then enabled the person with the RDF equipment to establish the approximate range and course of the aircraft.

Dowding quite quickly grasped the full potential of Watson-Watt's experiments and saw it as his best chance of solving the problem of where to find the enemy. Work was still needed on the project, and Dowding, when still Air Member for R&D, and after seeing how the system would hopefully work, immediately put forward a case to the Treasury for £10,000 – an immense sum in 1935 – and got it!

Now as C-in-C Fighter Command, Dowding was seeing the results of his support for RDF, approval having been given during 1936, for the construction of the first RDF stations. The first such stations were erected along the eastern approaches to the Thames, as the potential enemy, Germany, would need to approach London from that direction, across the North Sea, from its homeland bases. Later a 'chain' of 20 RDF stations was approved and built, each with its own 250-foot high masts. Later still a whole line of RDF masts stretched around England's southern and eastern coastlines, and all were operational by 1940.

By then, Dowding, with his new fighters, his new aircraft locating device, later known more familiarly as Radar, and his ground set up, was ready and able to defend his country against the might of the German air force.

The New Fighters Arrive

The first of the Hawker Hurricane eight-gun fighters equipped 111 Squadron, based at RAF Northolt, not far from Stanmore, in December, 1937. Treble One was commanded by Squadron Leader John Gillan, who had taken command just two months earlier. Gillan was 31, a graduate of the RAF College Cranwell thirteen years earlier, an exceptional pilot and for him, the Hurricane was love at first sight.

One of his senior pilots was James Sanders, who had been born in England but brought up in Italy. In 1934,

Below: *Gloster Gauntlet (K5359) of 17 Squadron at RAF Kenley, 1937.*

Bottom: *K1955 Hawker Hart variant which became part of the initial batch of Demons. This machine served with 23 Squadron.*

Above: *Gloster Gladiator, the RAF's first biplane with an enclosed cockpit.*

Top left: *Gauntlet fighter at the firing butts having its synchronisation gear checked in its flying attitude. Note Aldis gun-sight of WW1 vintage.*

Middle left: *No.74 Squadron's first Gloster Gauntlet II, 1937, at RAF Hornchurch.*

Bottom left: *Hawker Fury IIs of 25 Squadron, in echelon, 1937.*

Below: *Hawker Hinds of 142 Squadron, the light bombers Fighter Command would have escorted if war had come in the late 1930s.*

Sanders, while still studying, became convinced that war with Germany and most probably Fascist Italy, was inevitable. With astonishing fortitude, he resolved that if there was to be a war, he wanted to fight it in the cockpit of a fighter aeroplane, so returned to England and joined up. By the summer of 1936 he was flying Gauntlets with 111, and by the time the Hurricane joined the ranks of the RAF, Sanders already had a number of flying hours in his log book.

The squadron, when they heard they were about to switch from the Gauntlet biplane to the new monoplane, looked forward to it, feeling somewhat honoured that they had been chosen to be the first Hurricane squadron. James Sanders recalls:

We took to them like ducks to water, finding them much easier than expected. We had John Gillan as our CO, who was a magnificent man and liked publicity. As a fighter squadron commander he was remarkable. He made us so enthusiastic about flying this new monoplane which at the time we all knew to be quite special.

We had been flying Gauntlets and even with them we were quite a well known squadron because we did all the flight aerobatics; but John expressed the new concept in fighter aircraft, in spite of some inadequacies. For instance, it was quite slow taking off and took time to gain height with its fixed two-bladed propeller. But we coped with that very well and all the pilots took to it at once. To begin with, I admit, that we may have kept the cockpit hood open a little longer than was necessary, but we had been used to open cockpits for a long time.

The early Hurricanes, of course, had the venturi tube system for the flight instruments for quite a long time

Above: *Flying Officer M. L. Robinson's Hurricane (L1564), 111 Squadron, 1938.*

Above left: *The Gauntlets of 19 Squadron's Display Team 1938, led by Flight Lieutenant Harry Broadhurst.*

Left: *Flight Lieutenant Harry Broadhurst AFC.*

Far left: *111 Squadron's display team in 1937, led by Flight Lieutenant Kennedy (centre), flanked by Pilot Officer M. L. Robinson and Flying Officer M. W. B. Knight.*

which made things a little awkward, especially at night. With this system, the instruments performed no function until one was airborne so the airflow could enter the venturi tube [situated on the port side of the fuselage, near the side of the cockpit]. Then we got the three-bladed metal prop which made quite a difference.

The two test pilots at Brooklands, where we collected the first Hurricanes, were George Bulman and Philip Lucas and they were marvellous and enthusiastic; but we did find it difficult to get the Hurricane off at Brooklands with the two-blader, and could only just about clear the old high-banked racing track.

I remember some things we discovered by trial and error, or by chance. In early 1938 I landed the first Hurricane at RAF Tangmere, the home of 1 and 43 Squadrons who still flew the Hawker Fury IIs. The CO there had asked us if we could fly down and show them a Hurricane. Tangmere was like a billiard table, especially for landing the Fury, which was a beautiful little aeroplane. In a strong wind you'd take off in a Fury, climbing steeply and the wind would gradually blow you backwards as you gained height, so by the time you wanted to level out, you could find yourself still over the airfield!

I landed my Hurricane there and at the end of the runway my starboard undercarriage leg collapsed. Of course, all the 1 and 43 Squadron boys were standing watching me – Caesar Hull, Fred Rosier, Kilmartin, Johnny Walker and so on. All immediately threw their hats in the air and cheered!

Fortunately the prop didn't touch the ground so we were able to lift the wing onto a tressle, got the wheel down and it was only then that we realised for the first time the undercarriage hydraulics were not perfect. There had been a slight air-lock, so from then on we had to pump the undercarriage down solid before landing. We didn't know that until this happened to me.

The pilots of 111 Squadron were well aware they had a fast fighter on their hands despite the slow take-off speeds. With Gillan always on the look-out for publicity for his squadron, it was decided to see what the Hurricane could do flat-out. On 10 February 1938, he took off for Turnhouse, Scotland, and back, but a head wind curtailed his outward journey. However, after refuelling at Turnhouse he decided to take advantage of the conditions and headed south with a strong tail wind.

Gillan's speed was recorded at an average 408.75,

covering the 327 miles in just 48 minutes, the engine speed having remained above 2,950 rpm throughout the flight. The flight of course was well recorded and the story was in the newspapers the next day – Gillan had seen to that. However, what is not generally known, is that it was not Gillan who met the Press, as James Sanders relates:

'Baldy' Donaldson (Flight Lieutenant J. W. Donaldson, one of the three famous Donaldson brothers) was a hilarious character, in charge of the Station Flight at Northolt in 1938. He was a real clown. When John Gillan flew from Edinburgh to Northolt, we'd already done it the day before, Michael Robinson, Sydney Darwood, me and a couple of others, in order to test the route. John, of course, was after more publicity, if he could put up a record time for the flight. He had, therefore, rung up Air Ministry as soon as he landed at Northolt having already arranged to meet the press boys in London.

Baldy, who was a flight lieutenant, beat him to it. He too had telephoned the press and made it known that Gillan would now give the interview at Northolt! He got into Gillan's office after Gillan had headed for town, having borrowed one of Gillan's spare squadron leader uniform jackets and when the press turned up, proceeded to give the interview about the flight! So all the things that then appeared in the newspapers all came from Baldy Donaldson. He was later reprimanded by the AOC!

The First Spitfire Squadron

It was not until August 1938 that the RAF took delivery of its first Spitfire Mark I at 19 Squadron, based at Duxford under the command of Squadron Leader H. J. Cozens. One of his pilots was George Unwin, an NCO pilot. He remembers:

We in 19 Squadron were proud of the fact that for many years we had been, and still were, the squadron that won all the trophies, so as soon as 111 Squadron had 12 aircraft, they came and beat us up at Duxford, where we still had Gauntlets. Needless to say, some twelve months or so later we returned the compliment and beat up

Northolt when we could muster 12 Spitfires.

Awaiting the first Spitfire, we were very apprehensive. Pilot's Notes did not exist in 1938 and all the information we had was a piece of quarto paper on which was written such gen as stalling speed, climbing speed, cruising revs and temperatures. Jeffrey Quill [Supermarine's test pilot] delivered the first one and put up such a wonderful show of aerobatics that we were somewhat reassured.

After half a dozen flights one felt at home in the cockpit and realised what a lovely flying machine we had. The only worry was take-off, as the first Spitfires had a two-bladed fixed pitch propeller which was of course, in coarse pitch. For the first month at Duxford there wasn't a breath of wind to assist the take-off run and every inch of Duxford was needed to get airborne.

In those days, development flying was carried out by the first squadron to receive a new aircraft type. K9789 was selected for intensive flying up to 500 hours, in order that a maintenance schedule could be produced as the result of all the wear and tear after this amount of flying. Only a few of 19's pilots were allowed to carry out this flying and I was one of them, as was my great pal, Sergeant Harry Steere.[1]

It was in this field that we really put it over on 111 Squadron. Despite the fact that they had about 12 months' start on us, we finished our 500 hours before they did and what's more we did it on K9789, the one we started on! Evidently when they reached somewhere in the 200s, someone broke the aircraft. No damage at all was done to K9789 – but on its very last trip (flown by Harry Steere) the undercarriage started to collapse as he taxied in. Fortunately the ground crew were awaiting the aircraft and managed to keep the wing high enough from the ground to prevent the prop being damaged.

As far as I can remember, no one had any trouble flying this lovely aircraft. I had been flying fighters for three years when we got the first Spitfire but had never flown anything so easy and smooth, yet completely without a vice. The novelty of having a canopy, flaps and a retractable undercarriage all helped to add to the enjoyment. As the world now knows, as a fighting machine it was the best of its era.

Top left: *Flight Lieutenant J. W. Donaldson at RAF Northolt, with James Sanders' sister. He stole some of John Gillan's thunder!*

Left: *One of 19 Squadron's first Spitfires, K9795, 1938.*

[1] Later Flight Lieutenant Steere DFC DFM. A former Halton apprentice, he was killed on 9 June 1944 serving with the Pathfinder Force.

CHAPTER 3

Preparation

THAT SIR HUGH Dowding had a fine grasp of most situations and was able with almost single-minded determination to go for the correct solution to any problem, is now accepted, but there were times when his thinking was clouded by circumstances, and had later to be changed.

On 7 May 1937, he gave a lecture at Uxbridge, and it is interesting at this stage to understand what he thought of the future, just ten months after taking over as C-in-C Fighter Command. His feelings about the new single-seater fighters that were now replacing the biplanes in his squadrons are particularly revealing. In part he said:

The great handicap of the old types of fighter was that they had insufficient individual superiority of fire, could not attain concentration of fire when flying on a parallel course and were driven to attain concentration of fire

Treble One Squadron at Northolt, 1937, L to R: Mortimer, Sergeant Smith, Sergeant W. L. Dymond, Flying Officer M. L. Robinson, Pilot Officer J. G. Sanders, Pilot Officer R. G. Dutton, Squadron Leader J. Gillan, Pilot Officer R. P. R. Powell, Flying Officer S. Darwood, Pilot Officer S. D. P. Conners.

by synchronised attacks from different directions. These manoeuvres required a high degree of training and generally involved deflection shooting with a consequent loss of accuracy.

The increased performance of the modern bomber is rendering these tactics obsolete, mainly because deflection shooting at high speed targets tend to become very inaccurate. The time for each attack tends to get shorter with increasing speeds and the flight path of the attacker assumes a sharper curve. Also, of course, the timing and position of manoeuvres is more difficult and the time required to repeat each attack becomes longer and longer.

Further, the streamline monoplane of the future will be unsuitable for prolonged dives at steep angles. Speaking, therefore, on the single-seater fighter for the moment, the tendency is to increase fire power to the maximum extent possible and to attack from dead astern or with slight variation from that direction, imposed by the enemy's slipstream or invited by the disposal of his control surfaces.

There is a further development of the single seat fighter, now only in the experimental stage. A machine has been built with wing guns capable of being offset laterally in three positions up to a maximum of 18 degrees. The main object of this will be to enable concentration of fire to be obtained from single-seat fighters flying on parallel courses; it might also be used to enable fighters to attack a formation outside the slipstream. The range of the attack must next be considered. The object is to create a beaten zone of lethal density (about one bullet in every 3-4 square feet) in the minimum time. The determination of this range is still a matter of experiment but this is very largely settled by the fact that it is impossible to hold the sights steadily on a target when flying in the turbulent air created by the enemy's slipstream. Experiments carried out at Northolt have led to a tentative conclusion that 400 yards is about correct but this, of course, varies with the armament of the fighter, the type of bomber and the closeness of the formation being attacked. I want you all to pay special attention to this point during your affiliation exercises this year and to give me the results of your experiences at the end of the training season.

I now want to say something about bombers escorted by fighters. Single seat fighters, apart from the fact that their endurance is generally inadequate or extremely ill-adapted to act as escort for bombers, can only shoot straight ahead and therefore unless the attacking fighters are accommodating enough to go for the bombers without first attending to the escort, the latter can do nothing without losing touch with the formation which it is their duty to protect. The tactics of the attacker should be to make a small detachment from his force,

Treble One's first Hurricanes landing at Northolt in 1937. John Gillan leading, with James Sanders in nearest machine, L1549.

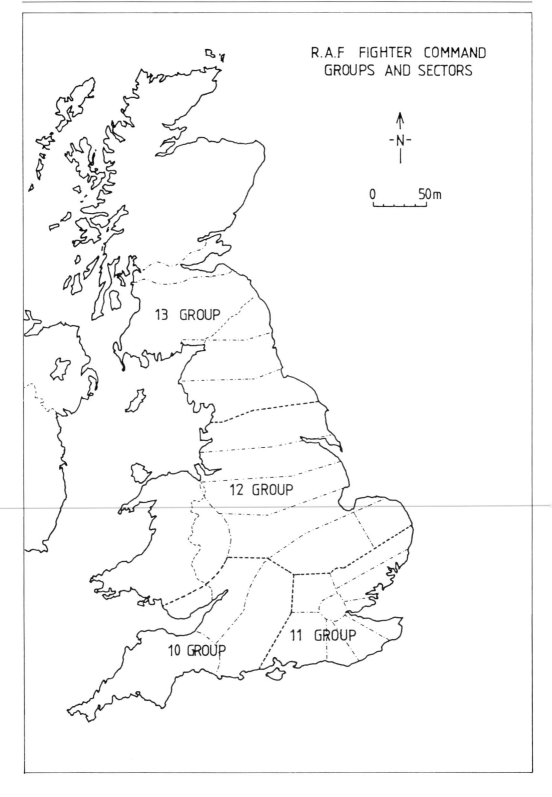

R.A.F FIGHTER COMMAND
GROUPS AND SECTORS

-N-

0 ____ 50m

13 GROUP

12 GROUP

11 GROUP

10 GROUP

to open fire on the escort from the rear. The escort will be compelled to turn and fight, thus losing touch with the bomber formation. The main body will then have an unobstructed opportunity to attack the bombers.

If, however, the enemy were to adopt a policy of constructing armoured fighters of an adequate endurance, and with their main armament firing astern, these might constitute a very effective rearguard to the bomber formation.

Considering now the tactics and formations which are likely to be adopted by the enemy, there are three broad alternatives:

(a) Send over large numbers of individual aircraft, trusting to numbers to break down any system of reporting their approach and to confuse the defence so that the majority would perhaps escape without any encounter by our own fighters. It is extremely improbable that he would adopt such tactics in good visibility and if used at all, would be restricted to periods of bad weather and at night time.

(b) to employ large numbers of formations each capable of putting up good defence by cross-fire from its own guns and hoping that the defending fighters would be so continuously engaged that during considerable periods they would be on the ground re-arming and refuelling. Our preparations are made largely with the idea that the enemy will adopt tactics of this nature.

(c) To send over a hammer blow of every available machine as nearly simultaneously as possible trusting that our defending aircraft even if all engaged simultaneously, will be inadequate through lack of numbers and that a large proportion of the attacks will not be engaged at all. I do not know how probable this contingency is but it is obviously one for which we must be prepared. For this purpose our fighter strength must be exceptionally flexible and our defensive line must be capable of reinforcements at various points. If such an armada were to fly in great depth on a narrow front it would be very difficult to bring large numbers of single seat fighters into action against it by attacks from astern since only the rearmost formations would be vulnerable. This in itself constitutes a reason, if reason is needed, for keeping up practice, attacks involving deflection shooting from above, below and the sides. Once thoroughly broken up, a column of this nature would tend to become disorganised and to afford easy targets for individual fighter formations.

Right: *Sergeant George Unwin (left) with Sergeant Jack Potter, Duxford, 1939. (Note 19 Squadron's pre-war codes, WZ)*

Below: *Camouflaged Gladiator of 65 Squadron, ready for war.*

Operations Room at Bentley Priory, ready for war by September 1939.

Chain Home radar. The three towers on the left are the transmitters; those on the right are receivers.

Towards the end of his lecture, Dowding said:

In order to disabuse your minds of the idea that it is always necessary to climb to a position above and behind the enemy before starting an attack, often this will not only be unnecessary but extremely inadvisable since you are doing nothing except lose time and advertise your presence. If you find yourself below the enemy then approach from below to the optimum range which will usually give the best effect and may result in complete surprise.

It is not necessary to try to analyse everything Hugh Dowding said at this lecture, but one or two points are revealing. That it was thought that single-seat monoplanes would be unsuitable for prolonged dives must have had some influence on the planning of future tactics. It is interesting, too, that thought was going into guns firing at some angle-off the line of flight in order to try to overcome the need to attack from dead astern. This obviously didn't progress very far, but one wonders what influence this line of thought had on the development of the Defiant aircraft, which only had rear-firing guns.

The mention of escorting fighters is also revealing. It has to be remembered that immediately prior to the war, and indeed right up till the fall of France, it was envisaged that if Germany did attack Britain, its bombers would come from Germany, across the North Sea. Because of this, there would be very little chance of their being escorted by single-engined fighters – they would simply not have the range. By the same token, the RAF's bomber tactics were being developed without thought of any single-seater escort, hence the well-worn phrase, 'the bomber will fight its way through.'

The considered enemy tactics, certainly (a) and (b), proved very accurate in their assessment. The possibility of the hammer-blow, however, could not be ignored.

What Dowding was alluding to when he spoke of 'armoured fighters of an adequate endurance and with their main armament firing astern' was the idea of twin-engined fighters, which was gaining ground in air force thinking. If single-seat, single-engined fighters hadn't the range to escort bombers over long distances, then perhaps a twin-engined fighter with greater fuel loads might be the answer. Britain, France and Germany were all working on this idea, which would eventually bring forth the Blenheim fighter, the Potez 631 and the Messerschmitt 110.

The Blenheim, of course, was a private venture supported by Lord Rothermere, proprietor of the *Daily Mail* newspaper. When the Bristol Aeroplane Company designed and built this 'fast commercial aeroplane' which the RAF were to use as a bomber, its potential as a twin-engined fighter was also seen. Appearing at a time when the RAF were looking for just such a fighter, it ordered 150 straight off the drawing board. When the first service types reached the RAF squadrons in 1937, they caused quite a stir, for this 'fighter' could outpace all the contemporary biplane fighters.

Unfortunately, Germany, like Britain, was fast re-

Observer Corps (later Royal Observer Corps) post, responsible for reporting all hostile aircraft movements inland over Britain.

Above: *Pre-war concern over long-range escort fighters produced the Blenheim 1f (this machine is of 219 Squadron) . . .*

Left: *The Royal Observer Corps' centre which received and co-ordinated the reports from the numerous posts around the country.*

equipping its front-line squadrons with single-seat monoplanes, and against them the Blenheim 1 did not shape up too well. And with just one fixed .303 gun firing forward, and one movable Vickers 'K' gun in a dorsal turret, it wasn't about to do much harm to an enemy bomber, although this was later increased by a pack of four ·303 guns in a ventral position on the pure fighter version, the Mark 1F.

Germany's Messerschmitt 110 seemed a much more promising bet with its speed, range and heavy armament of four 7.9mm machine-guns in the nose and a free moving 7.9 gun in the rear cockpit. Subsequent versions carried cannons. Hermann Göering, head of the new Luftwaffe, thought highly of the new fighter, but like most twin-engined fighters of WW2, it was not a success in its primary role. The main difficulty was always that the need to carry large fuel loads and heavy armament, in order to carry out their tasks, caused the very problems that resulted in their overall poor performance.

At the conference, Dowding also referred to the need for high muzzle velocity guns in order to overcome the expected armour in bombers. Cannon armament even now was under consideration, he said, but thus far the problem was the limiting factor of ammunition – just 75 rounds could be carried which would be fired off in just six seconds. 'It has yet to prove itself,' he said, 'over the machine-gun to compensate for loss of fire power.'

Another revealing thought about how the RAF viewed the new modern fighters was the belief that 'the high speed of the modern fighter aircraft would make it impossible to carry out synchronised attacks with fixed guns from different directions, involving as such forms of attack do, sudden changes of course and deflection shooting.'!

The Set-Up

By 1938, when the new monoplane fighters were beginning to arrive in Fighter Command, Dowding's organisation, after much experimentation, trial and error, etc., was roughly as follows:

No.11 Group, with its HQ at Uxbridge took control, both operationally and administratively, of all areas south of a line set east and west through Bedford. To the north of this line became 12 Group's territory. Through lack of resources, both groups' coverage of certain areas far to the west or beyond York became limited. Later, 10 Group would be formed to cover the south-west, 13 Group the north and finally 9 Group for the north-west and 14 Group north of the Tay River.

The groups were sub-divided into sectors, each with its own airfields, the main one known as the Sector Station. Early warning would come from two sources,

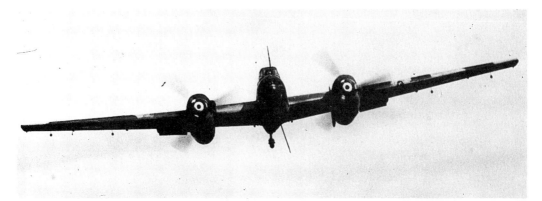

. . . the Messerschmitt 110, for Germany . . .

. . . and the Potez 63, for France.

RDF (Radar) for information of enemy aircraft beyond the coastline, and the Observer Corps for reports of aircraft once they had crossed inland. The set-up was that the RDF stations would report to a Command Operations Room, where the information would be displayed on a large table map. Other RDF station reports would help to correlate ranges and direction, thereby fixing the exact position (more or less) of the hostile force. Once established, the position would be relayed to the Group Operations Room, where it would be displayed on their table map, although the group's map would only cover their immediate area and not the whole country as on Command's table. The Group Commander or Group Air Controller would then judge the airfield or airfields in his Group in the best position to intercept the raid, (assuming they had squadrons available), passing the information to the airfield or airfields who in turn would put the required number of fighters into the air. Each airfield had its own control room and Air Controller who would guide his fighters by radio.

At least Dowding could now envisage interception of an enemy force. With RDF and the Observer Corps organised and becoming more proficient week by week, one of his main problems was being solved. That was he would no longer have to worry about where the enemy was and he could send fighters to them and not have to have them using up precious time and fuel flying about trusting to luck that the raiders would be found. All RDF stations, of course, pointed seaward. Once the hostile aircraft had crossed inland from the British coast, they could only be plotted by the men of the Observer Corps, weather conditions permitting.

In order that duplication, mixing up of friendly and hostile RDF plots and so on, be sorted out prior to any scramble of any fighters, a room was set up in the basement of Bentley Priory, below the Command Operations Room, which had been built in the former great dining-room. Here all the information would be 'filtered' before anything went onto the large map above. This became known as the Filter Room, and was the brainchild of Dowding's new Senior Air Staff Officer (SASO), his right hand man: Air Vice Marshal Keith Park MC DFC.

Keith Park was a New Zealander, and a former two-seater fighter pilot in the First World War, in which he had won the MC and bar, DFC and Croix de Guerre, and shot down, with his various gunners, 20 German aircraft. He was appointed SASO to Dowding's Command on 1 July 1938, when he was just 46 years old.

The only plots which did not have to go through the Filter Room were those from the Observer Corps. Their observations went to their own Observer Centres and then on to Group Ops where they were forwarded to Command. This was because there was no need to filter their plots which were straightforward reports of sightings and needed no correlation with other information.

This all took time of course, and the first 'real life' trials failed to make any real impact as regards interception. But slowly the system built up, the men and women involved becoming more and more proficient until by 1939, fighters could be directed onto 'targets' most of the time.

However, in 1938 there was still much to do, and there were signs of increasing unrest in Europe. Another problem Dowding had was whether he had the time to sort out all his Command procedures, tactics, and have all his squadrons converted to Hurricanes and Spitfires before a shooting war started. It would be a close call, and he knew it.

CHAPTER 4

Planning for War

BY THE SUMMER of 1938, the two Fighter Groups had a total of 30 squadrons on strength, 19 in 11 Group, 11 in 12 Group. Predominant were the Gloster Gauntlet aircraft (ten squadrons) and Gloster Gladiator (five squadrons with one converting to Hurricanes). Hawker Demons equipped eight, although one was converting to Blenheims, and there were still three squadrons flying Fury fighters. There were just three squadrons equipped with the new Hawker Hurricane (111, 56 and 87) while 19 Squadron, still had Gauntlets but were converting to Spitfires. One squadron had Blenheim 1fs.

Of these squadrons, five were Auxiliary Air Force units, all with either Demons or Blenheims. The Command's order of battle in September 1938 was as follows:

No.11 Group

Squadron	Base	Equipment
32	Biggin Hill	Gauntlet II
79	Biggin Hill	Gauntlet II
29	Debden	Demon
85	Debden	Gladiator/Hurricane
87	Debden	Hurricane
25	Hawkinge	Gladiator
600	Hendon	Demon/Blenheim 1f
601	Hendon	Blenheim 1f
604	Hendon	Demon
54	Hornchurch	Gladiator
65	Hornchurch	Gladiator
74	Hornchurch	Gauntlet
3	Kenley	Gladiator
17	Kenley	Gauntlet
111	Northolt	Hurricane
56	North Weald	Hurricane
151	North Weald	Gauntlet
1	Tangmere	Fury
43	Tangmere	Fury

No.12 Group

41	Catterick	Fury
64	Church Fenton	Demon
72	Church Fenton	Gladiator
19	Duxford	Gauntlet/Spitfire
66	Duxford	Gauntlet
46	Digby	Gauntlet
73	Digby	Hurricane
607	Usworth	Demon
608	Thornaby	Demon
23	Wittering	Demon
213	Wittering	Gauntlet

James Sanders, 111 Squadron 1938-40, helped establish the Hurricane as a first class fighting machine with Fighter Command.

Joe O'Brien was a flight commander with 23 Squadron in 1938, flying the new Blenheim fighters at night. He was killed in the Battle of Britain commanding a Hurricane squadron.

Operating Blenheims at night was never easy. The pilot of this 219 Squadron machine tried a variation of the 'three pointer', without success.

It was this force with which Dowding very nearly had to go to war that September, for that was the time of Munich, following Germany's march into the Sudetenland. On the 30th of that month, Prime Minister Neville Chamberlain returned from his talks with Adolf Hitler, waving his piece of paper, and saying: 'I believe it is peace for our time.'

This appeasement by the Allied governments, allowing Hitler to occupy the predominantly Sudeten German territories of Czechoslovakia, may be seen as an act of shame, but it certainly gave time for the British to make its almost last minute rush to rearm. If Europe had stood up to Hitler, perhaps WW2 might have been averted, but we shall never know for certain.

What Dowding now knew for certain was that every moment was precious if he was to have anything like

a fighter force with which to defend the British Isles. It still looked a formidable task. The latest proposed scheme was that Fighter Command should, by March 1939, have some 500 Hurricanes and 300 Spitfires in service, and that was just six months away. Having the aircraft was one thing, but the pilots, existing and new, had still to be trained on them, and know them inside out.

James Sanders remembers Munich and the early training on their Hurricanes:

We were at Sutton Bridge at the time of Munich and were ordered to move back to our dispersal points at Northolt and have our guns cocked. It was the first time we'd ever flown our Hurricanes with guns cocked. We expected, that if war had come, we'd have been fully

The opposition. The Heinkel 111 bomber, and . . .

. . . the Dornier 17, known as the 'Flying Pencil'.

Dowding's opposition on the ground: (L to R) Erhard Milch, State Secretary of the German Air Ministry; Hugo Sperrle, who would command Luftlotte 3 in the Battle of Britain; Adolf Hitler; Hermann Göering, head of the Luftwaffe; and Albert Kesselring, commanding Luftlotte 2. The occasion is their presentation of Field Marshal batons by the Führer.

operational for a surprise attack.

You have to remember that in the early days we had no pilot's notes – the Hurricane was too new. We were learning as we went along and although a beautiful aeroplane, it was still very different from our old biplanes. Most of the pilots on 111 Squadron were very experienced, but new pilots were joining us and other squadrons all the time, and it took more than a few hours' flying to gain the experience we had built up over months if not years.

Another pre-war fighter pilot who recalls the difficulties is Myles Duke-Woolley. 'Duke' had joined the RAF in 1935 as a Cranwell cadet and in late 1936 went to 23 Squadron at Northolt. Although flying Demons, he saw the arrival of 111's Hurricanes before his squadron moved to Wittering in May 1938, where later that year they converted to Blenheim fighters.

When the new monoplane fighters came in 1938, there wasn't anyone to write-up combat manuals on them, because nobody had got any clue. The only books that were lying around were all on biplanes.

In the mid-war years, when a biplane came in to supersede another biplane, it usually went off to be flown by people for some months who would prepare what became Pilot's Notes. All this would precede the arrival of the aeroplane on squadrons. When the monoplanes arrived, many of the old sweats imagined that this was just another type of flying machine.

When I first sat in a Blenheim, having previously been piloting Hawker Demons, I quickly realised we were into an entirely new 'ball game'. First thing there was a very detailed instrument panel, a gyro compass and right down in the bottom corner was the turn and bank indicator. Mark you, I was delighted we had the turn and bank, because if things went wrong at night, at least I had this to help me get back.

So really, since WW1, biplanes had steadfastly replaced biplanes, each one a little faster or with some slight difference in handling, but then suddenly we got flaps, retractable undercarriages, later variable pitch airscrews, enclosed cockpits, oxygen, etc. We never used oxygen in a biplane – one never bothered to go high enough! We did do what was called a 'battle climb', a rapid ascent to around 25,000 feet, but only once a year! Otherwise we never flew higher than 10,000 feet.

I had two years at Cranwell, two years with 23 Squadron, then suddenly we had Blenheims. I think it was then that the pilots began to draw apart from the staff. Whether the Air Staff people wanted to try to be

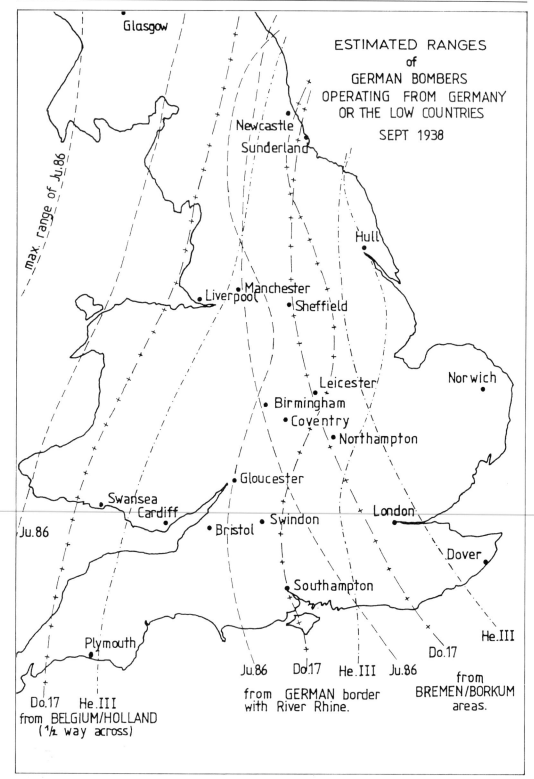

ESTIMATED RANGES
of
GERMAN BOMBERS
OPERATING FROM GERMANY
OR THE LOW COUNTRIES
SEPT 1938

Glasgow

max. range of Ju.86

Newcastle
Sunderland

Hull

Liverpool • Manchester
• Sheffield

Norwich

Leicester
• Birmingham
• Coventry
• Northampton

• Gloucester

Swansea
Cardiff

Ju.86

• Bristol • Swindon

London

Dover

Southampton

He.III

Do.17

Plymouth

Ju.86   Do.17   He.III   Ju.86

from
BREMEN/BORKUM
areas.

Do.17   He.III
from BELGIUM/HOLLAND
(½ way across)

from GERMAN border
with River Rhine.

Hurricane I of 111 Squadron with fixed two-bladed propeller.

Spitfire I showing the new three-bladed, variable pitch propeller.

helpful I don't know, but what I do know – they hadn't flown monoplanes! There weren't any for them to fly unless they managed to borrow one or perhaps one appeared in a Station Flight somewhere. Then they had to read what notes there were and very quickly realised it was much more complicated than they might have imagined. They had been used to just climbing in an open cock-pit, have some airman show them the tapes etc., and off they went. If they did fly a monoplane, all they did was get off, fly round the circuit and hope they could get it down again. But this wasn't operating it as a weapon of war.

For one thing the guns were in the wings now. On many old biplanes it was still the thing to have two guns whose butts were in front of you. We carried the 'Hide-headed hammer' with which we would be expected to clear any stoppages. It was the standard tool. If a gun

jammed you hit the cocking handle. If you were in the middle of a combat you were expected to fly off to one side, hold the stick between your knees, hammer away, open the breech, sort out the ammo belt, then re-cock the gun and get back into action! And this is what we had in 1938 when we very nearly went to war with Germany. Fortunately, at about the time we were to equip with Blenheims, we'd flown down to the West Country and my fellow flight commander and I had gone to Bristols and had managed to scrounge some handling notes. We certainly didn't get any when the aircraft finally arrived. When we did get the notes – and I've still got my original copy – they were dated June 1939, and we had received the aircraft the previous December!

By that time we had been flying them for about six months and had even begun flying them at night. Even this was exceptional, for normally one just didn't fly at

Spitfire pilot, (left) showing early reflector gun-sight and anti-mist panel on side of sliding hood. And (right) a section of three Hurricanes in line astern. The second and third aircraft flies just below the one in front to both avoid the slipstream and to keep a careful watch to avoid collision.

night pre-war. It was far too dangerous. Too much risk of the aircraft being damaged!

Fighter Command Attacks

Expecting hostile aircraft to approach from the west, unescorted, hopefully, Fighter Command had already begun to develop fighter tactics and attack plans to combat the raiders. In theory it would work well. The bomber or bombers would be located and the fighter leader would assess the type of attack necessary, form up his men, give them the appropriate order and that would be that.

One has to remember, too, that in the immediate pre-war RAF, the majority of squadron commanders were long-serving career officers, set in their ways and guided 'by the book'. If Air Ministry or Command sent down certain instructions to his unit, then it was his job to implement them, not question or interpret them in another fashion. As Myles Duke-Woolley explains:

In the pre-war airforce, a squadron leader had usually to be at least 30 years old before being put in command of a squadron. This was one of the reasons we lost so many senior chaps in the early part of the war. And as they got 'bumped off', so the 'Powers' looked around for another 30-year old, which meant perhaps dragging some chap out of training or a staff job, giving him a quick hour or two on a Hurricane or Spitfire. He'd arrive at his squadron, imbued with the old six Fighter Command attacks, which had been developed pre-war but which were now absolutely useless.

The Fighter Command Attacks had been developed when I was in 23 Squadron, for it was us in our Demons, who flew in formations to be attacked, in order for them to be devised and written. We were still at Northolt then, in 1937 when 111 Squadron still had their Gauntlets. They acted as the attackers.

The chap who wrote them up was Tiny Vasse, who actually flew in the rear cockpit of my Demon to see what it was all about, and to get the 'feel' of it all!

I remember, too, there was also a train of thought at one stage that things were developing so fast that it was believed the pilot would be too occupied to fire the guns and from this concept came the Defiant. I don't think Dowding liked them but in the end he had to have two squadrons of them.

In one paragraph of the 1938 directive for Fighter Command Attacks, there is a sentence that reads: 'Squadron Commanders are not to practise forms of attack other than those laid down, unless they have been specially authorised by Headquarters, Fighter Command.' Little wonder, therefore, most squadron commanders adhered to the book, and few flight commanders chanced their arm with new ideas. To be fair, however, squadrons were encouraged to forward ideas and suggestions to HQFC, but it probably had to be a brave chap who might do so.

This 1938 directive instructed:

Wave Attack. A series of attacks by successive waves of fighter aircraft, i.e.: single or other – e.g.: three aircraft attacking singly in three waves. Six aircraft attack in two by three – two waves/three aircraft attack.

Optimum Range. Roughly defined as range attacker has greatest advantage: lethal density must be attainable in reasonable time. For training purposes during the coming

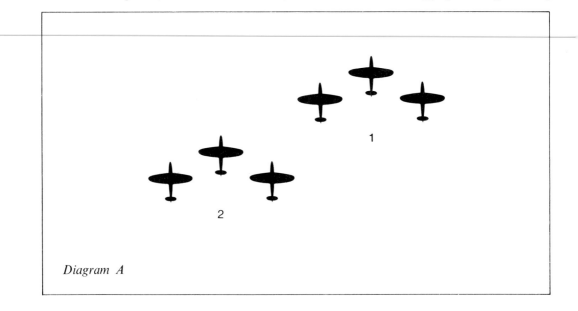

Diagram A

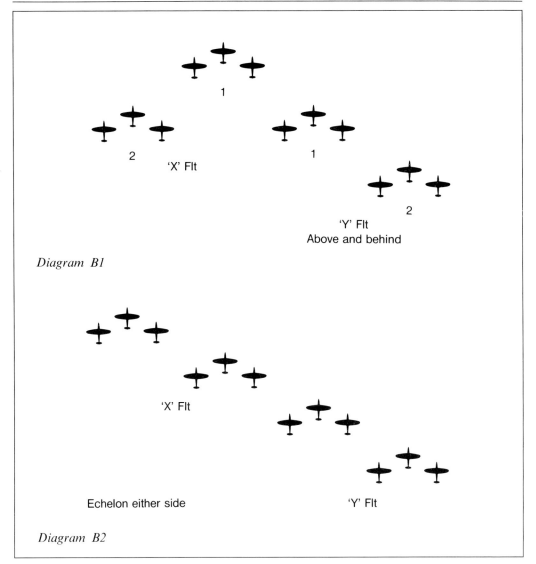

Diagram B1

'X' Flt

2

1

1

'Y' Flt
Above and behind

2

Diagram B2

'X' Flt

Echelon either side

'Y' Flt

year, optimum ranges assumed to be:
  1. Attack from astern – 400 yards
  2. Attack from rear guns – 'No allowance' position
     – 500 feet vertical interval
  3. Attacks from rear guns other positions – 200 yards

Search and Cruise Formations
Flight
(see diagram A)
Squadron
(see diagrams B (1) & (2))
Messages. First:
'Stand by for No.__ attack.' or 'Stand by for attack' if
leader unsure of which attack to deliver.
Second: 'No.__ attack, Go.'

No.1 Attack. A succession of single aircraft attacking from astern against a single bomber aircraft. Section forms line astern, (stepped down) 800 yards in rear
of aircraft. Section Leader closes to Optimum Range –
400 yards – opens and maintains fire at this range, breaks
away downwards and to flank. Number Two and Three
in turn close to Optimum Range and fire when proceed-
ing aircraft breaks away. (Attacking from slightly below.)

No.2 Attack. A succession of single aircraft attacking from astern against a single bomber aircraft. Leading Section forms line astern 800 yards in rear of flank
of bomber formation. Advance to Optimum Range at
400 yards. (Three fighters fan out each behind a target.)
(If second section, they close on other flank bomber and
close to Optimum Range and fan out, etc.)

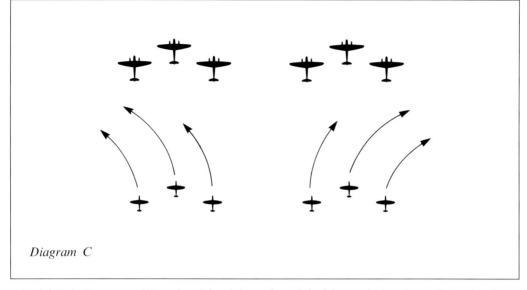

Diagram C

No.3 Attack. Two waves of three aircraft in echelon attack. One single-seater flight versus three bomber aircraft in vic formation.
(see diagram C)

Two-seater attacks
(A) – One Flight of six aircraft. One two-seat flight versus three bombers in vic formation, below and behind, rear gunners firing up and over.
(see diagrams D (1), (2) and (3))
(B) – One wave of six aircraft, one two-seat flight versus three bombers in vic formation. Ahead and below, singly or in formation. (However, this is not practicable in Defiant, as pilot cannot see backwards and upwards as in the Hawker Demon.)

The other three main fighter attack formations were all fairly similar depending on the circumstances. Needless to say, everything being trained for here fell flat if there were escorting fighters present. Note too that everything seemed to depend on the bomber or bombers obligingly flying along, taking little or no evasive action so that the attacking fighter(s) could make his approach, fire, break away and either return or be followed by his wingmen.

In broad terms the tactics being instilled in the minds of the fighter pilots in late 1938 was that in most cases the approach should be made from behind and slightly below, closing to around 400 yards. Guns should be harmonised at 350 yards for the Hurricane, or 250 yards for the Gladiator. Gauntlets, on the other hand, employed against fast bombers were to try for a range of 300 yards before firing, closing at top speed. Pilots were expected to continue firing as long as they could keep their sights on the target or until the aircraft was shot down or the guns were empty. For slower bombers, the Gauntlet pilots could adopt any appropriate method of attack.

The Demon pilots had to adhere to Fighter Command Attacks 'A' or 'B', only bringing their front guns into action, as for the Gauntlets, when the rear gun was empty or their gunner knocked out. This latter point, one wonders, may have had some influence on not giving the Defiant any front guns when they came into service in late 1939.

Sector commanders, if war had indeed come in 1938, were told to use their Gauntlets and Demons mainly at night, if they had a choice, due to their limited firepower. With the difficulties of later wartime night fighting or even flying, with a Hurricane or Spitfire, one wonders what the biplane pilots thought of this in 1938!

The day biplane fighters were told that with a bomber's greater wingspan, the fighter would have more 'elbow room' in formation. So, as a general principle they should endeavour to match machine for machine in the 'waves' which they send in to attack. (There was no mention of return or cross-fire from the bombers.) It was conceded that this principle might not hold good when attacking box formations, but, said Command, 'so far as is known, Continental nations have not so far adopted this type of formation.'

There is little doubt that much thought had gone into fighter tactics in the late 1930s when a war was beginning to seem inevitable. Just how much the producers of such tactics knew of 'modern' air warfare, the aeroplanes or merely the 'facts of life' remain a mystery.

The acid test, of course, would be when the realities of war tested the plans to the limit.

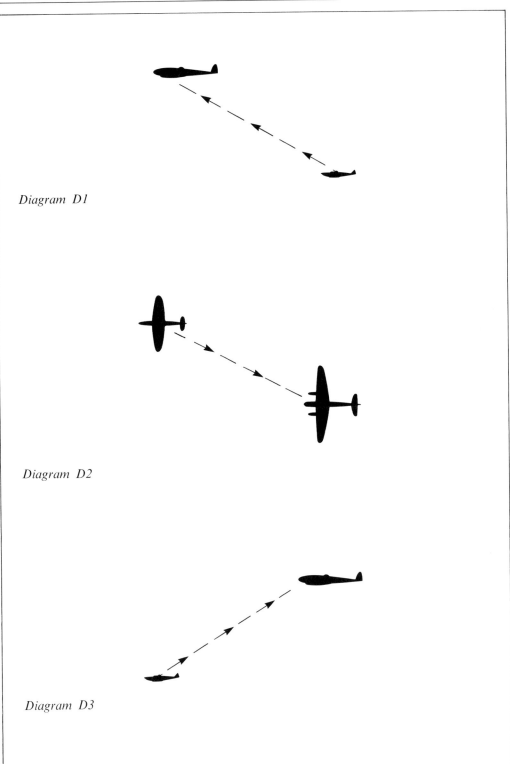

Diagram D1

Diagram D2

Diagram D3

CHAPTER 5

The Last Year of Peace

BY LATE 1938, Air Marshal Sir Hugh Dowding had much of his Command in place. There were still many improvements to make, decisions to be made, new technology to refine, aircraft to be supplied, but the structure was firmly established.

His right hand man, Keith Park, was working well, and his two Group Commanders, Air Vice Marshals E. L. Gossage and T. Leigh-Mallory were building up the team. Ernest Leslie Gossage CB CVO DSO MC, was 48 and had served with distinction in WW1. After the war he commanded the School of Army Co-operation. In recent years he had been SASO at HQ ADGB, SASO in Iraq in 1934 and AOC Aden 1935 before taking command of 11 Group the following year.

Trafford Leigh-Mallory CB DSO, was the same age as Park (46) and, like Gossage, his early career had been spent in Army Co-operation. He had what some called a somewhat haughty manner, and was a man of 'driving egoism'. Certainly he knew where he was going – to the top, if he had anything to do with it. Both commanded their Groups in different ways, Leigh-Mallory usually to the fore in writing letters to his C-in-C. This may have been his way of maintaining an 'up-front presence' to both his superiors and his contemporaries. He certainly formed some definite views and one of them was: 'if you're not known you are forgotten'; Leigh-Mallory was certainly not going to be forgotten.

One problem for Dowding, and he had many as a commander tasked to defend Britain, was where that defence line might start and end. Obviously the German Luftwaffe would attack across the North Sea, but would some of his fighter strength need to go to France in the event of war, just as the Royal Flying Corps had sent men and aircraft to France in August 1914. If so, this would deplete his home defence force, which was still below the size he envisaged, or indeed had been promised; it would stretch his command plan, and if the

new war progressed in a similar way to WW1, the main battle zone would be on the Continent, not England. In that event, part of his fighter force would undoubtedly be hived off and be under some other command. With Germany's ability to attack Britain from Germany as well as fight a war on the Continent, Dowding's reduced home defences would be stretched.

With the political situation far from improving following Munich, a conference in April 1939 agreed that if the political conditions came to demand it, four Hurricane squadrons should be earmarked as available by the summer, for despatch to Northern France. Park pointed out that by June 1939, Fighter Command would only have 21 fighter squadrons equipped with modern fighters, and that Dowding would probably not agree to 20% of these being sent out of the country. Park had also to point out to the Conference that the existing Hurricane squadrons were not yet trained nor fully equipped for air fighting against enemy fighters, which was true. As we have already seen, the emphasis was on fighter versus bomber action, against unescorted bombers.

The only aircraft Park could see as being suitable for France were four Gladiator squadrons, but the problem here was that this number would be unavailable owing to additional Gladiator requirements for the Middle East. When Park was then questioned about the suitability of Blenheims for day fighting against enemy fighters, he had to admit that in his opinion – and he was not alone – the Blenheim, even when fully equipped with five forward firing guns, would not prove suitable for this type of work.

France herself, was short of fighters, and the Government there felt that if war came it would be a repeat of 1914 but on a much larger scale, with the sudden invasion by massed divisions of troops, spearheaded by tanks, armoured vehicles and motorised transport which would sweep through the Low Countries. As it turned out, they were right on method if wrong on timing. The consensus was that this tactic, heavily supported by the German Air Force, would be mounted in order to eliminate France before turning attention to Britain.

Britain could help with bombers, although to be effective they might well have to use French bases, but unless some arrangement was made to operate RAF fighters from France, Britain faced the spectacle of 500-600 perfectly good fighters, sitting in the south-east of England, unable to contribute to the issue – an issue on which the fate of Britain would undoubtedly depend.

Dowding could see the difficulty, of that there is no doubt, but with limited resources he had to fall back on his prime role, that of defending Britain, not France. When Dowding read Park's notes from the Conference, he wrote a note to Park, with a copy to the Director of Plans, that: 'You had better tell Air Ministry that unless I get some decisions on this matter, I propose to take no preparatory steps.'

What was exercising Dowding's mind, too, were the estimates of the scale of German bombing attacks on this country that the Air Staff had prepared the previous autumn. It was thought that the Germans had in the region of 1,400 bombers. In the worst scenario, it was thought that the Germans could deploy 720 bomber sorties in one day, dropping some 940 tons of bombs on British towns and factories. During the first two months of a war, daily sorties would probably be in the region of 400-500, dropping 500-600 tons. This would gradually fall off when allowing for rates of wastage.

The range of all German bombers were not known for certain, especially that of the Heinkel 111 bomber. However, the only light in this dismal tunnel, was that it was felt that the main German thrust would be against Czechoslovakia, with France making preventative counter-attacks. Therefore, the Luftwaffe would not be able to spare the whole of its long-range bombers to attack Britain. Even so, a map was prepared, showing the estimated ranges of Luftwaffe aircraft from Germany, which clearly showed the problem. The map gave the ranges if bombers attacked from Germany itself (Borkum/Bremen areas), from the Rhine border, or from occupied Belgium and Holland. There was still no suggestion of Germans being able to operate over England from France (see map).

Against this Dowding now had 29 front-line squadrons, each with an establishment of 14 aircraft; i.e. 406 fighters if all were serviceable at once! Of these, four were Auxiliary squadrons. Returns showed he had another 106 fighters in immediate reserve, but his stores reserves were nil.

On the good side was the knowledge that he had five RDF stations working, with another three mobile units in operation. The five permanent stations covered a line from Dungeness to the Wash, while the mobile units

were assigned to the north, the Clyde and Forth areas.

Other defences were not so well provided for, as AA guns, light AA machine-guns, balloons and searchlights were well below the approved establishment levels.

Nevertheless, Dowding's command structure, while not perfect, was in good shape and, what is more, he was in total command. 'Suggestions' could be put forward to him, but in the main he was left alone to do as he saw fit. It was perhaps this that helped him the most in his single-minded approach to problems. And this power did not corrupt as it might have corrupted a lesser being, for Dowding was meticulously fair in all his dealings, totally dedicated to the task in hand, and, with the faith in his God, would achieve everything necessary to make the defence of Britain possible.

Tactics Reviewed

Meanwhile, the 1939 version of Fighter Command Attacks had been distributed to the squadrons, with little change from earlier versions. They were now standardised as follows:

No.	Fighters	Target	Direction of Attack
1	Section SSF	1 bomber	From astern
2	Section SSF	1 bomber	From below
3	Flight or Section	3 bombers in vic	From astern
4	Flight or Section	3 bombers in vic	From below
5	Flight or Section	3 bombers in vic or echelon	From astern
6	Squadron	9 bombers in squadron	From astern
A	Section free gun ftrs	3 bombers in vic	45°x below & astern
B	Flight free gun ftrs	Bombers in Sect astern	From astern

Breakaways after single seater fighter attacks will not be downwards but by throttling back and simultaneously turning outwards to a flank.

Opening ranges – training purposes:
Eight gun fighters	– 400 yards
Blenheim	– 400 yards
Gladiator	– 350 yards
Gauntlet	– 300 yards

There were now the beginnings of some arguments in the gun patterns of the monoplane fighters, whether harmonisation or a 'spread' pattern should be adopted. Dowding favoured the spread of fire from the eight guns, a sort of shot-gun effect. Perhaps he was only too aware that the average fighter pilot was not a great shot and that the Dowding Spread gave the optimum chance of inflicting damage. Against this, some pilots who were perhaps better than average in air gunnery were advocating that the eight guns should be harmonised so that the bullets converged to a spot ahead of the fighter. In the main the Dowding Spread continued although there was a gradual change to harmonisation by the more successful pilots.

Man of Iron

The Command Operations Room at Bentley Priory was deemed too vulnerable to attack from the air, so a new underground room was designed, work starting early in 1939. The site chosen was the sports field to the east of the Priory, despite protests from the local residents. A huge crater was scooped out of the earth, in which a large windowless structure was built. It says much for the contractors that the Ops Room was complete and operational by November.

Dowding's fighter airfields, too, were expanding in number, from just seven in 1936 to 11 at the time of Munich. When the war started there were more than 20 in the two main groups.

Yet, however one looks at it, Dowding's task was huge. As far as was known, the German Luftwaffe could and might strike anywhere, from London to the Scottish Highlands, as well as inland to Birmingham, Manchester, Liverpool or the Clyde shipyards. In 1939 he was also given the job of protecting the Naval Base at Scapa Flow. He therefore needed to stretch his meagre force right up the length of Britain. To defend London was a major task, but to do so too dramatically would leave other towns and cities exposed to the disasters of modern aerial bombardment. And the spectre of these attacks were very real to the general public. Everyone fully believed London and other important cities would be utterly devastated by bombing and populations killed by gas attacks. The recent film *The Shape of Things to Come* from the book by H. G. Wells, graphically illustrated Wells' belief that a future war would bring colossal destruction from the air and change all life as had been known in peacetime Britain and the world.

To add to Dowding's difficulties, there was again talk of sending fighters to France in the event of war. There was still the tacit agreement to send four fighter squadrons to France immediately war started, and following Anglo-French talks in March 1939 the Chief of Air Staff, Sir Cyril Newall, decided that six additional fighter units should be established on a mobile basis by the beginning of the new year, in order that they could be rushed to France at a moment's notice if it became imperative to do so. Newall did add that this would be conditional upon the situation in Britain, but the proposals alarmed and worried Dowding.

Here Dowding began what was to become his famous defence of his fighter force against depletion in a foreign air conflict. He wrote to Air Ministry on 7 July 1939 asserting that the loss of ten fighter squadrons to France would gravely imperil the defence of the British Isles. He had calculated that by January 1940 he would have 25 Regular squadrons equipped with modern fighters and 14 Auxiliary squadrons in various stages of efficiency. As the Air Staff had estimated that it would need 50 front-line fighter squadrons to defend the country adequately, he was already 11 short of that figure, even if all the Auxiliary squadrons were as efficient as the Regular units. If the ten were taken from his command, he would be down to 29: i.e. 21 short of the agreed establishment!

However, the politicians also had their juggling act to perform and had equally to try and keep their options open. For the previous two years at least, it was always an open question whether Germany would try to knock out England, or to knock out France first, so a plan to combat either, or both, had to be maintained.

Dowding had his third group, No.13, formed in August 1939, its HQ based at Newcastle. However, his own position seemed to be precarious. In 1938 he had received a letter from Newall that his services as C-in-C would not be required after June 1939, by which time he would be 57. In fact his successor, Air Vice Marshal Christopher Courtney, had been told he would take over on 1 July. This retirement date was later changed to the end of 1939, by which time Dowding had already made arrangements for his departure. Then this date was put back further, to March 1940.

Dowding was not unhappy at this for it gave him more time to have everything in place before he handed over his command, but the date was continually reviewed, especially after the war began. To change commanders then was inadvisable in the short term.

As the summer of 1939 wore on, it soon seemed inevitable that war would be not a possibility but a fact. On 24 August, some RAF reservists were called up. On the airfields, slit trenches were being dug, gas masks were issued, buildings painted in green and brown camouflage.

Most of the young fighter pilots were eager to get on with it, working on the basis that if war was inevitable, the sooner they got at it the better. For the older generation who had seen it all before in 1914-18, there was little to get enthused about. Many thought it would be over soon, with every possibility that Britain would be smashed into surrender, her cities in ruins, her people starving – those who survived the bombs and the gas.

The more optimistic thought it would be a long war, but one which they reckoned they could win. It might last two or three years, perhaps even four as WW1 had lasted, but few imagined it was to last six years.

Finally on 1 September, German forces attacked Poland. For all the political words over recent years, it had finally happened. To many fighting men it was a frustrating time, for Poland was so far away that there was little one could do to help. 'Sabre rattling' failed to worry Hitler, and Britain and France would soon settle down and accept the changing face of Europe as it had done in 1938. All that could be done was to read the newspapers or listen to the radio bulletins and hope that gallant Poland would stand up to the onslaught and give Hitler such a tough time that he would recant and pull out. It was not to be.

CHAPTER 6

The Phoney War

DOWDING LOST HIS four squadrons. Those selected were Nos. 1, 73, 85 and 87 – all Hurricane-equipped. The first two would form part of the Advanced Air Striking Force, being the fighter cover for the light bombers of the RAF (Battles and Blenheims) who were also going to France. The latter two would form part of the Air Component, attached to the British Army.

Dowding had visited 1 Squadron at Tangmere on 1 September and had said to its CO, Squadron Leader P. J. H. 'Bull' Halahan, that if they indeed had to go he was to take just 12 aircraft and pilots. In an equally dramatic tone he made it clear that Halahan could expect no reinforcements! The four units were out of the country within four days of war being declared.

As Dowding had 39 front-line squadrons when war was declared, this reduced his force to just 35, 17 short of the 52 deemed to be essential for the defence of the British Isles.

Fortunately the skies over Britain did not immediately darken with wave upon wave of German bombers carrying bombs and gas. In fact the sky remained strangely empty. There was an initial panic when two Frenchmen who were joining the Allied Air Mission chose to fly to London without giving prior warning, and their light aeroplane was picked up by RDF, which caused the first air raid warning. As this happened within only a short time of Chamberlain's speech on 3 September, everyone in London thought this was it.

As late summer changed to autumn one began to wonder if there was a war on at all. There was a flurry of activity in the far north when German bombers tried to attack ships in the Firth of Forth, producing the first clashes between the RAF and the Luftwaffe. Little damage was done although it confirmed that Dowding had to keep his fighter force stretched to the limit to cover the whole country.

Spitfires of 602 Squadron brought down the first hostile raider, a He111, ten miles east of North Berwick on 16 October, during a morning attack on ships by the Forth Bridge and Rosyth. On 13 November the first German bombs fell on British soil, on the Shetlands. In point of fact there were a number of actions over Scotland and the north in those first months, perhaps confirming that when the Luftwaffe finally got on with it, they would come from the east.

Everywhere else it was quiet. However, Dowding wasn't grumbling, even if his young pilots were getting even more frustrated. They had a war but nobody was fighting, but Dowding was fighting, fighting to strengthen still further his total force before the storm broke, for it surely would.

But it seemed to be one step forward, two steps back. He still had the threat of Newall's compliance to send up to six more squadrons to France if it became necessary, and then in mid-November, Dowding was informed that 607 and 615 Squadrons would be going to France. They would be used to attack any low-flying bombers while the Hurricanes would attend to the high bombers and the fighters. At least 607 Squadron had seen a bit of action: three Gladiators had shot down a Dornier 18 flying boat on 17 October while operating from Acklington. Dowding had to let them go, but at least it was not another two Hurricane squadrons.

Unease at Home

Dowding's commander of 12 Group, Leigh-Mallory, often wrote to Dowding with a barrage of questions and suggestions, at the same time ensuring his own back was covered. With Dowding pressed for time to secure the best for his Command, his patience must at times worn thin in replying to the many letters written to him. Leigh-Mallory wrote to him on 24 October 1939, from his Hucknall base:

Dear C-in-C,

I feel most uneasy about the number of squadrons

at present in 12 Group. I have, up to the present, lost three squadrons to the Field Force; number 616 permanently to No.13 Group, and now number 19 Squadron sent north to reinforce 13 Group.

In the last Command Battle Order no less than four of the squadrons shown under No.12 Group are non-effective as far as I am concerned. They are:

19 Squadron – attached to 13 Group,

616 Squadron – now belonging to 13 Group,

229 and 222 Squadrons – neither of which has any aircraft.

In addition, 46 Squadron is standing by to go out to France.

2. We have recently been faced with a phase, in which the Germans have been attacking coastal objectives. It seems to me from watching the international situation that we may be approaching very near the time when Hitler resorts to entirely different methods and begins to bomb military objectives in Great Britain itself, such as Rolls Royce at Derby and various shadow factories and aero-engine factories in the Birmingham, Wolverhampton and Coventry areas. If such an attack develops my position is a most precarious one.

3. I only have seven day fighter squadrons at the present moment. Of those, 610 and 616 cannot be regarded as more than 50% efficient when compared with the regular squadrons. They are a very different propo-sition to 602, 603 and 607 Squadrons, which were all in a very much more advanced state of training. That leaves me five reasonably well-trained squadrons with which to meet a really intensive attack on the Midlands. If one counts 610 and 611 together as equalling one squadron, it gives me a total of six.

4. With the big area I have to defend and the weight of attack which may be delivered against me, I wish to place on record that I think this inadequate.

Yours sincerely,
Trafford Leigh-Mallory

Dowding noted on the bottom of Leigh-Mallory's letter that he had spoken to him, while Keith Park noted in the file that the AOC of 12 Group appears to have overlooked that 264 and 266 Squadrons were at Sutton Bridge, and that 141 Squadron with Gladiators was trying to re-equip with Blenheim fighters as a priority. Also that 19 Squadron was about to be returned to Duxford.

One has to sympathise with Leigh-Mallory or any commander at this time for all were short in some ways, but Dowding could well have done without having to sort out his commander's problems, all of which he knew perfectly well. He knew for instance the range of the enemy's aircraft.

The Luftwaffe had a variety of aircraft to fight its

Some officers of 1 Squadron. To the right is Squadron Leader P. J. H. 'Bull' Halahan. To his right are his two flight commanders, Peter Walker and G. H. Plinston. Far left is 'Boy' Mould. They were among the first to go to France in 1939.

war. The bombers were all twin-engined medium types, the Heinkel 111, Dornier 17 and Junkers 88. Its lethal dive bomber was the Junkers 87, known more familiarly as the 'Stuka'. Its two fighters were the Me110 twin-engined long-range machine and the much vaunted Messerschmitt 109E.

It was the Me109 that gave the gravest concern for it would be the machine the RAF pilots would have to fight in order to get at the bombers. Would the Hurricane and Spitfire be a match for the 109? It was a question that needed to be answered. Perhaps some comfort came on 24 September when the RAF heard that a 109 had been shot down over the new Western Front by a French pilot flying a Morane 406 fighter. Hit in an air battle, the 109 had crash-landed at Rimling and the pilot had been taken prisoner. Although damaged, the 109 was mostly intact. Its wing guns (two) carried 550 rounds

Top left: *Gladiators of 615 Squadron take off from Croydon for France, 15 November 1939.*

Middle left: *Pilot Officer P. W. O. 'Boy' Mould, 1 Squadron, shot down a Do17 on 30 October 1939, the RAF's first victory in France in WW2.*

Bottom left: *Heinkel 111 shot down over Scotland, 28 October 1939. Brought down by pilots of 602 and 603 Squadrons, it was the first enemy aircraft to fall on British soil in WW2.*

Below: *Spitfire of 602 Squadron, Royal Auxiliary Air Force. Note starter trolley in foreground, plugged in, and the pilot's parachute placed ready on the port elevator.*

of ammunition, its fuselage guns (two) 250 rounds, made up of armour-piercing, tracer and incendiary bullets; the ratio being 4-1-4. What was also interesting was that the fighter carried no armour and did not have a bullet-proof windscreen.

Aircraft Armour

Protective armour had been talked about for some time, but the general opinion at Air Ministry was that it was not too important; after all, when attacking bombers, any return fire, it was believed, would be deflected from the pilot by the huge Merlin engine in front of him. It was envisaged that it would be sensible to have the front section of the windscreen reinforced and made bullet-proof, but that was all.

In 1938, Dowding was still of that opinion, but in June he was persuaded that due to the low-set nature of the Merlin engine, there was a tiny gap between the top of the engine and the bottom of the windscreen. This exposed the pilot's throat and upper chest to return fire, except for some limited protection by the header tank and other obstructions. Still, it was not until a meeting in July 1940 at Hawkers that it was agreed to install a small 4 or 6mm piece of armour plate atop the fire-proof bulkhead to close this gap in Hurricane fighters. This decision was also sent to Supermarine, although the Spitfire pilot sat somewhat lower.

Bullet-proof glass had first been requested in 1936 and six windscreens had been tested on Gauntlets and six on Gladiators. But by 1938 the RAF had still not received a general issue. Delay, it was said, was due to problems of development, laminations of the glass, supply of the correct materials, etc.

What had not helped the cause, was that in 1936,

First casualty in Britain – a rabbit killed by a falling bomb on the Shetlands, 13 November 1939. First bomb to fall on British soil in WW2.

when cannons had begun to be discussed, there was a strong feeling that cannon fire would miss the target, owing to the slow rate of fire, less ammunition and the speed of the aircraft! This was another reason that the ·303 gun was so strongly supported.

That same year Dowding had been worried by reports of German bombers being armoured which might make his coming eight-gun fighters ineffective. In the light of this, Dowding kept his options open and allowed the development of the cannon to continue. But again, thinking at the time clouded the issue. It was strongly felt that a cannon could only produce sufficient velocity when fired through an airscrew boss. Wing-mounted cannons would cut down the velocity to something inadequate.

Armour was being fitted to RAF bombers, to pro-

Heinkel 111H brought down by 43 Squadron, south-west of Whitby, 3 February 1940. It was the first German brought down on English soil.

tect the pilot. It was the same theory about the fighters, but in reverse. If a fighter needed no rear protection because the pilot attacked a bomber from the rear, by the same logic the bomber pilot needed rear protection from the attacking fighter. In order to give protection, armour plate was deemed the answer and a company was asked to produce a working model. However, the first sets supplied were of an amazing weight, something like 250 pounds! It was so heavy that it altered the bomber's centre of gravity and had to be placed further back, almost negating the reason for having it. Sense finally prevailed, the manufacturers admitting they were using a 'belt and braces' theory. Later back armour was produced and supplied that was around 30 pounds, while for fighter aircraft it was 45 pounds, thickness being standardised on 4mm.

The war had not been going very long before back armour for fighters was being strongly urged, especially by the fighters in France, both French and British, who were coming into contact with German fighters.

In a Secret memo from Air Ministry to No.1 Mission in France, dated 9 October, it was stressed that in view of the number of German fighter squadrons in the area opposite Metz and the tactics they were employing, it would be desirable to operate Hurricanes in strength rather that in small formations. Since there were only four squadrons of Hurricanes in France, acting as two independent pairs, the word 'strength' must be open to speculation.

However, by October 1939 it was agreed that all Hurricanes be equipped with back armour, at a rate of 20 sets per week, rising to 30 sets by the end of November. It was to be a sensible decision!

Lessons of Early Combats

Although there was no massive air fighting in the first months of WW2, there were a number of actions and skirmishes, mostly in France and a few in the north of Britain. By October, enough information had been gleaned for Fighter Command to feel there was nothing wrong with the harmonisation or spread of the 8-gun fighters at the ranges that had been laid down. However, Dowding was now saying that attempts to bring down an enemy aircraft from very close range, i.e. closer than the spread pattern, might fail because the bullet cones would have no chance of concentration and the streams of fire might miss altogether.

It is amazing to think now that such things were discussed and the findings issued to fighter squadrons. Dowding also thought that some pilots were attacking too fast and over-shooting the target. 'Keep cool,' was his advice, 'there is no hurry. You have an hour's petrol and only 18 seconds fire capacity. Go easy on the throttle; wait till you get your sights on and keep them

The tail fin of the same Heinkel (of II/KG.26) showing the effects of the 'Dowding Spread'. The bomber was shot down by Peter Townsend and his section.

on.' Good, sound advice, unless the fighter pilot suddenly found he had a Messerschmitt fighter on his tail. So was, therefore, Dowding advocating that a pilot sit behind a formation of enemy bombers, amidst the crossfire from the rear gunners, and keep cool?

There was some strange advice given out early in the war, none more so than that which appeared in a Bomber Command Tactical Memorandum (No.10) dated 29 December 1939. It was written by Air Commodore N. H. Bottomley, SASO at Bomber Command, and had followed the disasters met by Wellington bombers during daylight shipping searches in the North Sea and off Wilhelmshaven on 14 and 18 December 1939. On the first date, 12 unescorted Wellingtons found some vessels but were attacked by enemy fighters which shot down five of the bomber force. On the 18th, 22 Wellingtons reached the target area and again found some ships, but they had been picked up by German radar. Intercepting fighters shot down 12 of the Wimpys. These two actions, which had cost the RAF 17 bombers from a force of 34, sent a shock wave through Bomber Command and the Air Ministry who had firmly believed that the modern bomber with its power-operated gun turrets would be able to fight its way through any opposition. Strange thinking really, when on the other hand Fighter Command had been training for years in the firm belief

Another early Luftwaffe casualty, a further He111 of KG.26 brought down on 10 February 1940. Note under-gun gondola.

Squadron Leader A. D. Farquhar receiving the DFC from King George VI at Drem on 26 February 1940. Commanding 602 Squadron, he had several early successes, and with George Proudman, with cannon, brought down yet another He111 on 22 February.

that they would be shooting down German bombers with ease, using their well practised attack formations.

Then came Bottomley's Memorandum, with an amazing opening analogy:

The rear ship [HMS] *Exeter*, 64 [guns], was left separated out of due support of those ahead and received in consequence the fresh broadsides of the first five of the enemy and the remaining close action on both sides, assailed by two and at least by three opponents, two 50s and one 64. When the third approached, the master of the ship asked Commodore Richard King, whose broad pennant flew at the masthead, 'What is to be done?' 'There is nothing to be done,' replied King, 'but fight on till she sinks!'

1. That is an account of a naval action fought in 1782. If some proof were needed of the enduring nature and general application of principles of war, we have it in that quotation and in all the major air actions we have so far experienced in this war and those particularly during the month of December, fought in the Heligoland Bight.

2. In all these actions, crews have found the greatest security against enemy fighter attack when they have not allowed themselves to be 'left separated out of due support of those ahead.' Even the heaviest close range attacks have been successfully withstood when aircraft have kept 'shoulder to shoulder'. Generally speaking, those who have succeeded in reaching their objectives, in performing their tasks and in returning home safely are those who have been able to maintain close and unbroken formations. The greatest losses have been inflicted on the enemy whenever they have been confronted with those crews trusting in their concerted firepower, have maintained the same secure, tight and unshaken formations.

3. In the action on 18 December over Wilhelmshaven and the Heligoland Bight, the enemy again and again attempted spectacular attacks at great speed from various quarters, closing to short range in desperate efforts to bring down the ordered array of their sections. His losses were greatest when he was bold enough to face concentrated fire of the tightly packed sections, holding together in spite of AA fire and in spite of those shock tactics.

4. Whenever we have sustained losses from fighter

Flying Officer George Proudman, 65 Squadron, attached to 602 for cannon trials. Killed in action over the Channel, 7 July 1940.

attacks, they have been due to the inability to provide the mutual support which only close formations can give. It was from stragglers that Messerschmitts took their toll – those aircraft which were thrown out of the turn or those who were left behind due to inconstant speed.

5. We have many lessons to learn from the army as well as the navy. If a soldier leaves a gap in the defences, he leaves in jeopardy his fellows and his conduct may be criminal. If a pilot voluntarily fails to keep station he not only risks the lives of his crew but he endangers the lives of his section or possibly the entire formation. If the section leader has no regard to station-keeping of his section and streams away from them, he equally endangers all his fellows. Security in formation as in the operations of any force, rests upon mutual support and mutual confidence. This mutual dependence is one of the first principles of the operational bomber aircraft and it must be clearly realised and acted upon by all. If we develop this mutual support and this mutual trust, the morale of our formations will stand on a firm foundation. 'Shoulder to shoulder.' should be one of the watchwords of Bomber Formations.

How the surviving Wellington crews received that missive can only be guessed at, but it certainly showed how out of touch some commanders were in the ways of modern warfare. No pilot willingly dropped out of formation and all knew the dangers if it happened, but if damage to engines or control surfaces by concentrated attacks by fast enemy fighters could not be avoided, then what else could he do. No, the policy was wrong, and if the lesson wasn't learnt then, it would soon be learned in France. Little wonder that the RAF quickly went over to night bombing for raids on Germany.

If Dowding read this, he may have had some reason for optimism that his fighters might indeed prove more than a match for the Luftwaffe's bombers. So where one Command was rapidly beginning to re-think its own strategy, another was rubbing its hands with glee. If only the RAF could get to grips with the enemy bombers.

CHAPTER 7

Invasion in the West

THE SEVERE WINTER of 1939-40 did nothing to help Fighter Command's training plan nor did it help those squadrons in France who were exposed even more to the elements. The only bright aspect was that by the end of 1939 Fighter Command had claimed a total of 15 enemy aircraft shot down over Britain, virtually all in the north, but had lost one Spitfire, a machine of 41 Squadron, hit by a German rear gunner off Whitby. The pilot, Norman Ryder, had survived a ditching.

On the political front the situation had not improved. There was a fear now that Hitler might turn his attentions to Scandinavia in his search for war materials such as iron ore. It would also mean yet another springboard from which to launch aerial attack upon Britain, especially in the north. In view of this possibility, Dowding was asked, in February 1940, to send three fighter squadrons to Scandinavia, two of them Blenheim squadrons.

Dowding was like the little Dutch boy holding his finger in the dyke. With a Command still below establishment, he had been asked to send six squadrons to France (four Hurricane and two Gladiator), earmark another four to be immediately ready to go to France if a situation developed; four more had been assigned to assist Coastal Command in trade protection (convoy work) and two squadrons had to be assigned to a new sector at Middle Wallop. With four squadrons having to be left in north-east Scotland, two at Wick and two on the Aberdeen coast, and with an additional commitment to send five more squadrons to the Wick Sector for Fleet protection, he was being stretched to the limit. Dowding wrote to Air Ministry:

I regard with apprehension the proposal to withdraw

In command of 11 Group, Fighter Command, in 1940, Air Vice Marshal Keith Park often visited his squadrons in his personal Hurricane, to keep abreast of what was happening.

three squadrons for a Scandinavian Expedition for a number of reasons.

1. The first is the intrinsic difficulty of sparing three effective squadrons from the line.

2. The second is that the maintenance of three squadrons in active operations and in close range of enemy fighters will constitute an added drain on the aircraft output.

3. The third is that we cannot enter this commitment with a limited liability but that irresistible pressure will be brought to increase the number of fighter units.

4. The fourth is that the Blenheim is an entirely unsuitable type to engage against the German Air Force at short range. It was asked for by me as an interim home defence night fighter for use with AI. It is an altogether unsuitable type to pit against the Messerschmitt. It has unprotected tanks and no armour and its speed and manoeuvrability are quite inadequate to enable it to even bring its main armament into action against German fighters. It must rely on the single back-gun. We have already learned from Bomber Command, that the Blenheim falls an easy victim in these circumstances. I do not underestimate the importance of attempting to deny the Swedish iron ore supply to Germany but the letter [sent to me] certainly over-emphasised it. It is not within my province to discuss whether we are likely to win the war by stopping the Swedish ore supply to Germany but it is my duty to point out that we may lose it by opening yet another source of dispersion and wastage of our fighter resources.

Once again he was overruled and he had to assign 23,

263 and 604 Squadrons but then the two Blenheim units, 23 and 604, were withdrawn to have armour and self-sealing tanks fitted. This left just 263, which had been formed in October 1939, taking some of the Gladiator aircraft from 605 Squadron as that unit slowly converted to Hurricanes.

The following month, March, Dowding received instructions that 3 and 79 Squadrons would operate from Manston in the event of hostilities in France, which now seemed likely to begin in the spring. These would support 46 and 501 Squadrons who would proceed to France (Lille) in that event, remaining there for the 'required period'!

It was late the previous year that James Sanders, still flying with 111 Squadron, ran into some trouble. One Sunday morning he decided to see if he could take off in a Gauntlet and immediately he became airborne pull the fighter into a loop and then roll off the top. It was a spectacular manoeuvre and he had practised it on clouds so felt confident he would manage it. He chose the Sunday as it would be quiet, but on landing discovered he had been seen.

Told to report to the Group Commander, AVM

The famous 'vics of three'. A squadron of Hurricanes on patrol. This style of formation looked nice but was a 'gift' for Luftwaffe pilots.

Gossage, he discovered that not only had he been seen by his station commander, and himself, Gossage, but also by the C-in-C, Hugh Dowding! There had been a conference of which Sanders knew nothing. Fortunately Gossage knew Sanders' mother, but there had to be some form of punishment so when Gossage asked the young pilot what he should do with him, Sanders asked to be sent to France. Bearing in mind that Sanders was now a very experienced Hurricane pilot with something like a 1,000 hours on the type, the RAF did indeed send him to France, to 615 Squadron – who were still flying Gladiators!! Perhaps the punishment was to be sent to an Auxiliary Squadron!

Sanders actually had a crack at a German in a Gladiator, at the end of December:

An X-Raid turned up when I was on the aerodrome about to do a weather test. It was very bad weather, with a lot of cumulus cloud about but I got very high and saw this German He111 scudding in and out of the clouds. It was very difficult but I gradually got relatively close to it and fired quite a lot of ammunition at it. It finally disappeared in the cloud and when I got back, found that, not having worn gloves, I had slight frost bite to my fingertips. Our CO was, of course, quite keen to see if the German had come down but I couldn't say if I'd got it or not.

The Gladiator was an absolute toy. Bags of power in it, it could turn and was quite reliable. It could be landed on a penny – a beautiful little aeroplane, carrying four machine-guns.

Expansion Continues

In February 1940, Gossage became Inspector-General of the RAF; his place as OC 11 Group was given to Keith Park. Meantime, No.10 Group under command of Air Vice Marshal Sir Christopher Quintin Brand KBE DSO MC DFC, whose HQ was at Box, Wiltshire, was added to the Command. Brand, a South African, had been a fighter pilot in WW1 and also a successful pilot during early night-fighting sorties. He had been knighted in 1920 following a pioneer flight to the Cape with Pierre Van Ryneveld. Of his 12 victories in WW1, five had been shot down at night.

The deadly Messerschmitt 109E day fighter. Here the armourers load the twin 7.9mm machine-guns mounted on top of the DB engine. Note too the muzzle of the 20mm cannon through the propeller boss. The 109 is also up on trestles in order to test-fire the guns in line of flight.

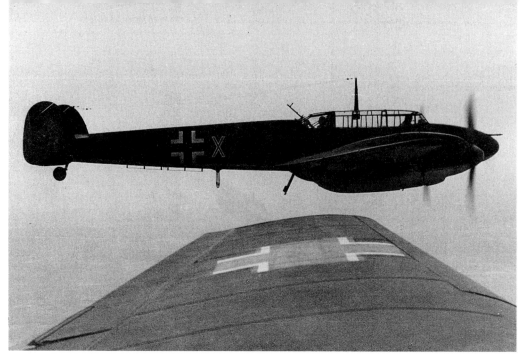

The twin-engined Messerschmitt 110 fighter was a disappointment for the Luftwaffe, as, like the RAF Blenheim, it was no match for single-seater opponents. This aircraft is of ZG.76.

Two of the RAF's first 'aces' of WW2, Newell 'Fanny' Orton DFC*, and E. J. 'Cobber' Kain DFC* (New Zealand). Both fought with 73 Squadron in France. Kain died in a crash in June 1940, Orton was killed in action in 1941.

Meantime, other squadrons were re-equipping with monoplanes, such as 92 Squadron. One of its pilots was Pilot Officer Allan Wright:

Having flown Blenheims over the winter of 1939-40, mainly at night, with no guns, no radar and in fact no radio, it was all pretty hopeless. Trying to find our way back to the airfield was absurd. So when we began to re-equip with proper aeroplanes – Spitfires – we were immensely relieved. Most of us felt it was better to fight during the day when one could at least see what was going on.

However, we had no pre-training. We flew up to Birmingham in an Anson and there were our Spitfires outside a hangar. Having been quickly shown over the cockpit, we took off one by one. The amusing thing was in seeing the aircraft as they left the ground, undulating up and down as each pilot, holding the stick with one hand, was busily pumping up the undercarriage with the other! Then we had to learn to fly them and practise the Number One Attacks, Number Two Attacks, and so on. Roger Bushell, our CO, was a tremendous chap. He was the father of the lads when the squadron was formed at Tangmere. He trained us and gave us the right feeling and taught us to be independent – to do things and not to have to look to somebody. It was due to him that when the squadron went to Biggin Hill in September and went through three COs very quickly, we became known as the independent crowd. We managed without a CO because we'd had that training; we knew what to do and I think we did it very well.

Other squadrons were coming along. 253 Squadron was formed from a whole pilot course from No.2 FTS Brize Norton. Initially they had been trained on twin-engined Oxfords in order to convert to Blenheims, but in the event they got two Magisters and a couple of Battles, and were soon going over to Hurricanes. Dowding was eager to get as many Hurricane and Spitfire squadrons as he could, and 253 was formed by using spare equipment from a number of other Hurricane units. They got their Hurricanes but as can be imagined, the other squadrons donated their oldest machines!

Norway

In April came the German invasion of Norway, commencing on the 9th. First Denmark was overrun without a struggle, then German airborne and naval forces landed in Norway. British counter-measures surprisingly did not include air support. By mid-April it was evident that some fighter support was necessary to combat the German aircraft, and so the already assigned 263 Squadron went aboard the carrier *Furious* and headed for a frozen lake airstrip at Lesjeskogen. Its CO was none other than John 'Baldy' Donaldson who had been

at Northolt when 111 Squadron received its first Hurricanes.

They did not last long. Attacked from the air, most of the Gladiators were destroyed on the ground and the survivors, moving to Aandalsnes were soon unserviceable and to had to re-embark and return to England on the 26th. The squadron returned to Norway on 22 May as part of the plan to recapture Narvik where it was joined by Hurricanes of 46 Squadron, commanded by Squadron Leader K. B. B. Cross. Despite some spirited fighting, both units were soon hard-pressed and then had the task of covering the British withdrawal. This was completed on 8 June, the surviving fighters having been flown onto HMS *Glorious* – despite the fact that Hurricanes had never before made any deck landings on a carrier. Tragically *Glorious* was sunk the following afternoon by the battlecruiser *Scharnhorst*. Only Cross and his flight commander Pat Jameson survived from 46 Squadron, and the story was later circulated that Baldy Donaldson, having been rescued by a German destroyer, was so rude and contemptuous of his captors that they threw him back into the sea.

It had been a stupid campaign from the start, but the final outcome for Hugh Dowding was that he was minus two squadrons, but by this time he had much more to worry about. Even before the return to Norway, the 'balloon' had gone up in France.

The Battle of France

On 8 May, 1940, the AASF HQ in France had written to Air Ministry saying that it was essential for all fighters earmarked for France should have back armour. The fighter versus fighter war was hotting up. The following day the forces in France were put on full alert for a possible invasion of Holland preceded by the occupation of the Netherlands Islands and Texel, with a possible airborne assault on Texel aerodrome. Requests for bombing support by the light bombers of 2 Group were made to help if the assault came. That same day, 504 and 151 Squadrons were put on alert to move to France at short notice to replace 46 (this was before they were sent to Norway, of course) and 501.

Unlike previous warnings, this one proved correct. At dawn on 10 May, the Phoney War ended and the Germans' *Blitzkrieg* began. British and French airfields were attacked by swarms of low-flying bombers and fighters, while German paratroops landed at the airfields in the Hague and Amsterdam. Further to the rear, German troops and panzer units crashed through the borders into Holland, Luxembourg and neutral Belgium. The Hurricanes of both the Air Component and the AASF were in the forefront of the battle from the beginning.

The pilots of 615 Squadron were busy converting to

Those Hurricanes in France not lost in action had to be destroyed by evacuating RAF personnel. Here five Hurricanes have been blown up by ground crews. Empty petrol cans in foreground.

Hurricanes by this date but were quickly thrown into the action. James Sanders remembers:

The squadron began converting to Hurricanes at the end of April and had not completed doing so by 10 May. At the time of [the attack on the bridges at] Maastricht, Joe Kayll and I had to fly up to locate an airfield in Belgium to operate from. I got into a Gladiator and he went off in a Hurricane. He flew to Morsel while I went to Evere on the east side of Brussels. I got into Evere and had just landed when I noticed it was full of Germans, so I rapidly shot off and keeping on the deck, headed for home. The next morning we all flew to Morsel in our Hurricanes arriving before our ground-crews, so had to start our own aeroplanes and so on.

It was difficult for the poor Auxiliary pilots in 615 to convert onto the new monoplane for the pilots were not terribly experienced. When 111 Squadron had converted in 1938 we were all very experienced pilots anyway, so found little difficulty, but for the 615 chaps it was a very different story.

The fighting was bitter and despite the tremendous odds, the RAF pilots put up a magnificent show. Daily they met the hordes of bombers, dive bombers and escorting or free-ranging fighters, but in the end they were just overwhelmed. The armies too on the ground were being pushed back river by river. The light bombers of the AASF, sent out in penny-packages to attack bridges, tanks or mechanised transport at low level, were shot out of the sky. The gallant Battle pilots and crews had almost no chance against the deadly ground fire and if

they flew at altitude, fell prey to the 109s. The first air VCs were won by two of the three crew of a 12 Squadron Battle which led a virtual suicide attack against road bridges just to the west of Maastricht. It was hopeless.

Churchill, the new Prime Minister, and his war cabinet were forced to promise help to the French who were falling back on all parts of the front. Dowding was requested to reinforce the fighter units already in France and had to comply. In a desperate attempt to preserve some nucleus of his squadrons, he organised reinforcements by 'composite' squadrons for short periods of time, while being supported by RAF squadrons flying across daily to fly and fight, but not to remain in France overnight.

These 'composite' squadrons were made of two flights from different units but operating as one. The pure logic behind this is obscure for not only did the two units not know how the other worked, they mostly didn't even know each other. Therefore they could hardly be expected to operate effectively as a single unit. Dowding later wrote:

This was done under the impression that the loss of eight half squadrons would affect me less than that of four entire squadrons, because it was supposed that I should be able to rebuild on the nuclei left behind. But this assumption was incorrect because I had neither the time nor the personnel available for purposes of reconstruction.

Keith Park, as 11 Group Commander, taking the brunt

More smashed Hurricanes, their backs broken by explosive charges, are left behind by the retreating air force in France.

of the battle from the British side, was also at a loss to comprehend the sense of this action by his C-in-C. All he could see was his already under strength command being slowly whittled away in a battle few thought could be won.

Dowding now asked Churchill to confirm that he would stop any further Hurricanes being sent to France and he seemed to get the PM's agreement. Dowding wrote to Park on the 15th:

We had a notable victory on the 'Home Front' this morning. Any orders to send more Hurricanes were cancelled. Appeals for help will doubtless be renewed, however, with increasing insistence.

I do not know how this morning's work will stand the test of time; but I will never relax my efforts to prevent the dissipation of the Home Front fighter forces.

The 'good news' came after Dowding himself had been present at a meeting of the War Cabinet, where there seemed to be a threat of resignation by Dowding if the policy of draining his fighter force into France continued. Whatever had or had not been said or recorded about this meeting, Dowding had his respite.

Park, however welcome this news was, had his own problems. He wrote to Command HQ on the 17th:

For future temporary requests for BAFF [British Air Forces in France], may whole squadrons be despatched to avoid the present situation whereby 14 flights of different squadrons are operating as composite squadrons overseas and at home, under squadron leaders who know only half the pilots in their formations and are separated

from their Headquarters flights? For example, 111 Squadron has one flight in France, another flight at Kenley and the Headquarters flight at Northolt with consequent dislocation of maintenance and administration.

Meantime, Dowding had, on 16 May, followed up his agreement with Churchill with a letter to the Under Secretary of State at Air Ministry. It was a very bold move from a very courageous man, full of conviction. There was no shilly-shallying. Dowding knew what was right and knew what he had to do and to achieve. The letter is not new to history but is so important that there is no apology for reproducing its contents here, yet again:

Secret   16th May, 1940
Sir,

I have the honour to refer to the very serious calls which have recently been made upon the Home Defence Fighter Units in an attempt to stem the German invasion on the Continent.

2. I hope and believe that our Armies may yet be victorious in France and Belgium, but we have to face the possibility that they may be defeated.

3. In this case I presume that there is no one who will deny that England should fight on, even though the remainder of the Continent of Europe is dominated by the Germans.

4. For this purpose it is necessary to retain some minimum fighter strength in this country and I must request that the Air Council will inform me what they consider this minimum strength to be, in order that I may make my dispositions accordingly.

5. I would remind the Air Council that the last estimate which they made as to the force necessary to defend this country was 52 squadrons, and my strength has now been reduced to the equivalent of 36 squadrons.

6. Once a decision has been reached as to the limit on which the Air Council and the Cabinet are prepared to stake the existence of this country, it should be made clear to the Allied Commanders on the Continent that not a single aeroplane from Fighter Command beyond the limit will be sent across the Channel, no matter how desperate the situation may become.

7. It will, of course, be remembered that the estimate of 52 squadrons was based on the assumption that the attack would come from the eastwards except in so far as the defences might be outflanked in flight. We have now to face the possibility that attacks may come from Spain or even from the north coast of France. The result is that our line is very much extended at the same time as our resources are reduced.

8. I must point out that within the last few days the equivalent of 10 squadrons have been sent to France, that the Hurricane squadrons remaining in this country are seriously depleted and that the more squadrons which are sent to France the higher will be the wastage and the more insistent the demands for reinforcements.

9. I must therefore request that as a matter of paramount urgency the Air Ministry will consider and decide what level of strength is to be left to the Fighter Command for the defence of this country and will assure me that when this level has been reached, not one fighter will be sent across the Channel however urgent and insistent the appeals for help may be.

10. I believe that, if an adequate fighter force is kept in his country, if the fleet remains in being and if Home Forces are suitably organised to resist invasion we should be able to carry on the war single-handed for some time, if not indefinitely. But, if the Home Defence Force is drained away in desperate attempts to remedy the situation in France, defeat in France will involve the final, complete and irremediable defeat of this country.

I have the honour to be, Sir,

Your obedient Servant.

H. C. T. Dowding

Some servant. Some Man!

Even as this was written, Churchill was in France talking with the French and was shocked to learn that they had no strategic reserve to support the crumbling battle front. The French again asked for support in aircraft, especially fighters. Churchill, shocked, and eager to try to boost the French morale, immediately sent a telegram to the War Cabinet to consider urgently reinforcements of fighters.

Dowding's letter pulled everyone up abruptly. His strategy of words was marvellous. He was placing the ultimate burden of responsibility on their shoulders and if the war was lost, the blame would be placed squarely on them. Politicians don't like that.

The Chief of the Air Staff, Newall, now gave full support to Dowding and the order was given. No more fighters for France.

The squadrons now in France since the beginning of the war, and thus away from Dowding's defensive command, were as follows:

Date	Squadrons
7 Sept 1939	1 and 85
9 Sept 1939	73 and 87
15 Nov 1939	607 and 615
11 May 1940	3, 79 and 501
12 May 1940	504
16 May 1940	1 Flight from each of 56, 601, 253, 111, 229, 213, 242, 245

The Battle of France had gobbled up nearly 200 Hurricane fighters, some 25% of Fighter Command's strength. Just as important was the loss of pilots, the vast majority being Regular Air Force personnel, including squadron and flight commanders. Given time, both could be replaced but while aeroplanes could be produced, the quality of pilot experience would take a good deal longer to achieve.

Dowding had saved the rest of his fighters from being thrown into the pit of defeat in France. The test now was to see if he could defend the British Isles with what little remained.

CHAPTER 8

Dunkirk and the Channel

SIR HUGH DOWDING'S dramatic yet successful retention of his fighter forces within Britain sounded a death knell for France. Those RAF fighters that may have been sent to France would only have prolonged the inevitable fall of Britain's ally, which finally came in mid-June.

Meantime, with the British and French line cut, German advance troops and armour pushed through to the Channel coast near Boulogne to begin the threat on Calais. Surrounded on all sides, the British Expeditionary Force in the north was pushed into a pocket around the seaside town and port of Dunkirk. By the evening of 24 May, German Panzer units were just 15 miles from the town where they were halted by Hitler's express order. Unwilling to have his armour travel over the soft sandy soil around Dunkirk, and wanting to save his tanks for the final battle with France to the south and west, the Führer's order to halt saved the BEF.

Operation Dynamo – the evacuation of as many British and foreign troops from Dunkirk as was possible over the next few days – was put into action on the 26th. The hope had been to extricate something like 45,000 troops, but the miracle of Dunkirk permitted 338,226 Allied soldiers to be returned to England. Göring, Hitler's Luftwaffe chief, had promised to destroy the troops remaining in Dunkirk with his air force, thereby saving the tanks and German troops a bloody land battle. They failed in this impossible task and good weather and the 'little ships' saved the situation. What Dunkirk gave to Fighter Command was its first real clash with the German air arm.

Not that the fighting in France prior to and especially after 10 May had not seen RAF and German aircraft in action. Far from it, but the Dunkirk evacuation

Göering talked Hitler into letting his Luftwaffe blast the evacuating forces on the Dunkirk beaches. One of Hitler's first mistakes of the war was to agree.

Dunkirk 1940. Small ships ferry men out to a larger vessel, while a line of army trucks form a makeshift jetty into the sea. Abandoned vehicles litter the beach.

La Plage de Dunkerque: the debris of war, all that is left of the evacuating BEF.

Fighter Command flew scores of sorties over Dunkirk and the French coast. Here a Hurricane is rapidly rearmed for another sortie.

saw for the first time, RAF fighters in an offensive yet defensive action, for which none of the pilots had been trained.

Keith Park's 11 Group again bore the brunt of operations, for Dunkirk and the French coast were directly opposite south-east England. If Dowding was worried about his lack of total defensive forces, Park had similar if reduced problems, for at no time during the nine days of Operation Dynamo was he to have more than 19 squadrons under his control. That meant in total 228 Spitfires and Hurricanes if, each squadron had its full operational number of twelve fighters available. Often of course, they did not. Battle damage and casualties meant that squadrons might take off with anything from eight to eleven fighters.

Even if Park had 228 all the time, it was impossible to cover the whole area of the evacuation for every moment of daylight. He had to cover the ships going to and from France, defend the beaches from attack by German bombers, help protect RAF bombers making attacks on the enemy troops edging forward around the perimeter of the town, and send fighters inland to engage German aircraft on their way to the battle zone. Unlike the army or navy, Park had a third dimension in which to fight, height above the battle. To patrol too high

would let the bombers and dive bombers have a free hand in attacking ships and the beaches. Too low and he would miss the higher flying bombers, be subjected to flak from around Dunkirk, and run the risk of attack by enemy fighters from above.

The RAF fighter pilots now found themselves in a battle anything from 40 to 60 miles from their bases, flying across open water, out of range of their radio connections with base, and fighting an aggressive enemy for the first time, who had the scent of victory in its nostrils.

It is a well-known fact that whatever training or belief in one's practised battle tactics are, they can only be proved or disproved in actual combat. The RAF's tactics were now to be put to the test.

Flying in four sections of three, in lovely vic formations, the RAF fighter squadrons started to fly out in just squadron strength to meet and engage the enemy. The pilots were about to discover just how wrong and antiquated their vic formations were. The RAF had been flying sectional vics for many years, with the twelve aircraft of a squadron flying in four vics to make a nice pattern. That was the problem – it looked nice, especially at air shows. The theory behind the close vics was that the leader, whilst climbing, often through cloud which usually dominated the British weather, could count on his two well tucked-in wingmen, staying with him when they finally broke into the sunshine above. When all four vics emerged into the sunlight, the squadron could quickly form up and not spend time in trying to locate stragglers. In some of the pre-war air displays, the three aeroplanes sometimes were tied together in order to show how well the two wingmen stayed close to the leader. Spectacular, but not relevant to combat situations.

This dominance of the close vic prevailed with the monoplanes and with the increased speeds, made it essential that the two wingmen keep a close eye on their leader to avoid collisions. In a battle situation, therefore, only four of the twelve pilots would really be searching the sky for hostile aircraft, while the other eight, although shooting glances to the left or right, were more concerned with staying in formation. Over Dunkirk, these tactics soon showed their weakness, when Me109s came diving down from the sun to slice through the nice, neat vics.

For most of the squadron and flight commanders, the latter of a slightly older generation, who had trained and kept by the book, and were leading their units into action for the first time, a rude awakening was in store. There were no nice fat bombers lumbering along waiting to be shot down in nice Number One Attacks, etc., but fast-

Flying Officer Bryan Wicks of 56 Squadron, fought in France and, after being shot down, escaped into Dunkirk and managed to return to England. He was killed over Malta in 1942.

jinking bombers, or dive-bombers, with very hostile and agile fighters with them. There was no lining up to have a go, one fighter after another. It was all sudden rushes, with one's head swivelling round watching for the 109s which always seemed to be around.

Allan Wright, flying with 92 Squadron, recalls:

Dunkirk, when one thinks of it now, was a terrific shock to the system. We had only received our Spitfires in March, were declared operational in May and went to Northolt. We did a flew scrambles from there, climbing up to vast heights to chase some recce aircraft, then it was Dunkirk.

We flew to Duxford, then straight over and I was just flying along and saw some aeroplanes go by. I thought they looked different and to myself said, Oh, they look like 109s! Then someone yelled out '109s!' and everyone disappeared. I remembered thinking the 109s looked very pretty, then flew back to base.

Afterwards I realised I'd been pretty lucky for my best friend had been shot down, and the CO was taken prisoner after our next patrol, so one soon learnt.

Bob Stanford Tuck joined us just before Dunkirk and he could certainly put a Spitfire through its paces. I remember once seeing him come screaming down and pull out about 300 feet and I just couldn't imagine being able to stand the 'G' he was obviously pulling.

Casualties were inflicted on the Germans, but the losses were high. On the first day of Operation Dynamo, the RAF lost 11 fighters shot down or force-landed. Three pilots were killed, two wounded and another taken prisoner. One squadron commander was amongst the missing. The next day 20 fighters were lost, with one squadron commander dead and four flight commanders shot down. And so it went on.

Whatever the training, one had to survive the first clashes with the enemy to gain the experience to remain alive in high speed combat. The commanders at Air Ministry or at Command, might have survived their war of 1914-18, but things happened so much faster now. Pilot Officer R. N. H. Courtney, flying a Hurricane with 151 Squadron, was in action for the first time over Dunkirk:

Over the town we saw a number of Me109s well above us. Ken Newton asked the CO if we could break away to engage them and we climbed up towards them. I was about to attack one when I was shot down by another behind me which I had not seen. The Hurricane was badly damaged and I was wounded in the back of the neck and in the right leg. It was difficult to see because of the glycol and petrol which began spraying into the cockpit and eventually I had to bale out. I was picked up by a corvette and eventually found myself in Ramsgate hospital.

Some of 54 Squadron who saw action over Dunkirk. L to R seated: Flight Lieutenant James 'Prof' Leathart, Flying Officer A. W. A. Bayne, Flight Lieutenant M. C. Pearson; Standing: Flying Officer Colin Gray, Pilot Officer Bob Blake, Pilot Officer George Gribble. Max Pearson was killed over Dunkirk on 27 May and Gribble force-landed on the beaches on the 25th but got back by boat.

The Me109s were now operating from captured French airfields not far from the battle area and could put up scores of fighters, whereas the RAF fighters came to the area in penny-packages in order to give the maximum amount of cover. Therefore they were usually outnumbered and had the additional worry of having to retain sufficient fuel to return to England. For most of the evacuation, a pilot could always force land on the beaches at or near Dunkirk, but that would mean having to try and get on a ship back to England. Many did just that, but the aircraft was lost the moment it touched down, on wheels or belly.

In order to try to combat the numbers of 109s, Fighter Command began to send out squadrons in 'wings' of two, or perhaps three squadrons, but again there were difficulties. There had simply been no training in multi-squadron flying and so absolutely none in multi-squadron combat techniques. The late Humphrey Edwardes-Jones, then commanding 213 Squadron, once told me:

Apart from the ludicrous situation of nobody knowing how the other squadrons in the 'wing' operated, there had been no training in flying such wing formations. It was a case of trying to learn as we went along. Even so, it was usual, once we had flown across the Channel as a wing to split up and patrol independently. Some of the squadrons could not even cloud-climb, and when forced to do so were invariably in loose formation.

Each squadron took it in turn to lead the 'wing' but with little or no organisation or guidance on how to operate, it became a bit of a shambles. I once found, for instance, that due to losses in one squadron, a flying officer was leading his squadron, and therefore, the wing! It seemed that it was just a case of it being that squadron's turn to lead and nobody in authority had checked to see if they had a suitable leader. I soon changed that!

We were also pretty busy. I was usually up before 4 am each day, sometimes flying as many as four patrols. Our day ended at dusk but with debriefing, a decent meal, checking on my squadron's serviceability for the next day, etc., it was usually about midnight before I got to bed.

Using two or three squadrons at a time may have helped in the numbers game, or at least should have, but the main result was that Park could not put up fighters all

Convoy battle. First phase in the Battle of Britain was attacking British shipping in the English Channel, July 1940.

the time. There were, therefore, gaps in the air cover, and the Germans seemed to learn quickly. Obviously observers behind Dunkirk could see when the sky appeared relatively clear of the RAF, which was when it seemed the German dive-bombers came in.

Another problem was that often the RAF fighter squadrons could not talk to each other, as their radios carried different frequencies. Even with the numbers and if the 'wing' had stayed together, the radar picture at these distances from southern England, did not give an accurate picture, and with radio range being at the limit, even if a plot of a large enemy formation could be seen, a warning might not be picked up.

At this stage of the war, squadrons always tried to operate as a twelve-man formation (that's how they had been trained!) and so if one squadron was down to one or two below that magic number, it would borrow pilots and aircraft from the other squadron or squadrons sharing their base. Thus they flew as composite squadrons, for later the other squadron too would borrow a pilot or two from the first squadron. This was also a problem, for the pilots were not familiar with the other unit's way of doing things.

Replacements of battle losses did little to help initially. To replace a lost pilot was not difficult, but the new pilot would now be coming from an OTU or pilot pool, and therefore have no squadron experience at all.

There could be no question of just sitting him in a Spitfire or Hurricane and sending him out with the next patrol just in order to make the number up. He would be deemed non-operational for several days usually, until his flight commander, having had him 'worked out' by another pilot, and managed a few more 'hours on type' to be recorded in his flying log book, thought he was ready.

Replacement aircraft, too, were not in short supply, but it took at least 24 hours if not more, to make the new aeroplane operationally ready. The ground crews had to check it over, harmonise the guns, fit certain items of equipment which the fitters and riggers would find hanging up inside the airframe. The radio needed to be checked out and correctly crystallised. There was also the paper work. 11 Group's aircraft usually came via No.41 Maintenance Group, but they had to receive demands, in triplicate, before a fighter could be assigned. Then a ferry pilot had to fly it to the squadron's base.

Spitfire aircraft had never been sent to France, Dowding had been emphatic on that, and during the evacuation, Spitfire pilots were ordered not to overfly the French coast. Some did so in the heat of combat, but Dowding did not wish any of his Spitfires to fall into enemy hands. Thus the Hurricanes took the brunt of the casualties.

Some squadrons were pulled out of the battle, to be

replaced by others, either because of casualties or the unit's pilots, who may have been fighting over France prior to Dunkirk, needed a break. In all, 31 fighter squadrons passed through Park's 11 Group during the period of the evacuation, but the best average was just 16 for any one day, so the earlier mentioned available figure of 228 was in reality reduced to a possible maximum of just 192.

Dunkirk officially ended on 3 June. Fighting continued, to the south and west, until France finally capitulated on 21 June. There were still a handful of RAF fighter squadrons in France, being steadily forced back until the remnants either flew their Hurricanes back to England, or the aircraftless pilots and their ground personnel, found a ship to bring them home.

The fighting from 10 May to 3 June cost the RAF the now accepted figure of 432 Hurricanes and Spitfires. To put this another way, this was the equivalent of some 20 squadrons! So it was essential that Dowding had stopped the flow of fighters into the bottomless pit that had been the Battle of France.

Statistics can make for dull reading, but figures here, to understand fully the problems facing Dowding and his Command are of interest. During the Dunkirk evacuation, the RAF flew 3,561 sorties of which 2,739 were by Fighter Command. An official figure of 106 RAF aircraft were lost during those nine days (26 May–3 June), although it is almost impossible to reconcile those figures today. Three hundred and ninety Luftwaffe aircraft were claimed shot down, later reduced by Park to a possible 258, with 119 probables and damaged. Captured documents after the war would indicate a figure of 132, including those claimed and shot down by the Royal Navy.

Fighter Command lost 52 pilots killed, five Defiant gunners killed, eight pilots captured and 12 pilots and air gunners wounded. Of these, three squadron commanders and six flight commanders had been killed, one of each taken prisoner, with more than a dozen section leaders and senior NCO pilots lost. More fortunate were 39 pilots who had either baled out over the sea or force-landed in France, being rescued and brought home.

Taken as a mini-campaign, Dunkirk was a victory, not only for the Army in terms of survival, but for the Navy in its rescue mission and the RAF for its aerial defence of the beaches and convoys. The old army remark, 'Where was the RAF?', is now largely understood to be false. If Fighter Command had not been there, then most of the rescued would have ended up in prisoner of war camps.

England Alone

With the fall of France and when the last Allied soldier was taken from that ill-fated country and brought home, Britain was alone. To many it was a depressing and deeply shocking feeling. To others it was a moment of realisation that, while alone, we would fight on regardless. Others felt we would be better now, fighting by ourselves with nobody else to worry about. Dowding could only look at his recent losses, the smallness of his Command, and hope to providence that his fighter pilots could turn the scale of battle in Britain's favour.

On 10 June, with France still in the fight – just – Fighter Command's order of battle read like this:

In France: Hurricane squadrons, 5 (two as servicing units)

In Britain: Hurricane squadrons, 19 (operational, 17)
Spitfire squadrons, 22 (operational, 19)
Defiant squadrons, 2 (operational, 2)

Day fighters:

Production:	April	May
Hurricanes	169	240
Spitfires	60	64
Defiants	17	22
Reserves:	7 June	9 June
Hurricanes	247	133
Spitfires	21	6
Defiants	12	11

Pilots from Operational Training Units in June were 71, of whom 13 were posted to squadrons by 5 June. July output will be 120.

With fighting continuing in France until 21 June, Britain was given some breathing space before Hitler turned his attention to any major hostilities against her. Even at this stage, Hitler hoped, if not expected, Britain to sue for peace, once France had fallen. And why not? With all of Europe in German hands, Britain was totally alone with little prospect of immediate help from any of her Commonwealth partners.

A large proportion of her army may have been spirited away from Dunkirk, but most if not all of its heavy equipment had had to be left behind. War materials and food to keep the island race going would have to be brought in by sea, and with all the French ports now under German control, the deadly submarines of the German Navy would make that task a major one. But as always, the German leadership underestimated the British doggedness.

Fighter Command, during late June and early July, reformed its war-weary squadrons from France, replaced battle casualties from both France and Dunkirk, trained its new pilots with a real urgency and awaited Hitler's next move. This must surely be an air assault as a prelude to invasion of southern England.

Just as in September 1939, the fighter pilots were keen to get on with it, especially the young replacements, as yet untried. The older hands had faced the Messerschmitts, Heinkels, Dornier and Junkers, and while they had individually survived so far, many of their comrades had perished in France or above the beaches. They now faced the prospect of a long battle with an enemy bomber force which now had its fighters available for escort duty. If the pilots hadn't at first realised the problem this gave them over Dunkirk, Command certainly knew that this would be a major issue in the coming conflict.

Testing Skirmishes

As July began, so too did German reconnaissance flights over the Channel and over the coastal ports. The skirmishes began above the green-grey waters, with German bombers trying to sink coastal shipping, and test out the RAF defences. Some of the battles were bitter with losses on both sides, but the RAF could ill-afford the losses at this stage. Perhaps it would have been better to call in all coastal shipping in the Channel rather than expose it to attack, but then the British don't think that way. It was the English Channel and nobody was going to stop us using it, was probably the thought.

The pilots lost over the Channel in July and early August could possibly have been avoided but they weren't. So finally, with the August sunshine bathing southern England in a glorious summer, Britain's finest hour was about to begin.

CHAPTER 9

Air Battle Over England

SO MUCH HAS been written on the Battle of Britain that there seems little point in going over it in much detail. For Fighter Command it was its greatest battle and the pilots who fought it have found their niche in the history of the war as well as their place in the history of the twentieth century.

As Churchill was to immortalise them in the House of Commons in his perhaps, most famous speech, they became 'The Few'. Just how few is easy to state but difficult to imagine. At 9 am on the morning of 2 July 1940, Dowding had the following numbers in his three main Groups:

	Spitfires		Hurricanes		Defiants		Blenheim IFs	
	Sqds	a/c	Sqds	a/c	Sqds	a/c	Sqds	a/c
11 Gp	9	107	13	142	–	–	4	38
12 Gp	5	60	6	72	1	12	2	20
13 Gp	6	84	4	58	1	13	1	12
Totals:	20	251	23	272	2	25	7	70

Just twelve days later, on the 14th, the table showed:

10 Gp	2	29	2	26	–	–	–	–
11 Gp	7	79	12	134	1	12	3	30
12 Gp	5	60	6	76	1	12	2	18
13 Gp	5	65	5	80	–	–	1	16
Totals:	19	233	25	316	2	24	6	64

On 24 July, with the full might of the battle about to begin, Dowding had a figure of just 996 operationally serviceable fighter aircraft of all types, but with just 603 available for operations. When he saw the disparity in these figures, the Secretary of State found it difficult to understand why more aircraft were not available for operations. Fighter Command HQ had to explain that an aircraft without pilot or crew could not be regarded as available for operations and that the limiting factor was trained pilots.

The Establishment as laid down for Spitfire and Hurricane pilots was 1,248, whereas at this date Fighter Command had only 1,132, i.e. short by 116. Of the 1,132, 159 had not yet reached full operational standard, so the true figure was 973. In this case the operationally fit aircraft, it could be argued, was the same: 973.

Another answer to the discrepancy lies in number returns. Each squadron, despite its complement of aircraft, would state that it had, where this was true, 12 operationally fit aircraft. i.e. the usual number required for a squadron patrol/sortie, each manned by a pilot whom the squadron commander assessed as being combat ready. So that if he had 14 aircraft ready, he would still only send in a return stating 12 (whether he had 14 operationally fit pilots or not). If on the other hand he only had ten operationally fit aircraft, even if he had 14 fit pilots, the return would still only show ten.

On 27 July, for instance, squadron returns showed that 660 aircraft were immediately available for Ops, as against 966 serviceable. The discrepancy, therefore, of 306, equalled ten non-operational squadrons of about 120 aircraft, and 54 operational squadrons having returned a figure of 12 aircraft each = 648. A few squadrons had in fact stated a few above 12 (13 or 14) which accounted for the other 18. In these squadrons there were just under 850 aircraft. Another factor was that each squadron would have pilots on leave or sick (usually leave would be ten days in each three-month period).

Because of the disparity of these return figures, squadrons had to give actual figures with effect from 15 August, i.e. their basic 12 plus all other aircraft serviceable, whether they had pilots to fly them or not.

When it started, the main weight of the German assault came from the south and south-east. The Luftwaffe had

Spitfire I being rearmed and made ready for the next sortie. Note the gun patches have yet to be stuck over the open gun ports in the wings.

now taken over most of the former French Air Force aerodromes and landing strips, and their obvious first target would be to destroy the RAF fighter force in order to mount a successful invasion. Air supremacy over a large area of southern Britain had to be a first prerequisite for such a bold step.

Following the Channel battles of July, the German's main air assault began on 8 August, directed against Fighter Command and especially its fighter airfields. As we now know, these assaults so very nearly achieved their aim and although no fighter station was put out of action totally and probably would not have done, it was a desperate situation. On several occasions, returning fighters had to be diverted to nearby airfields when their own were littered with debris, unexploded bombs or holed runways and landing fields.

The adversary: the Me109E.

Aircraft, and personnel too, were hit on the ground, buildings, hangars and maintenance workshops put out of action, but the airfield personnel put up superhuman efforts to clear the airfield and fill in bomb holes within the shortest space of time in order to get their base fully operational once more.

Finally, at the start of September, a lost German bomber dropped his bombs on the outskirts of London, and Churchill reacted to this by sending Bomber Command to attack Berlin. This in turn caused Hitler to direct Göering to bomb London, and force the British people into submission. It was hard luck on the city and its inhabitants but it took the pressure from (mainly) Park's 11 Group fighter airfields which undoubtedly cost the Luftwaffe the battle.

The final phase of the day battle came in October to December, when the weather turned wintry, curtailing bomber operations. Now the Me109 and Me110 fighters began to come over carrying bombs to drop almost indiscriminately on London or other targets. The damage they could inflict was minimal, but these fighter-bomber sorties needed to be engaged and in that deadly winter sky, casualties to both sides were again heavy. After that, the night blitz began in earnest, continuing to May 1941.

So Few

No.11 Group bore the brunt of the Battle of Britain. Park had to juggle his few fighter squadrons in order to give the maximum cover and to inflict the maximum damage with the minimum hurt. Radar by this time had become the great ally, and on most occasions, much to the German's annoyance and surprise, they usually found the RAF fighters waiting for them. Only on a relative few occasions were they able to bounce climbing Hurricanes or Spitfires.

Each sector station was given its targets by Command, who would in turn 'scramble' the best situated squadrons to take off and engage. In the beginning, squadrons generally flew in single units, so that it was not uncommon for 12 fighters to be sent up against 50 plus enemy aircraft or even more. As the battle progressed, so controllers, wherever possible, would try to match a raid with two squadrons, perhaps even three if they were lucky, but it was not often achieved.

For the controllers, who were themselves still learning their trade in the light of real situations, it meant judging precisely the right moment to send up their fighters. Too soon and they would have to land and refuel before engaging. Too late and they would find themselves underneath the raiders – and the fighters!

If at all possible, they would try to arrange it so that a Spitfire squadron would be above a Hurricane unit to engage the Me109s, enabling the Hurricanes to have

a crack at the bombers, but again circumstances, such as weather, cloud, wrongly-estimated heights, or free-ranging Me109s, might not make this achievable. The Germans too would launch feint raids which would turn back, so that the RAF defenders would have to land to refuel, thus being still on the ground when the real raid approached.

It took a while for it to be appreciated that these free-ranging Me109 formations were of no danger in themselves, and when identified either by radar or by the fighter squadrons, Park gave orders for them not to be attacked, for this generally cost the defenders a fighter or two, even if a couple of 109s were brought down. The Germans might think this good arithmetic, but the RAF could not afford it.

A further look at the numbers, just for 11 Group, as at 17 August, makes interesting reading:

Airfield	Sqdns	Available Hurricanes	Available Spitfires	Remarks
Tangmere	43	12		
Tangmere West	601	11		
Hampnett	602		10	
Kenley	64		9	
Kenley	615	9		3 sections
Croydon	111	8		
Hawkinge	615	3		1 section
Hawkinge	610		12	
Biggin Hill	32	12		
Gravesend	501	7		
Hornchurch	266		5	A Flt only

The targets: formation of He111 bombers over England.

Airfield	Sqdns	Available Hurricanes	Available Spitfires	Remarks
Hornchurch	54		7	B Flt only
Hornchurch	600			6 Blenheims
Rochford	56	12		
Manston	65		7	A Flt only
North				
Weald	25(B Flt)			3 Blenheims
North				
Weald	151	12		
Debden	257	12		
Martlesham	25(A Flt)			4 Blenheims
Martlesham	85	12		
Martlesham	17	12		
Northolt	1	10		
Northolt	1(RCAF)			forming
Northolt	303			forming
Tangmere	FIU			
Totals:		132	50	13 Blenheims

Keith Park could, of course, call on the neighbouring Groups, Nos.10 and 12, for support, and he often did. No.10 Group had just eight squadrons plus one Blenheim unit and another with Gladiators. Quintin-Brand, of course, had to use his squadrons to cover the whole of the south-west, including Bristol and Exeter, so could generally only spare squadrons based near to 11 Group's western border.

Leigh-Mallory had 11 squadrons, plus two Blenheim and one Defiant unit. The Blenheims, of course, were not used in day fighting in any of the Groups, and after Dunkirk, where they had an initial success, the Defiants too had been pulled out of day operations. 12 Group was working on the Big Wing theory, which over the last few years has been the cause of much speculation about the tactics that it employed. The leading light behind the Big Wing was the famous legless pilot, Squadron Leader Douglas Bader, CO of 242 Squadron. Bader, supported by his AOC, was advocating the use of several squadrons, three and sometimes five, which would form up north of the Thames, gain height to be above any raiding force, then fly south to engage the enemy in force.

This was fine in theory, and occasionally it worked, but in the main it took too long to form up, climb and head south, so that by the time it got there, the raid was probably on its way back home, and/or had been broken up by the 11 Group squadrons.

Park could not afford the luxury of forming up two or three squadrons. His tactics was to hit as many raids as possible as soon as possible. By attacking and split-ting up the large German formations, he hoped to dilute the number of bombs hitting a target, his airfields, and

once split up raiders became easier prey for his fighters.

In the main, therefore, each squadron was, in its own way, left to fight the battle as it saw fit, or as the squadron commander dictated. Some of the squadrons were still being led by senior commanders who continued to fly as per the book, while other units, who were between COs, or who had more far-thinking flight com-manders, were quickly revamping the old formations and tactics in the light of present circumstances. It is now accepted that Park handled his squadrons extremely well given the difficult circumstances that he faced.

The 12 Group Wing, of course, took time to form up. Even if it was called upon early enough the time element was always crucial. The theory was sound but this time element was usually against it. By the time the three or five squadrons had gained height and formed up in order to head into 11 Group's battle area, the Germans had invariably bombed, been attacked by Park's own fighters, and were on their way home again. This was no use to Park and he made no bones about it, which caused some acrimony between the two group commanders, which perhaps Dowding should have sorted out better than he did.

The suggestion has even been made that the com-mander of 12 Group, by insisting on the Big Wing theory and thus delaying his squadrons getting into action, reduced the number of enemy aircraft that might have been destroyed had he sent his fighters into the battle straightaway. By the same token, 11 Group's casualties might have been lessened. At the time it was thought that the Wing's kill-to-loss ratio was proving a point, but the claims were over-optimistic and the losses small because by the time the Wing got into action, the 109 pilots were short of fuel and heading for home.

What Leigh-Mallory did not know, until much later, was that Dowding and Park were among the very few people to know of the Ultra intelligence data (breaking of the German 'Enigma' code) which on occasion gave them an idea of the enemy's intentions. By late September it was through information from Ultra that Churchill knew that Hitler's invasion plans had been called off, when it became clear that the special inva-sion HQ was being disbanded.

By and large the old RAF attack formations were gone, and some squadrons were beginning to see the dangers of the old sections in vic. They had seen the German fighters were usually in twos or fours, and some RAF leaders were beginning to fly in similar ways. There was also a strong train of thought that the most effective way of breaking up a close formation of German bombers was to attack from head-on rather than from the stern. The whole subject is large and complex but some men-tion here of some of the tactics is appropriate, as this theme will run throughout this book.

Waiting for the scramble. Roger Boulding, Henry Szczesny, Johnny Freeborn and H. M. 'Steve' Stephen of 74 Squadron.

Pilots of 43 Squadron during the Battle: L to R: Sergeant J. Arbuthnott, Sergeant R. Plenderleith, Sergeant H. J. L. Hallowes, Flying Officer J. C. Simpson, Squadron Leader P. W. Townsend, Pilot Officer H. C. Upton.

Squadron Leader Michael Crossley DSO DFC, 32 Squadron, claimed 22 enemy aircraft shot down in 1940.

Flight Lieutenant E. J. 'Jumbo' Gracie DFC, 56 Squadron in 1940. Later fought on Malta, but was killed in 1944 flying from the UK.

James Sanders, who was still with 615 Squadron following the Battle of France, where he had won the DFC, was in the thick of the action:

Attacking bombers on your own, or even just two of you, was, I felt always a very deadly thing to do as you caught all the crossfire, which would get you every time. So many pilots, intent on their attack, didn't realise the crossfire was so dangerous. The answer was to attack from the front. I used to expound this theory because, having practised it, I found that if we were to distract the leaders and break them up, the rest would not know what to do with their bombs.

We tried this in the Battle of Britain a number of times. We did it on a formation coming up from Selsey Bill towards Dorking. I was going down towards the leaders, while Tony Eyre and Keith Lofts covered me with an attack from the back. I think they claimed one each though my section didn't claim any, but I think 11 bombers came down. So one never knew if you'd hit them when shooting from head-on but you broke them up. Another thing, of course, was that the 109 escorts were always above and at the back, waiting for a Spit or Hurricane to attack from the rear, so an attack from the front thwarted them too.

Flying Officer Allan Wright, still flying Spitfires with 92 Squadron, would end the battle with the DFC. He could appreciate James Sanders' tactics but recalled it wasn't always that easy:

You could only make head-on attacks if you were vectored from the ground and then, considering the difficulties, you'd be extremely lucky. When a whole mass of aircraft is heading in, you've got to see them at least 10 miles away to be able to turn in, then you've got to be very accurate when the closing speed is something like 600 mph!

If the enemy formation makes a turn at all – even just two degrees – then everything is altered and the angle is increasing. Then again, seeing aircraft at a distance one isn't sure which way they are going, which slows up the decision factor.

As early as July 1940, the Air Fighting Development Unit (AFDU) at Northolt were advocating the use of head-on attacks when opportunity presented itself, as: (a) it would be most difficult for enemy fighters to interfere with the attack; (b) the enemy aircraft were very vulnerable from ahead, and short bursts of 2-3 seconds should be sufficient to destroy them; and (c) some successes had already been obtained with head-on attacks in individual combat.

James 'Prof' Leathart was CO of 54 Squadron in 1940, having fought over Dunkirk prior to the Battle of Britain. He had won the DSO for his rescue of the CO

Flight Lieutenant Frank Carey DFC* DFM, served with 43 Squadron in the Battle of Britain, later seeing action in Burma. One of the greatest exponents of the Hurricane.

of 74 Squadron from Calais in an unarmed Magister in May. He recalls:

I had joined 54 Squadron when it was equipped with Gladiators and almost daily we carried out No.1 and No.2 attacks, etc., and during summer camps we did have live practice with deflection shooting at drogues, albeit at much lower speeds than the Luftwaffe flew. We continued these standard attacks when we got Spitfires in 1939.

However, we never had time to do any live firing and I am sure that initially we allowed too little deflection against Me109s etc. But the battle over Dunkirk taught us a lot and how to fight the Battle of Britain. It was about this time that 'De Wilde' ammunition replaced the old tracer. Tracer gave us a false impression, but De Wilde gave a flash on impact so you could see your hits.

We in the 11 Group squadrons had to take on mostly the fighter escorts of 109s and 110s in the Battle, which were much more dangerous than fire from bombers' rear guns. We could have done with more help from 12 Group, whose mass wing took so long to form up, that the escorts had all gone home by the time they got on the scene of battle.

George Unwin and 19 Squadron had also cut their teeth over Dunkirk and were far more ready to react to the Battle over England, and quickly changed their tactics.

Our first trip over Dunkirk, Squadron Leader Steven-

son carried out a No.1 attack on several Ju87 dive bombers. Having to throttle back considerably because of the slow speed of the targets, we were sitting ducks for the 109s above. The outcome was the loss of all three of the leading section. That was the end of the Fighter Attacks 1, 2 and 3; from then on, especially during the Battle of Britain, we went in fast and out fast, although we continued to fly in vics of three aircraft until we realised that whenever we got on the tail of a 109, another of his mates would be behind. In other words, flying in pairs was the answer both from the protection angle and the ability for quick manoeuvring. A few more experiments gave birth to the finger four, i.e. two pairs and this formation was used from then on.

By late 1940, it had also been found that a successful harmonising of a fighter's guns on a point at 250 yards instead of the spread pattern of 400 yards was proving much better in action. Many of the successful pilots had already found this out for themselves. Air to air shooting was as much an art as anything else, and the false belief that because one was a fighter pilot one could automatically shoot well was becoming only too evident. The odd thing was there was very little training in air to air firing, nor had there been. George Unwin, who gained his share of success in the battle, winning the DFM and bar, remembers:

At our pre-war 'practice camp' usually at Sutton Bridge

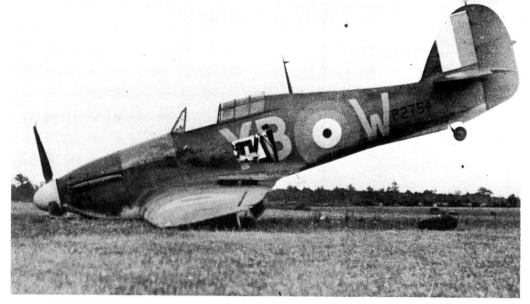

Above: *Hurricane of 17 Squadron in 1940, having had its undercarriage whipped off.*

Top right: *Flight Lieutenant Eric Lock DSP DFC*, 41 Squadron. Of his 26 victories, 24 were claimed during 1940.*

Right: *Two other high-scoring fighter pilots in 1940 were the New Zealand duo in 54 Squadron, Al Deere and Colin Gray. Both ended the war with the DSO DFC* (Gray getting a second bar) with scores of 21½ and 27½ respectively. Both became wing leaders.*

on the Wash, for two or three weeks each year, we fired off 100 rounds in each of two guns in a Gauntlet at a target towed at 100 mph. It didn't seem to be of any consequence whether or not you hit the drogue. No action, to my knowledge, was ever taken to improve any-one's shooting no matter how bad it was. For the rest of the year you didn't even fire your guns! One would have thought that being able to shoot would have been an essential qualification of a fighter pilot, but there it is!

Myles Duke-Woolley was now flying Hurricanes with 253 Squadron, having survived the Blenheim (see Chapter 12):

We soon went over to pairs after I joined 253 and we really started to develop this. I was finally operating in pairs above 30,000 feet which in Hurricanes was abso-lutely unheard of. But I got them up there and dived them 2,000 feet, which put on 20 mph. Once you'd got the tail up and in a correct flying attitude, you could hold the speed and at 30,000 we were cruising at much the same speed as the Spitfires. We bounced the odd German fighter formation up there.

That wasn't all he achieved. Myles tells of the occasion he found himself above the 12 Group Big Wing:

In late September 1940 there was an argument in progress about the method of re-enforcing 11 Group from 12 Group. Leigh-Mallory was in favour of large formations, Park of 11 Group, favoured the small mobile

formations. Both were constantly looking for ammu-nition to support their arguments.

Very often in those days, liaison between groups was not watertight and one never knew before take-off that the 12 Group 'Balbo' would be in the area. The inci-dent I remember was when I was leading 253 on a stand-ing patrol over Canterbury. Normally these patrols were at about 15,000 feet but I seized the opportunity for practice and we were at 28,000 feet in our new formation.

Huns were reported to be approaching our area but no more precise information was given about direction, height or numbers. We accordingly increased height to 31,000 feet and seeing nothing to the east and south, I gazed north, almost immediately seeing a black mass bearing down from that direction. I soon recognised them as the 12 Group Balbo but they looked so deter-mined that I felt that they might lead us to something interesting, so turned in behind them as some sort of involuntary top cover. Feeling friendly disposed myself towards them I never thought they would mistake us for a German formation but I forgot to realise that our formation was still unpublished, that Hurricanes just didn't operate at 30,000 and the 109 did look rather like a Hurricane from certain angles.

The Balbo, of course, did mistake us and thought they were about to be bounced, so they orbited. I thought they were orbiting to intercept 'my' raid and orbited too. When the Balbo straightened out to climb – 'engage' – me, I naturally followed suit. They equally naturally had

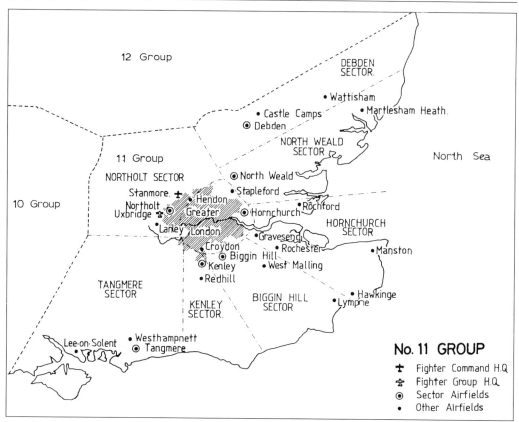

12 Group

DEBDEN
SECTOR.

• Wattisham

• Castle Camps   • Martlesham Heath.

◉ Debden

NORTH WEALD
SECTOR

North Sea

11 Group

NORTHOLT SECTOR

Stanmore. ✝   ◉ North Weald
                          • Stapleford
10 Group   • Hendon
Northolt   ◉ Rochford
Uxbridge ⚜ ◉ Greater   ◉ Hornchurch
          • Lanley London   HORNCHURCH
                  • Gravesend   SECTOR
                • Croydon • Rochester   • Manston
          ◉ • Biggin Hill
          ◉ Kenley   • West Malling
          • Redhill
TANGMERE   BIGGIN HILL   • Hawkinge
SECTOR   KENLEY   SECTOR   • Lympne
                  SECTOR.

Lee-on-Solent • Westhampnett
          ◉ Tangmere

No. 11 GROUP

✝   Fighter Command H.Q
⚜   Fighter Group H.Q
◉   Sector Airfields
•   Other Airfields

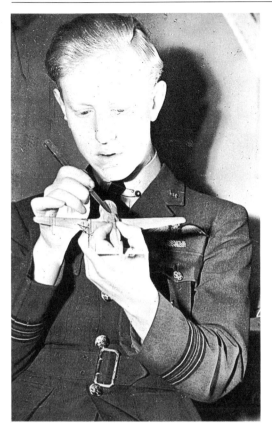

no intention of climbing up on a straight course to be bounced, thus for some minutes there was a complete stalemate until the Balbo started to get short of fuel and retired in good order to the north, whilst we returned to the coast.

About a fortnight later I read a letter from 11 Group, in caustic terms, analysing the operation of the Balbo. I remember about eight of its trips were mentioned, the main point stressed being the comparatively short effective time on patrol. With some horror I then saw one trip described and the remarks in roughly these words:

Below left: *Two pilots of 74 Squadron who claimed Biggin Hill's 600th victory of the war. Flight Lieutenant J. C. Mungo-Park* DFC*, *who was killed in 1941 and Flying Officer H. M. Stephen* DSO DFC, *who claimed 22½ victories in 1940.*

Left: *James 'Ginger' Lacey* DFM* *shot down 23 German aircraft in 1940, 17 of them in the Battle of Britain. He went on to claim a total of 28 during the war.*

Below: *Pilots of 504 Squadron. L to R: Flying Officer P. T. Parsons, Flying Officer M. E. A. Royce, Sergeant C. Haw, Sergeant F. Haywood, inspecting trophies from a German raider. Note another bullet-riddled trophy over the door.*

Above: *Flying Officer M. Royce, Sergeant C. Haw, Flight Lieutenant T. Rook and Squadron Leader John Sample, 504 Squadron, 1940.*

Below: *Flying Officer 'Scruffy' Royce* DFC*, 504 Squadron, talking to his rigger and fitter, RAF Filton, 1940. He retired as a wing commander.*

Right: *504 Squadron 'Scramble'! Pilot Officer H. N. Hunt, Flying Officer M. Royce, Flight Lieutenant A. H. Rook, Pilot Officer P. T. Parsons, Sergeant C. Haw, Sergeant 'Chan' Haywood. Tony Rook, Charlton Haw and Haywood later served in Russia.*

'. . . six squadrons attempted to patrol for 50 minutes in Canterbury area but mistook an 11 Group squadron, also on patrol, for German aircraft and returned in disorder to their bases!'

The story got around Kenley and was received with huge delight by ground crews as well as pilots. I remember feeling myself that my innocuous patrol report could link me with the 11 Group report and that if any fur was flying I was possibly going to be in the middle somewhere!

Rest and Recuperation

In order to keep his whole force intact, despite casualties and fatigue, Dowding tried to ensure that squadrons were frequently taken out of the front line and sent north for a break. Often the squadrons first to go were those who had suffered severe losses, or those who had, in addition, been in the south longer, perhaps having flown since Dunkirk in 11 Group actions.

As the battle progressed, he developed his idea of 'C' Squadrons, those which he sent north to rest, and there he had new pilots assigned to these units so that the few experienced pilots which remained could impart training and knowledge to them. These new pilots would then be posted down to other units in the south as replacements. The Class 'A' Squadrons were those in the battle area fed by the Class 'C' units.

This came into effect on 8 September, continuing until 1 December, when more OTUs were formed, although some training still needed to be undertaken at squadron level. 'B' Squadrons were those in the other groups, who were fully operational but less active due to their location.

The experienced pilots in the 'C' Squadrons continued to maintain an operational stance, in case hostile aircraft came into their area, but in the main the squadrons were effectively non-operational as a unit. As an indication of the numbers involved, on 1 November 1940, there were 21, wholly or in part, Class 'C' Squadrons situated in 9, 10, 12 and 13 Groups. Of the total of 550 pilots on strength, 230 were deemed as operational if the need arose, while 320 were non-operational and under training.

At the height of the battle, the OTU courses were of two weeks duration with final training on the 'C' Class units. At the beginning of November, with the slackening of the air fighting, the OTU courses were increased to four weeks.

CHAPTER 10

Lessons from the Battle

IN 1950, MYLES Duke-Woolley was a wing commander serving at RAF Acklington. He was asked by Air Commodore Theodore McEvoy, a wartime commander, with, amongst other things, 2nd Tactical Air Force, to write up his experiences in air fighting during 1940. 'Duke' wrote:

No. 253 Squadron had, on average, 17 pilots on strength and we always tried to have only 13 on the station; thus four were nearly always away at a time, on 24 or 36-hours leave pass. Squadron and flight commanders took time off when their personal aircraft were due for periodical servicing, either a 30-hour inspection or upon being perforated by a careless German! Thus, for example, I usually got a 24/36-hour stand-down every two or three weeks, during which time the usual pastime was to sleep for 18 hours to freshen up.

On normal days, the batman used to call me at 0445 hours and had strict standing instructions to call me again at 0450 and remove the bedclothes! A quick wash and breakfast followed. I never can eat so early in the morning but found from experience that this was the only meal before dinner, one could count on getting. So one ate heartily, although unenthusiastically.

We got to dispersal at about 5.30, varying of course with the time of first light. The dispersal was on the east side of Kenley airfield, outside the peri-track, south of the NE/SW runway and on the grass. 501 Squadron was dispersed around the north of the airfield. The ground crews on early morning readiness slept in the shelters at the back of the blast pens and hardly ever did we have less than 14 Hurricanes serviceable for first light.

Often the first sirens would go about six o'clock, usually for a recce aircraft and sometimes a section would be sent off. During October, usually all sorties except for standing patrols, were by section, to chase single bombers using cloud cover but before that time arrived, most sorties were by one or two squadrons, thus our first scramble was either a squadron, solo or as a

Wing, with 501 or 605 Squadron. With 605 we always used the same tactics and gained height on a westerly heading, turning back over Guildford, roughly at about 12,000 feet, thereby getting our height off to the flank of any incoming raid. The ground controllers in those early days, usually failed to appreciate the paramount values to us of height and background, trying invariably to make us gain height to the south. We had learned this lesson, however, by bitter draughts of unpalatable medicine and resolutely held to our tactics.

We would be down again by almost eight o'clock and the armourers would be on the wings before one stopped taxying, with belts of ·303 festooned round their necks. They used to get at it with a magnificent will. My own crew never failed to re-arm and refuel me within six or seven minutes at the outside and the whole squadron was turned round in about 15 minutes.

After our second landing we usually repaired to lunch but I never remember finishing it. Invariably I recall heaping my plate with all the nicest bits of meat and the best roast potatoes in view, settling myself down and off would go the Tannoy – '253 Squadron to Readiness!' I finally learned the trick of always taking the pie, if offered, and mashed potatoes, then making it back to dispersal with my plate and fork, eating as I walked or was driven in a car.

The other feature of those days sticks in my mind was the supply of new aircraft. I do not know the chain of command but the effect within the flight or squadron was extraordinary. If we had an aircraft shot up, say, at 1500 hours, we made no effort to repair it. We asked for a replacement and the machine was simultaneously notified as being fit or unfit to be flown away. The replacement would arrive by nightfall, usually about 1930 and the guns would be harmonised and the compass swung, that night. Although the aircraft would not be on dawn readiness operationally, it would be ready for an air test, complete with squadron lettering, by 0900.

In fact I recall in 253, the letter 'A' was extraordinarily unlucky and seven aircraft running in ten days were replaced until the flight sergeant begged me to ban it. We did and had no further replacements for nearly three months.

The squadron was commanded by Gerry Edge, who had been a flight commander in 605 Squadron. He was an Auxiliary and undoubtedly one of the unrecognised fighter wizards of the war. He pioneered the head-on attack and when he took over 253, it had lost four COs and flight commanders and a number of pilots in one week.

I would say the old Huns certainly tried hard but they did not like the head-on business. One could see the leader carrying on straight ahead but the followers wavering, drawing out sideways to the flanks and in some cases just plain leaving the formation. In one sortie with ten aircraft, we helped knock out 17 of a bunch of Dornier 17s. Not all were destroyed but left the formation in various stages of disrepair, some being destroyed and others winding up who knows where – we didn't stop to look, for they were closely escorted by 150-odd fighters.

Cannon Armament

RAF fighter pilots were well aware that the Messerschmitt pilots had a cannon firing through the propeller boss of their aircraft. The RAF, too, was no stranger to the knowledge that the cannon was a better destructive weapon than the Browning ·303 machine gun, but development of the cannon for the RAF had been slow and beset with mechanical problems.

At first the opinion was that a cannon firing an effective explosive shell would be too large and heavy to carry in a fighter, so work was not pursued with much enthusiasm. It was not until 1935 that the Air Staff took some notice of the Hispano-Suiza company's development of a 20mm cannon on the Continent. There was not, however, any great rush to equip the new monoplanes with cannon and it was not until the time of Munich that the Air Staff decided that the Hurricane and Spitfire could be so equipped.

However, early trials in both 1938 and 1939 showed a number of defects which caused gun stoppages and other problems. The first Spitfire to be fitted with two 20mm cannons was L1007, a machine which had initially been at the Aeroplane & Armament Experimental Establishment (A&AEE), since July 1939. This Spitfire was flown to Northolt in November 1939 and then allocated to 65 Squadron for trials under AFDU supervision (Air Fighting Development Unit).

As the few air actions that did occur in the early weeks of the war happened over Scotland, Pilot Officer G. V. Proudman was attached from 65 to 602 (City of Glasgow) Squadron in December 1939 for operational evaluation. He went with the suggestion that he fly as Number Two in a section, the section leader being the first to attack an enemy bomber in order to knock out the rear gunner, so Proudman could have an uninterrupted go with the cannon aircraft!

He had to wait till February 1940 before he could fire the cannons at an enemy aircraft. On the 22nd he took off with his CO, Squadron Leader A. D. Farquhar from RAF Drem and found a He111P just before midday off St Abb's Head. Farquhar attacked, wounding the rear gunner, then called Proudman in to do his bit. Proudman opened fire but then the guns jammed and stopped.

However, the Heinkel was going down, the pilot making a forced-landing at Coldingham. Seeing the crew scramble clear, taking their wounded gunner with them, Farquhar, fearful that the Germans would set fire to the bomber and destroy not only its secrets but any evidence of what cannon fire might have done, attempted to land nearby. Unhappily the Spitfire hit some soft mud and turned over; the Germans helped the squadron leader out but after they had set fire to their own aircraft.

On 2 March, Proudman had to make a wheels-up landing near Dunbar in L1007 and after repair it was sent to 19 Squadron when they began to experiment with cannon. George Proudman returned to 65 Squadron in May, only to be shot down by 109s over the Channel on 7 July.

No.19 Squadron received another cannon-armed Spitfire in June (R6261), followed later by others. There was no great improvement in reliability, with frequent stoppages. There was also a lack of spread' but that was due to the pilot's experience of the Dowding Spread with the eight ·303s. What was more of a disadvantage, with all the targets around, was that the cannon only gave a pilot six seconds of fire, as against 16-18 with the machine guns. However, what the pilots did like was the destructive power of the 20mm gun.

Dowding monitored 19 Squadron's experiences closely and was aware that some of the jamming problems resulted from the fact that to accommodate it in the thin wing of a Spitfire, the gun had to be mounted on its side. In August, another cannon-armed Spitfire arrived but this, in addition to two cannons, had four ·303 guns. This was an improvement in firing time, but the main armament continued to malfunction, so much so that the squadron complained that if they had purely ·303 armed aircraft they could be inflicting more damage on the Luftwaffe, and could they be permitted to re-equip totally with Spitfires with machine-guns only? This request was agreed to.

Meantime, 151 Squadron was undertaking the first cannon-armed Hurricane trials in combat conditions. Hurricane L1750, coded DZ-Z, was equipped with two

20mm guns. 11 Group Headquarters were asked to submit all details of combat with the Hurricane as soon as they came to hand. Flight Lieutenant R. L. Smith was assigned the aeroplane and with it he had a couple of inconclusive actions in July. Then on 13 August he destroyed a Dornier 17. Eagerly 11 Group Intelligence telephoned Dowding's new SASO, Air Vice Marshal Sir Douglas Evill, who immediately sent a memo to Dowding. He explained that Smith had blasted a Dornier which had immediately burst into flames. Rod Smith was asked to submit a report on the Hurricane, which he did at the end of August:

On 15 July Smith attacked a Do17 which was filtering through the tops of the cloud layer at 11,000 feet. Unfortunately the clouds were rather thick so he had difficulty in aiming his fire; he followed it in as it turned and dived. The last manoeuvre was made very rapidly – half rolled to the right, so he may have been out of control but cloud extended from 11,000 to 4,000 feet, so he was unable to contact it again.

On 11 July he was in a dog fight with Me109s. He attacked one from the beam which was being pursued by another Hurricane. He fired a short burst and broke away, narrowly missing the Hurricane.

When I looked again the 109 was going down in smoke but did not claim it as I thought the other Hurricane might have done the damage but I was so close I couldn't have missed completely.

13 August he led three sections to attack rear of three formations of 2-engined enemy aircraft east of Manston, 6.30, at 8,000 feet. Approached out of the sun having stalked them for 10 minutes. I opened fire at 300 yards from dead astern, firing into the mass of very tight Do17s. One immediately burst into flames in both engines and I transferred my aim to another which started smoking but the front panel of the windscreen was completely shattered, by, I believe, explosive cannon. This did not encourage me as I had glass in my eyes and everywhere else, so I returned to base. There were no stoppages.

The squadron had also received a four-cannon Hurricane in August, V7360, coded DZ-C. Rod Smith flew this on 22 August, and on the 24th fired two, one-second bursts at a diving 109 from 400 yards but claimed no hits. Smith found the four-gun fighter much heavier than one with eight ·303s and, like the two-gun model, suffered somewhat in manoeuvrability. The four-gun machine had the cannons fitted horizontally, but then the Hurricane had thicker wings. When Spitfires later had cannon, the guns were also placed right way up a slight 'hump' appearing on the top of the wing surface to accommodate it.

All these trials were useful in the event, for Fighter Command would, by 1941, be equipping all of its fighters with cannon armament, or a mixture of cannon and machine-guns. Some pilots were reluctant to change, notably Douglas Bader, but he was eventually converted.

The German Problems

While the general population of Britain imagined the Germans would be able to bomb towns and cities with impunity, Government and Air Ministry knew that this was untrue, at least, in daylight. German bombers (the Heinkel 111, Dornier 17 and 215, and the Junkers 88) were all medium bombers, not designed for attacking targets at long range. While they could and did reach targets such as Liverpool and Glasgow at night, they could not attack such targets in daylight except by flying in very cloudy conditions but only then as single raiders, not in a large formation. With long range targets too, their bomb load would have to be reduced so as to increase fuel levels.

The German bomber radius of action in daylight had to be limited by the distance their fighter escort could fly. While the Me109 was an excellent fighter, it was designed for close support fighting over land, ideal for such campaigns as Poland and France. With the battle against Britain, it had to fly over the Channel and back which limited its range, thereby curtailing its activities. The 109 pilots had just minutes in the combat zones and then, with one eye on the petrol gauges, had to fly and sometimes fight their way back across the Channel.

This became more of a problem in September when the attacks were switched to London, which stretched the 109 pilot's radius of action to the limit. Close escort to the bombers restricted the fighter pilot's main function of engaging RAF fighters. Having to keep station with the slower bomber speeds further restricted their activities as they had to burn up more fuel by continual throttle movements.

The twin-engined Me110, designed primarily as a long range escort for just these sort of actions, was almost totally out-classed by the Hurricanes and Spitfires. Often they had also to rely on assistance from the 109 pilots, or had themselves to fly in their famous defensive circles when engaged, thus leaving the bombers to fend for themselves.

The Germans' other bomber, or dive-bomber, the famed Junkers 87, was totally out of its depth against England. Again it was an aeroplane designed for a Continental land war, giving close support to the German Blitzkrieg tactics. In Poland and France it was the supreme weapon when used in support of troops and Panzer units. Against land targets in a sky still dominated by the RAF, it became highly vulnerable, its dive-bomber tactics making it easy to attack and difficult to escort.

Imaginative Ideas and Tactics

In the continual search for improved tactics, there were any number of ideas put forward to Command to try to keep at least one step ahead of the Luftwaffe. Air Marshal Sir Arthur Barratt, who had been in command of the BAFF in France, and who was by October 1940 commanding the RAF Staff College at Andover, wrote to Dowding concerning armament, armour and tactics. He had been talking to a test pilot who had been attached to a fighter squadron, and was putting forward the man's opinions:

The existing armament is good for the destruction of enemy single-seaters but it is rapidly becoming obsolete for use against bomber formations. Enemy bombers are now heavily armoured in the rear and it appears that the rear machines of their bomber formations are firing cannon aft. The armament of 8 x ·303 guns is, therefore, insufficient both in range and penetrating power for effective attack in the face of the rear armour and cross-firing encountered in these formations. It is apparent that our fighters must be split into two categories. (1) 'dog-fighters' for high altitude encounters with the escort fighters, (2) 'destroyers', for the splitting up and destruction of enemy bomber formations.

For the dog-fighters, a high rate of fire and good 'spread' is required for the snap-shooting at short range, which is the usual order in these engagements and for which the existing ·303 armament is satisfactory. For the 'destroyer', however, heavy projectiles with great penetrating power which can be fired from long range are essential and I consider that an armament of four Hispano cannons is the minimum to make it worthwhile putting a fighter into range of a fire which may now be expected to issue from the rear of the enemy massed formations.

It would be a mistake on policy to try to compromise between these two distinct armament requirements. The question of rate is of great importance. The 'dog-fighter' must be kept as light as possible to climb at high altitude; turning circle and general manoeuvrability will not be an operational necessity. Therefore considerable extra weight and wing-loading can be permitted in the interests of range and striking power and forward projective armament. The two differently armed fighters will operate in close co-operation; the 'dog-fighter' forming a protective escort to the 'destroyers'.

Let no one think that the days of the dog-fighter are over, or that massed formations of bombers can be broken by the fire of ·303 guns. Regard to protective armour, the fighters armed as destroyers will require very considerable forward protective armour against the fire of the bomber formations.

There are several points of interest in the letter, apart from Sir Arthur not appreciating fully the intricacies of 1940 combat. In some ways Fighter Command had been trying the tactic of 'dog-fighters' (Spitfires) to engage fighters, 'destroyers' (Hurricanes) to engage the bombers. Sometimes it worked, but the weakness in Barratt's argument is that in an imperfect world, the 'destroyer' would always be likely to run into enemy 'dog-fighters', and find itself at a distinct disadvantage if they were too heavily armoured and armed. By the same token, the more lightly armed and armoured Spitfires, would either have to ignore a bomber formation if they found one without their 'destroyer' units, or attack and risk the heavy defensive return fire Barratt acknowledges was present.

Later in the war the German fighters defending their own homeland against large formations of American four-engined bombers, tried just such a tactic, forming units of heavily armoured fighters with which to attack the massed ranks of Fortresses and Liberators. These *Sturmgruppen*, both 'heavy' (to engage the bombers) and 'light', to ward off fighter escorts, were introduced in the summer of 1944, the 'heavy' fighters also carrying two 30mm guns. They had their successes, but when the US Mustang and Thunderbolt fighters got in behind the *Sturmgruppen's* FW190s, they became an easy prey, especially as the German pilots had orders to continue their attacks and not attempt to escape.

As to the suggestion that the day of dog-fighting might be over, that argument was to arise continually as speeds of aircraft increased and it was believed the turning circle, so widened by these speeds, would render a dog-fight a thing of the past. Fifty years on we still have the dog-fight concept.

Had the Battle of Britain continued after the end of 1940, perhaps some of Barratt's ideas would have been considered – there were many stranger ideas discussed. However, although the pilots did not know it, the day battle over Britain had been won. Not that they even knew that it was to be called the Battle of Britain, in 1940. They had been merely fighting an enemy that had knocked out most of Western Europe and whose black-crossed aircraft were now bombing their country. For all they knew, once the winter had passed and spring brought better weather, the German Luftwaffe would be back to try again!

CHAPTER 11

Fighter Tactics

ALTHOUGH THE FIGHTER pilots did not know it, they had won what later became known as the Battle of Britain (a phrase unknown to the pilots in 1940). With the onset of autumn, the bombers no longer came over during daylight, except for the odd nuisance raider, the bombing having gone over to the hours of darkness. However, the Luftwaffe continued to fly against Britain, mainly in the form of Me109s and some Me110s.

These fighter sorties on their own did not constitute a threat, so the Germans began to carry bombs to drop, in the majority of cases, indiscriminately. They then had to be intercepted and engaged. Flying against these fighter and fighter-bomber missions became very dangerous, especially in the cloudy weather conditions that now prevailed, whereby RAF squadrons could be surprised while they climbed up from their airfields.

The battles that raged during these last weeks of 1940 were costly to both sides, and set the seal on what was to follow in the next year or two in the air, fighter versus fighter combat. Fighter Command, while far from down and out, had lost some 544 pilots during the summer air fighting. Replacements had and were arriving and despite the continuing daylight operations, time was now found to formulate in more detail the tactics which ought to be adopted and employed. What happened now was to begin to influence the future fighter conflict.

In Search of Perfection

Once the years of peacetime tactics training were found to have been totally useless in actual battle conditions, the race to find better fighter tactics was on. The fall of France changed everything overnight with the sudden realisation that enemy bombers would be escorted by the deadly Me109s. Gone was the nice theory of engaging juicy fat bombers with the RAF pilots queuing up to 'have a crack'.

Not that this realisation changed everyone's thinking, far from it. With each fighter squadron having its own leader with his own particular ideas on how to engage the enemy, it was generally left to him and perhaps his flight commanders to come up with the tactics they thought best.

Over France and Dunkirk most fighter pilots quickly discovered that the time-honoured vics of three were a thing of the past. Nevertheless, some squadrons continued to use this formation well into the summer air battles of 1940, often to their cost. Only slowly did the RAF pilots realise that the enemy fighters were flying in fours and twos; indeed, many combat reports in mid-1940 describe seeing Me109s in threes, the pilots believing that the Germans were flying in similar formations to themselves – the eye dictating what the mind wants to see.

The quick and far-thinking pilots not only realised their own tactical problems but came up with solutions. Pilots such as 'Sailor' Malan in 74 Squadron, Bob Tuck with 92 and then 257 Squadrons, Al Deere in 54 Squadron, had begun to see that flying in sections of four were better than vics of three, with the object of breaking this down into twos after a fight started. The initial problem was that once a fight started, it quickly turned into a free-for-all, each pilot fighting on his own, then breaking off to return home. In 1940 it was rare for a squadron, once it had been engaged, to return in formation, each pilot drifting back individually when fuel and or ammunition ran low.

As slowly the squadron sections changed from threes to fours, there came the question of how the fours should fly: in line astern, in line abreast or in echelon port or starboard. But whatever formation was used it was only a means by which the leader could get all his aircraft into a battle situation and be self-protecting. Once the attack began, or they were themselves engaged by enemy fighters, that was an end to the formation. Tighter control of the fighters in the air would come later.

One has to remember that once the Battle of Britain began, everyone was far too busy to co-ordinate, formulate or discuss what the best tactics might be, and, again, each unit was in some way experimenting. Even if one squadron believed it had found a good tactic it was not exactly possible for them to tell another unit, even if they shared an airfield with them. And HQ Fighter Command were far too busy to do so although occasionally some Intelligence on the subject might percolate down. Allan Wright:

As to Command or Group's role in passing down new tactics being adopted by other squadrons, such information would have been received by our CO and flight commanders; we pilots would have been concerned with their instructions, rather than where they came from. Our COs during September 1940 had little influence because they did not last long enough, except for Johnny Kent, who arrived at the end of the month.

Brian Kingcome, our 'A' Flight commander, was the most influential of our bunch. Bob Tuck, our other flight commander, who though a great fighter, did not 'give' very much. I succeeded him, but only for a week or so before being shot down myself.

The only change in squadron tactics I can remember being discussed was the gradual move from close formation with two weavers to the 'finger four' and two aircraft flying and fighting as a pair which evolved with this change. At the time I thought that each type of formation had its advantages and disadvantages according to circumstances. I don't think this change became mandatory throughout Fighter Command until well after the Battle of Britain when our role had changed from defence over Britain to offence over France.

A fighter sortie is essentially made up of two parts: seeking out the enemy and engagement. The first part was the squadron or later the wing leader's problem. I would not have known much about that in 1940. We pilots in general were directly concerned with the second part, and the tactics of: (a) one-to-one battle with fighters, (b) how to deal with the single bomber/recce aircraft, (c) the single fighter versus bomber formation.

During the Battle of Britain, engagement tactics were worked out within the squadron. I was not aware of any instructions from above. I doubt if guidance in this personal area was possible or desirable in the battle zone. No fighter pilot could be spared in 1940 to give up the fray for a while to tour other fighter squadrons. Who, at that stage, when we were all learning at the same time, would accept a pilot from another squadron as more qualified than one's fellows?

In general, the adoption of new tactics was slow rather than rapid.

Allan Wright's mention of 'weavers' shows how some thinking had progressed. The danger of a formation of Hurricanes or Spitfires flying towards a reported raid, was of being bounced by free-ranging Me109s. Whether still in vics or in pairs and fours, some squadrons decided to have a pair of fighters to the rear of the main formation on the look-out in case of a surprise attack. They generally weaved in a figure-of-eight manoeuvre, above and behind the others. This was fine in theory and on occasions it did prevent a surprise attack. However, the problems associated with this tactic was that quite often the weavers were the less experienced pilots, and because of their constant manoeuvring and turning, they ran out of fuel faster than the main formation (and owing to radio silence, often just broke off when running short of petrol); or they were picked off by attacking Me109s before a warning could be given.

Nevertheless, the 'weaver' tactic persisted for some time and was used over France until well into 1941.

Cross Section of Ideas

By the end of 1940, a number of front line squadrons had been asked to submit their methods of flying in formation to Command HQ. Nos.92 and 74 Squadrons were at Biggin Hill from September 1940; 92 reported:

The Squadron climbs in close formation of three sections of three in line astern; the fourth section splits up and its leader flies in a box of the third section while his No.2 and 3 come forward and weave under the leading section about 200 feet above. The method of weaving adopted is for the two aircraft to fly parallel to the squadron one on each side of it and about 600 yards apart. The first aircraft then turns and flies across the squadron towards the second aircraft, meanwhile keeping a lookout to the rear of the squadron.

As it approaches the second aircraft and starts to straighten out to fly parallel to the squadron again, the second machine turns and flies across to the opposite side of the squadron, again keeping watch to the rear: when it begins to straighten out, the first machine starts back across the squadron again.

In this way a constant watch is kept and the weaving aircraft find it easier to keep up with the squadron and use very little more petrol than other aircraft of the squadron.

No.74 Squadron:

The squadron climbs in three sections of four aircraft in line astern [the middle section slightly ahead], changing course according to the sun and weather, but making sure height is being gained away from the enemy fighters, then climbing on a zig-zag course the whole time.

At Kenley, No.501 Squadron noted:

Squadron climbs in three sections of four in line astern, the last pair weaving. Each four is sub-divided into pairs which work together, one to make the attack, the other to guard against surprise. The chief danger is from above and behind and the two weavers should be able to give the alarm in time. On receiving the warning, leader orders 'Squadron split', whereupon two of each section do steep climbing turns to the right and the other two a steep climbing turn to the left. These pairs then have a good chance of coming on the enemy before they can deliver a successful attack or get away.

From North Weald, Nos.46 and 249 Squadrons reported:

The following standard formation is used by both squadrons. The squadron flies with two sections of four aircraft in line astern – stepped down – followed by a pair of aircraft also stepped down. The remaining two aircraft weave, one below and one above the squadron and well forward. In these positions, the weaving aircraft are able to keep a good lookout and cannot be surprised and shot down without the knowledge of the remainder of the formation. The squadron has always worked on the principle of working in pairs if attacked and even when attacking bomber formations has split into pairs.

Another 'golden rule' which has been instilled into the pilot's heads is never to dive away if attacked from above but to turn to the right as steeply as possible. In the past six weeks it was found that with the superior performance of the German aircraft over ours at height, more particularly as the leader out in front found it difficult to see what was going on behind him, the squadron started to work in flights almost in line abreast about 1/4 mile apart, each flight having two weavers. In this way everyone can see what everyone else is doing and the pilots are already in pairs if need be. Also, each flight covers the other's tail if attacked from behind. When operating in pairs the squadron flies in line astern, each squadron adopting the formation described above. The second squadron flies above and behind the first.

In an experimental formation which these two squadrons have recently been trying out is described below:

The squadron flies in pairs of aircraft in echelon according to sun and weather conditions. There are two weaving aircraft, one above and one below, in each case well forward. The squadrons have not as yet had much experience of this type of formation but the following points have been discovered:

(1) All aircraft can rapidly form a defensive circle.
(2) The formation is flexible and bears a resemblance to hostile formations.
(3) It is highly manoeuvrable and can easily meet attacks from any point.
(4) On account of its wide front, it is rather difficult to cover adequately by the weaving aircraft.

This formation is standard in 605 Squadron, who have had considerable success in adopting it.

Meanwhile, at RAF Hornchurch, Nos.41 and 64 Squadrons considered:

No.41 Squadron climbs and patrols in pairs in line-astern. Formation composed of tactical or attack unit; No.2 of each unit being defensive on No.1's tail where conditions render this necessary. Rearguard action commences from ground about 1-2,000 feet above and below. Rearguards are changed after 30-minutes due to loss of efficiency in 'looking out', after this period is also due to petrol shortage.

Patrol Leader remains two or three lengths ahead of his No.2 to give more freedom of manoeuvrability if surprised from above. Squadron splits into pairs which evade without losing height. The No.1's of each pair are the six best shots. No.2 adopts position 3-400 yards behind and above No.1, unless or until individual attack is ordered, or unless a good target presents itself.

This formation has been effective and very adaptable to the 109 formations which are the usual and favourite target. Pairs pull away to the port or starboard and form up as a wide front of six spearheads with six aircraft in reserve (rearguards), are often unable to form up in time and act independently.

No.64 Squadron:

Squadron takes off and climbs to patrol height and carries out patrol in sections in line astern. The sections consist of two aircraft, each flight comprising three sections of two to avoid whip and unnecessary depths of sections; climbs onto patrol in close line astern. The rear pair maintain a rearguard by weaving one above and one below the squadron. The role of the weavers will be dealt with later on. On reaching patrol height the sections open out to a distance of about 5 to 6 lengths between each section. Sections are stepped down from the leading section and each section or pair flies at about four spans interval. This patrol formation is found very suitable and a thorough lookout can be maintained by all pilots. On sighting an enemy aircraft or on being unexpectedly attacked, squadron can turn very rapidly in either direction without losing cohesion. The essential being that whether countering an attack, the squadron never breaks down into smaller units than a pair.

Rearguard of the two weavers fly one above and one below the squadron, patrolling from side to side and crossing the line of the squadron directly above or below as the case may be, the leading section. The function of these weavers is to maintain a thorough lookout of the rear, both above and below and give immediate warning of a rear attack. To safeguard the weavers themselves from surprise they are instructed to make short zig-zag courses, and not to stray far to one side or in rear of the squadron.

The squadron is capable of climbing 2,000 feet a minute up to 20,000 feet, after which the rate of climb falls off until a maximum of about only 500 feet per minute is reached at 32,000 feet. Pilots are instructed to conserve oxygen up to 15,000 feet. At normal patrol heights of 23,000-30,000 feet, the leader of the formation flies at an IAS (indicated air speed) of 160 mph to 2,400 rpm and weak mixture. A patrol of 1 hour 30 minutes can be assured under these conditions.

No.602 Auxiliary Squadron at RAF Tangmere, reported:

At the beginning when the Me109 menace was not so great, the Squadron always used to fly in sections line astern with two weavers. It was found that this was very manoeuvrable and that provided the pilots stuck close together, the squadron could fly around with impunity after passing as near as 1,000 feet below quite large numbers of 109s.

Another fanciful idea put forward during November 1940 was the consideration of a Hurricane squadron patrolling with two Defiant aircraft to their rear and on the flank, but in front of the two weavers. Again one can see the basic logic of this: e.g., two Defiant gunners, facing aft, in aircraft which did not look so dissimilar to the Hurricane, ready to blast any would-be attacker with their four turreted ·303 machine guns, or at least give warning. Once again practicality overcame theory!

Yet another suggestion, and one which later historians would ask why it wasn't tried earlier, was to attack Luftwaffe airfields. It had to be known that the many French airfields taken over by the Germans were packed with aircraft, which daily raided southern England. Why were they not attacked?

In fact, some 2 Group Blenheims had tried on one or two occasions but suffered heavy casualties. The more important targets for 2 Group and Bomber Command in general, were the increasing volume of barges in the French ports which could only be there for an invasion force. Day fighters could not be spared to attempt any form of attacks on airfields and Fighter Command's night-fighter force was so small and untried it would have been foolish to risk crews and aircraft in some form of night intruder attacks. At night the enemy airfields would be completely blacked out and often night fighter crews over England had enough difficulty finding their own home bases without trying to find strange airfields over France.

The ordinary front line day squadrons, of course, were just too busy to be spared to attack enemy airfields, and Dowding could not risk his depleted force being depleted further. Even if some aircraft might have been destroyed on the ground, it was felt that these would easily be replaced whereas losses in RAF pilots could not be risked in this form of attack.

In December 1940, however, the first discussions took place concerning the possibility of raiding German bases at night, now that the night bombing of Britain was increasing. At least it was hoped that any such RAF intruding would it was hoped, be able to locate such a German base operating by seeing the airfield lights coming on, not to mention aircraft navigation lights as they either took off or landed.

No.23 Squadron based at Ford were first selected to try this method of attacking the enemy's night bombers, helped with navigators from 25 and 29 Squadrons. The squadron's Blenheim 1fs were not the ideal aeroplane but 23 Squadron was withdrawn from nightly interception patrols over England to begin raiding German airfields.

It was a reasonable tactic. The best form of defence has often been attack, and certainly the Germans at this moment, had the upper hand in the night war. As we shall see, Britain and Fighter Command were ill-prepared for any form of German night-raiding.

Dowding and Park Leave the Command

Air Chief Marshal Sir Hugh Dowding was retired as AOC-in-C on 24 November 1940. Park was moved from the command of 11 Group three weeks later.

There has been much emotive comment at both these decisions, the issue being slightly clouded by Dowding himself. The best that can be said is that at the time the issue was not handled in the best of ways thereby leaving a bad taste over the proceedings. However, Dowding was 58 years old and had been the C-in-C for four years. As mentioned in an earlier chapter, he had already been warned that retirement was due. That he had been the architect of victory in Britain's gravest hour is unquestioned. That it was his plans and ideas which developed the Command even to be half able to withstand the German onslaught is not in doubt.

If Dowding had been given the honours which he deserved, a Marshal's rank and a peerage at that moment, and Park had been rewarded too in some way, the replacement of these two valiant men would have been more acceptable. Neither men had made any great friends amongst the hierarchy in Government or at the Air Ministry. Both men knew exactly what was needed to defend Britain and went for it in a no-nonsense manner. That they were proved right in most of what they strived to achieve only made what enemies they had even more keen to see a change.

But change there was. Air Chief Marshal William Sholto Douglas was given the job of succeeding Dowding, while the Command's premier No. 11 Fighter Group, went to the career-conscious commander of 12 Group, Sir Trafford Leigh-Mallory.

Sholto Douglas was 47 years old in 1940 and had been Deputy Chief of the Air Staff at Air Ministry, for which he received the CB. He had a distinguished First War, winning the MC and DFC, and commanding one of the most famous fighter squadrons in France, 84, ending that conflict as a lieutenant colonel.

To the ordinary squadron pilot, Dowding had seemed a distant, aloof figure. Only afterwards did they begin to see him in a different light, by which time they had read or heard much of their erstwhile commander. Park had also been a difficult man to know, but at least he had been seen more often by his pilots, as he often flew into their stations during the battle, to discuss with them the problems they faced. Many an airman had wondered who this man with the white flying overalls was as he stepped down from his Hurricane, only to be set bolt upright when he took off his flying helmet and placed his AVM's cap on his head.

Sholto Douglas and Leigh-Mallory would be very different from their predecessors, but then too, the fighter war was to be very different. It had been basically a defensive force but it was now about to begin a very offensive war.

CHAPTER 12

In the Night Sky

FIGHTER COMMAND WAS certainly ill-prepared for a night war in the air, but then most of the major air forces in the 1930s gave little real thought to waging a war during the hours of darkness. For one thing everyone assumed a blackout would be essential, and so how on earth would any aviator be able to find his way about and actually land in pitch darkness?

This was a perfectly sound argument, but by the late 1930s, when war seemed inevitable, the Air Ministry had to face the possibility that Germany might attempt night bombing. So it began to consider ways of countering such a move. Hugh Dowding, too, thought that night bombing might be a distinct possibility and so progressed with the thought that the new Blenheim 1f fighters might provide the answer.

Others thought that if the worst came to the worst, day fighter pilots, on the 'lighter' nights might well be able to see sufficiently to locate the odd hostile raider, helped by ground searchlight beams. With the advent of a more reliable radio on the modern monoplanes, this too might help the pilot to be guided into the vicinity of an enemy aircraft which had been detected by the new RDF system.

There was a film which was released in 1939 entitled *The Lion Has Wings*. In this the theory that day fighters might be used with success against night bombers, probably allayed the fears of the general public! Nevertheless, men such as Dowding knew better, and among the many things he was trying to achieve in the immediate pre-war period, when time was fast running out, was to encourage the 'boffins' to produce a workable airborne radar. He knew that his day fighter pilots would be extremely lucky to find an enemy bomber in the darkness. Although not impossible, it would be like looking for a fly in a darkened Albert Hall.

What he needed was improved ground control to direct a night fighter equipped with radar into the vicin-

ity of a raider so that the airborne radar equipment could pick it up. Once the airborne radar had found it, the operator could guide his pilot onto the hostile, who would then shoot it down. As the war progressed this kind of procedure developed beyond the hopes of the pioneer radar people and of men like Dowding, but in the early days it was a very different story.

We met Myles Duke-Woolley in earlier chapters, firstly flying Blenheims on early night flying with 23 Squadron, before becoming a day Hurricane pilot. Once the war had started, he and his brother pilots had to face the task of not only flying at night on a regular basis, but be trained to find and intercept possible night bombers.

We hadn't the faintest idea how we were going to find a target; no idea at all! Initially we had no airborne radar and it wasn't until well into 1940 that 'Spike' O'Brien[1] told me that we had some electronics expert and instrumentation to see. He also told me he had volunteered yours truly to fly it around!

It was fitted into a Blenheim and it so happened that the 'expert' had been at Marlborough school with me and had been working on the first AI (Airborne Interception) gear. It was very heavy and I recall that no air gunner wanted to come with us!

We took off and climbed to 6,000 feet, then got ready to switch the 'gubbins' on. He said 'OK!' and switched it on. There was the biggest blue flash I'd ever seen which appeared to zip past me and shoot out the front windscreen. I said, 'Wow! If there had been an aircraft out in front of us we'd have burned him up!' But apparently this was not the intention, for he then said, 'I'm awfully sorry but it appears the set has blown up.'

The insulation had broken down completely; they'd

---

[1] Squadron Leader J. S. O'Brien DFC, killed in action leading 234 Squadron on 7 September 1940.

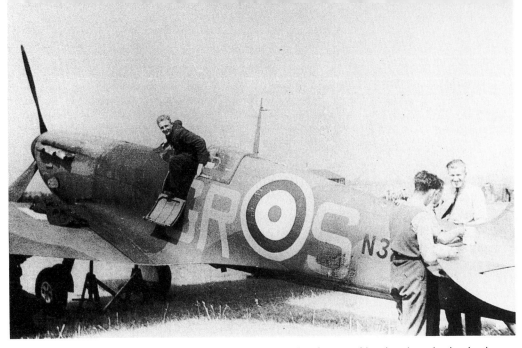

Flight Lieutenant Allan Wright DFC, flew with 92 Squadron, 1940-41.

Myles Duke-Woolley DSO DFC.

not taken into consideration the reduction in air pressure or something, but it had been spectacular – just like a ray-gun.

My friend reappeared about a month later with the 'mark two' and we flew this about quite a lot, and we did in fact make an interception one night. It was very difficult, as each time I turned, the enemy aircraft turned the other way and eventually we lost it. Then we picked up another one and he said it was flying away from us. I increased speed but still it was gaining on us; in fact it was pulling away from us fast! I couldn't go any faster myself, and the engines were getting jolly hot. Eventually I had to throttle back and later I discovered they hadn't put enough oil in the engines which hadn't helped. Then it transpired that this early AI worked just as well backwards as it did forwards so in fact what we'd been doing was not chasing a German but running away from one! So the AI disappeared for the second time whilst they got it to work just forwards.

We continued our night patrols – without radar – hoping to spot a raider or to see searchlight and AA fire activity which would at least direct us to the scene. Then came the night of 18 June 1940. I have never been so frightened in my life and was never so frightened again.

I was on patrol off the east coast, over the Wash. It was a gin clear night and Control called me up to say that German aircraft had been raiding the Midlands and some of them were coming our way. I looked to the west and could see a number of searchlights criss-crossing about, so called back to say that it looked as if the searchlights had somebody and should I investigate? I was told no, it was being dealt with, so I just watched. Then, about 10-12 miles away I saw a very small yellowy light going down, then it went out. Then

All-black Hurricane night fighter; 601 Squadron, 1941.

I saw a parachute, and suddenly realised that what I had seen was one of our intercepting aircraft going down on fire. Again I called Control, told them a Blenheim had gone down and that I was going to engage. After a short silence I was told to engage in my own time.

It was only then that I realised that we'd never had any real briefing on how to actually shoot an aircraft down! The only information we'd had was by some chap who had shot something down in 1918. The thing we'd been told to do was to rush up behind the bomber, close in to 100 yards and with our outstanding armament, blow it apart.

Closing in I began to realise I should also soon be fired at and that I had no armour protection in front of me. My fuel tanks were not self-sealing and the more I thought about it, the more I realised that I was going to live just long enough to get tangled with this German aircraft – about four minutes.

I'd been married just nine months, my wife had just given birth to our first child and I knew I was never going to see it. Then I was thinking furiously about how I was going to attack and perhaps get away with it. A plan occurred to me which I then imparted to my gunner. Fear was growing inside me; I found I could not speak and that I was sweating profusely. Then, quite suddenly, and something I still do not understand, I heard my voice speak and it was absolutely calm. I told Control I was in touch with the raider and would engage shortly. Then this same calm voice was asking my gunner if he had his parachute on. He said he hadn't, so this calm voice continued, 'They've still got a searchlight on him and what we're going to do is this. I'm going to keep to port until the light goes out, then I'm going to

come up in line astern of him at 100 yards and open fire with a five-second burst. If that doesn't work I'll come back and do another one. I shall then break away to port and shall come up under his wing and I shall want you to put bursts up into him. If that doesn't work, we'll have to go back and start again.' And that's what we did.

I flew alongside him – it was a He111 – about 500 yards away, until the last light flicked out, came in behind, put the sight on him and counted out five seconds as I pressed the gun button. I then broke off and looking where I'd been could see all these red flashes, which I later realised was the return fire from the German gunner. I then went in again, but after another long burst he was still flying along. I then flew underneath and let my gunner have a go but still he didn't appear to be hit or damaged.

All the time something kept nagging at me that I was doing something wrong. Then I suddenly realised that our guns were harmonised to 250 yards, from a point some feet below the sight. This meant that at 100 yards, the range I'd been told I'd blast him from the sky, I was hardly hitting him at all. So I deduced that I had to fly at least four feet higher for it to be more or less right. So I slid in again, aimed high up on the German's tail fin, fired and broke to port, but this time his return fire was much less, so I knew I was hitting him. I pulled in again and gave him seven seconds, but as we broke this time we were hit. There was a smell of cordite, a scream from my gunner, so I just flicked back to the left and the German disappeared.

My gunner, saying he'd been hit, caused me to look at my instruments but they all read 'zero' and rolling

Cannon-armed night intruder Hurricane IIC of 245 Squadron.

around somewhere behind me I could hear the oxygen bottle. We were around 20,000 feet; I knew my limit was 15,000 or so, so knew I had to get down. I was still amazed at my voice, talking so calmly. I asked my gunner, 'Where's the blood?', something I'd never normally have thought of saying! I could hear him panting, then he said it was all right, he'd only been hit in his parachute pack. A couple of bullets had come up between his legs, hit his chest type parachute which he had put on following my earlier enquiry. When I then asked him where the bomber was, he said, 'Oh, he's on fire!' I was now reducing height, drifting downhill, so called Control. I'd come down over the coast and was about ten miles inland when the starboard engine stopped but at least now I found I had proper control of my voice. I determined that somehow the feed to the engine had been cut, and so it proved as I crossfed it and successfully started it up, but my gunner confirmed we were losing fuel from the engine, so I shut it down. Some minutes later we landed safely.

The gear! Two night fighter Hurricane pilots of 486 New Zealand Squadron, Sergeant Leo Walker and Pilot Officer Les Weir.

This action had occurred on the night of 18/19 June, the first real full scale attack by enemy night raiders. In the event, 'Duke' missed being the first RAF pilot to destroy a German aircraft at night by just 30 seconds, honour going to another Blenheim pilot. On the same night, Flight Lieutenant Sailor Malan of 74 Squadron shot down two He111s – flying a Spitfire!

A number of pilots would have some success in night-fighting in Spitfires and Hurricanes. Although not designed for the job, they stood just as much chance of engaging the enemy as any other aeroplane not fitted with radar. Radar in fact did not begin to equip night fighter aircraft until well into September 1940. Six of the first came from the hands of Messrs Electrical and Musical Instrument Company, in Hayes, Middlesex, early that month.

Once fitted to Blenheims and then Beaufighters, night-fighting took on another face, but meanwhile the day fighter pilots helped to bridge the gap together with the Defiant crews. 'Fighter Nights' were organised, flown on nights when it wasn't really pitch dark, the fighters being given a certain altitude to patrol, so that fighters would be covering a whole area each at staggered heights.

Allan Wright, still flying with 92 Spitfire Squadron, shot down a night raider on the 29/30 August 1940, as he recalls:

We had a number of problems flying Spitfires at night, one being that we had no way of getting back to base, which made things a bit difficult. We had radio control but were not under radar control, although the radio only told us there was something there. Our only aid was three bunches of flares on the ground at different places, perhaps ten miles apart, to give us a rough positional fix and patrol area. We were operating from Pembrey and I recall one pilot on the squadron, losing his way but put black on red on his compass, couldn't contact ground control and ended up running out of fuel and baling out. He found himself about five miles from the Wash!

On 29 August I was told a Heinkel was heading for Bristol from the south east so flew in that direction. I then saw some searchlights which then collected on something, so went towards it. I told Control I'd seen it and was closing in when I was surrounded suddenly by exploding AA fire! I called Control, yelling at them to get the guns to stop, which eventually they did. Meanwhile, the searchlights had lost the raider but after hunting around for a bit, I spotted two glowing exhausts.

I crept in close so as to positively identify the thing but dropping under it I lost sight of the exhausts so had to come up to relocate them.

This went on for some minutes until I finally saw it was a Heinkel and opened fire. Then something began

to flicker in one engine so I had a go at the other motor but then I ran out of ammunition. My problem too was that the German was flying so slowly. It was a bit difficult to keep behind it but it was also difficult to keep the glowing exhausts in sight.

I went home and everyone was trying to find out if it had come down, and eventually a report did come in that a Heinkel was down but shot down by AA fire. I questioned this and later it was confirmed that it was full of ·303 bullet holes so I was awarded that one.

The Heinkel was from 3/KG27 which crashed at Hale, Hampshire, at 11 pm, the crew having baled out. James Sanders recalls a night fighter sortie in his 615 Squadron Hurricane. Over the radio came the voice of an Italian airman, but then James Sanders spoke fluent Italian so understood every word:

One night I was flying over Surrey when over the radio I heard an Italian pilot clearly saying that London was burning. There was a margarine factory burning at Dagenham I seem to remember, which could be seen for miles. The Italian must have been very close to me, for he gave his name and reported back that he was approaching the target. But he was over Ashdown Forest – miles to the south of London!

I was trying desperately to see his aircraft but couldn't, so I called him on the radio, saying in Italian that he was a bloody liar, that he was not over the target, which promptly caused him to drop his bombs which I saw explode in the Forest. I imagine he then headed for home.

I felt he must have been only about 100 yards from me, probably below, but I just couldn't see him. What was obvious, however, was that he didn't want to drop his bombs over London but was telling his base he was over it.

Stop-Gap Defiants

To help fill the gap in Britain's night defences, the now defunct Defiant two-seater turret fighter was pressed into service, although it too did not carry radar. Nevertheless, provided a crew managed to spot a bomber in the night sky it could have a crack at it, although, just as in day fighting, the pilot had still to manoeuvre his machine to allow his gunner to fire his four turret guns.

Christopher Deanesly, who had been flying Spitfires with 152 Squadron during the Battle of Britain and been wounded, ended up as a fighter controller at St Eval, when volunteers for a night fighter flight commander were asked for.

During the period from the end of September onwards the day blitz had almost ceased to be replaced by an intensive and successful night effort. Fighter Command had to act quickly as it had become obvious that Hurricanes and Spitfires (especially the latter) were ineffective against the enemy and expensive in casualties for night use under blackout conditions without VHF radios.

Not without difficulty six or eight Defiant squadrons were formed. Day squadrons had to post some of their pilots (air gunners came from the gunnery schools) to man the new units. Understandably in the climate of the time, squadron COs did not let their best pilots go. Partly as a result the new squadrons had a difficult time becoming operational.

Group asked for volunteer flight commanders for these night fighter squadrons. I put my name forward and was sent to a new squadron – 256 – which had been recently formed at Catterick and was now down at Colerne near Bath. We had Defiants but had very poor equipment. There was no VHF radio, the black-out was appalling, the living conditions were difficult and it was a terrible winter.

On the plus side the squadron had a good number of newly trained pilots and air gunners from New Zealand, Australia and Canada. They made a valuable contribution at a difficult time. For two or three months we did nothing except make mistakes and collect casualties. The same thing was happening to a Polish squadron (307) up at Blackpool. They were doing no good so Fighter Command decided the Poles had had too much of the fleshpots of Blackpool and it would be better to move them on. So 256 Squadron went to Blackpool (Squires Gate) and they moved to Colerne.

It had already taken us three months, January to March 1941, to become operational, with many casualties, men and aircraft. Once we went north, 256 never looked back and we started to intercept enemy aircraft and shoot them down (as did other Defiant squadrons during April and May).

During these two months with a better airfield, lighting and VHF radio we learned a lot and with improved experience and handling, both pilots and gunners could use their eyes. In the bright moonlight nights, particularly if bombers dropped incendiaries, it was possible to see them, provided one was at the same height. Once intercepted it was not difficult to shoot them down. One approached from below and the gunner was able to shoot almost vertically upwards with immediate and devastating effect.

To do this needed the ability to 'formate' as a day fighter pilot. After one successful combat there were clear marks on the propeller when I had run into the enemy's trailing radio aerial! The first success I had, we'd been called late one afternoon to move the squadron down to Ternhill near Market Drayton. There we were met by the groundcrew of my old squadron, 605, who rallied round and did our refuelling.

Later we flew patrols around Birmingham and I ran into two or three aircraft high up. It was a bright night and we could see them if they were quite near and with the aid of a good gunner, we shot one down. I had a remarkable gunner, a New Zealander by the name of Jack Scott. The bomber went down with one engine on fire.

Over the next few weeks we had some raids on Manchester and Liverpool and the squadron south of the Mersey, 96 Squadron at Cranage, had some successes. This went on for the first ten days in May but after that the Germans were withdrawn in preparation for the war against Russia.

The advantage of the Defiant was its power-operated turret with its four ·303 machine guns. If you could get beneath an enemy aircraft, the impact of the vertical fire was very effective. The difficulty with Hurricanes and Spitfires was that you were supposed to attack from behind but, of course, you had a tremendous number of bullets ricochet off, whereas if you got underneath you could get very near without being seen and the impact was colossal.

I followed one down one night. It was well on fire, then it suddenly it went out. I hadn't a clue whether I was over land or sea but later we heard it may have gone into a lake near Wrexham. We had no aids of course, except the general fact that it was moonlight and there were a lot of Germans about, but if we managed to get underneath one we could poke our guns right up to it.

During those weeks, Chris Deanesly and Jack Scott shot down four night raiders and received the DFC and DFM respectively.

Enter the Beaufighter

Whether Air Ministry was really caught out by the German night bombing offensive has never been really explained. Certainly it would seem a perfect example of ignoring the obvious course an enemy might take. This was especially the case of an enemy, Germany, who might be badly mauled, as indeed it was, in daylight operations. But wasn't this exactly what Fighter Command had been training for, to defeat an air assault by day? Wasn't it obvious, therefore, that such a potential enemy would resort to night tactics?

Only a few people, seemingly, gave night defence any real credence, among them Dowding who was trying to get development and production of airborne radar through as quickly as possible together with a suitable aeroplane to carry it. The Blenheim fighter had been little more than a stop gap for the real night-fighter aircraft, the Bristol Beaufighter, the design of which began in 1938. The prototype was ready by mid-1939, while the

Flight Lieutenant Christopher Deanesly DFC *and his Defiant air gunner Sergeant Jack Scott* DFM, *256 Squadron. Note four 'swastikas' by cockpit.*

first production model was delivered to the RAF in April 1940.

At the beginning of September 1940, the first Beaufighters went to 25 and 29 Squadrons, followed by 600 and 604 Squadrons the following month. At last the RAF had an aircraft capable through speed and armament to carry AI and be a threat to Luftwaffe night bombers. 604 Squadron achieved the first AI Beau night kill on 19/20 November, 1940, by shooting down a Ju88. The crew was John Cunningham and John Philipson; Cunningham later became one of the most successful night-fighter pilots of the war with 19 night kills and one day kill.

AI (Airborne Radar) worked on the principle of an echo which rebounded when it hit another aircraft. Working with two small radar tubes (screens), the radar operator, once contact had been made, could direct his pilot onto the plot. Once in visual contact, it was up to the pilot to attack and shoot it down.

The threat of night-bombing was always there but when it began in earnest in late 1940, developing into the massive blitz on London in the period up to the beginning of May 1941, Fighter Command was ill-prepared for it.

In January 1941 the Command had just six night-fighter squadrons – that is squadrons specially selected for night-fighting as opposed to press-ganged day fighter squadrons who would fly on the chance of meeting a raider. Each of the six squadrons, with a 7th forming, had 17 pilots. Recruiting for new night pilots was among RAF employed ex-civil airline pilots at the beginning of 1941, for they had both twin-engined experience and supposedly the temperament for long hours of flying around in the dark, seeking out a largely unseen prey. Output of night-fighter pilots from OTUs was just 12 per month, although this increased during the year.

There were many strange ideas about how night-fighters might be selected. Flight Lieutenant John Wray, a former day Blenheim pilot who was trying to get back onto operations, volunteered when pilots were being sought to become night-fighters. They were sent off to be tested by some team or other, carrying out vision tests. He recalls:

There were about eight of us in a room and we were seated in a circle, had some kind of blinkers placed on our heads, then they put the lights out. In the centre of the circle was a form of 'magic lantern' from which we were shown brief glimpses of such objects as aircraft, ships, hammers, car wheels and so on. We were unable to move our chairs from a pre-arranged spot and to stop us bending forward for a better view we were attached to the back of the chair by a clip on our collars. When the first images appeared I couldn't make too many out, so when the lady in charge passed by, I unclipped myself and leant forward for a better look! Even then I found it difficult.

When we finished and the lights came back on, I was told I had a score of 27 but the pass mark was 28 out of 30. Being so desperate to get back onto Ops I asked the woman what could be done. She was dead against any sort of fiddling but promised to add up my score again. This time it was 28 and I was in!

John finally went as a flight commander to 25 Squadron where he flew Beaufighters for 14 months. Another pilot to be involved in these sorts of schemes was Sergeant Pilot F. W. T. 'Bill' Davies, who moved from 32 to 245 Squadron in 1941. Bill remembers:

We were supposed to be night-fighters and getting worked up with Turbinlite Havocs but I never got involved in that dotty enterprise. We did do a bit of night formation, which was hazard enough!

We flew at night from Middle Wallop where 604 Squadron, with 'Cat's Eyes' Cunningham, were very much the blue-eyed boys. Having got their Beaus and early AI to work effectively they had shot down quite a number of Germans.

At Middle Wallop we were given night vision tests, consisting of trying to make out dimly illuminated objects. We were told that Cunningham was rated after his test as 'below average'!!

With a Little Help from Our Friends

Dowding seemed to have his fair share of people 'knowing' his business better than he or his immediate advisors. These people usually got to him via someone else at Air Ministry or even Winston Churchill himself. One example came from Admiral T. S. V. Phillips KCB, who was the Vice Chief of the Naval Staff, who wrote to Churchill over his concern at the night bombing of Britain and Fighter Command's lack of success to combat it.

Churchill, ever diplomatic, forwarded Tom Phillips' remarks to Dowding for comment. Whatever Dowding's reaction was at receiving this missive was certainly not reflected in his reasoned reply, although he was able to get in the odd jibe. One wonders at the reaction of Tom Phillips if Dowding or someone of similar rank and position had questioned Naval strategy? However, Phillips wrote in mid-October 1940, and Dowding's reply to the various points in his letter to the PM, are noted in italics. Remarks in square brackets are the author's:

1. There is no doubt that the interception of night bombers is the most important problem for us today. There is to my knowledge a very strong opinion among numbers of officers of the Airforce both on the higher and lower levels that more success would probably be achieved at the present time if the problem were tackled in certain additional and different ways. [One can imagine Dowding's reaction to this opening paragraph. Who were these 'officers of the Airforce'?]

(1) I think this is very probable.

2. The present methods are that Blenheims and Beauforts [sic] fitted with AI are used for endeavouring to intercept by the modern scientific methods. Defiants are also used for attempts at night interception without the use of AI. Apart from a very occasional individual, no eight-gun fighters are used for night interception. [The latter is unfair in the light of the effort the eight-gun day fighter pilots had recently put up and were continuing to put up.]

(2) This is an understatement. There is a specialist eight-gun fighter squadron in No.10 Group and a Hurricane flight has just been formed at Tangmere. In addition to this, flying is being carried out by eight-gun fighters when day Ops have not been arduous. The night before last, for instance, there was a queue of pilots waiting their turn in a Hurricane to see if they could 'wipe the eye' of the professionals.

3. With regard to AI of course, as this is perfected it should provide the ideal means of interception by night but the hard fact is that it does not deliver the goods today. At the beginning of the war, AI was stated to be a month or two ahead. After more than a year we still hear that in a month or so it may really achieve results. The Defiants have not proved themselves in this form of warfare. [They were not designed to do so!] I believe that the score today is two enemy aircraft shot down for five Defiants which have crashed.

(3) I cannot, of course, say that this statement was not made, but it was never made to me or by me.

4. In my view and in that of many Airforce officers [here they are again] I have referred to above, what we should do now, pending the perfection of AI, is to go back to simpler methods and to use our eight-gun fighters at night by specialising these squadrons in night fighting. We have at present no eight-gun fighters specialised in night fighting and I am informed that Fighter Command have expressed their unwillingness to specialise any such fighter squadrons because they state that

Top right: *Defiant night-fighter of 264 Squadron, 1941.*

Right: *Bristol Beaufighter with airborne radar (Mark IV AI) aerials.*

with the land battle still on hand they cannot afford to take any day fighter squadrons away from day work so as to specialise them in night work. [Perfectly correct. One could imagine the Navy's reaction if some ship or naval docks were hit by day raiders through a lack of day fighter cover!] The only occasions on which an eight-gun fighter goes up at night is when a few odd individuals who have not been employed by day, happen to be available. [Not strictly true and, in any event, most pilots were not trained for night flying, especially over a blacked-out countryside. Perhaps the Admiral should have tried it!]

(4) This represents my opinion. We have escaped being overwhelmed by mass attacks on the part of the German Airforce, but probably few people know by how narrow a margin.

5. This is clearly unlikely to achieve any success, as night fighting is essentially a matter in which specialisation is necessary. [Agreed.]

(5) See 2 above.

6. We have today some 65 fighter squadrons and in view of the far greater destruction that is being done in England today by night bombing as opposed to day bombing I cannot believe that we should not be justified in deflecting three (which I think is the minimum) eight-gun fighter squadrons to concentrate solely on night interception.

(6) See 4 above.

7. In the last war I understand that the night raiding of London was in fact stopped in about six weeks by the specialisation of two fighter squadrons in night fighting. [Not strictly true.] The problem is, of course, more difficult today because of the greater speed of the bomber and the greater height at which he flies, but the principles remain the same and I consider that everything should be tried today to deal with this most important problem.

(7) The principles are now quite different, and the method which achieved success at the end of the last war have proved to be quite ineffective.

8. Note. The situation seems to me to be somewhat analogous to that which existed last autumn and spring when our convoys on the East Coast were being attacked by German bombers. Fighter Command at that time were only willing to employ their modern scientific methods making use of RDF, R/T, etc, to intercept these bombers. Employed in this manner the fighters totally failed to achieve their object and the Admiralty pressed for a considerable while that Fighter Command should go back to simpler, bow and arrow methods and put their fighters with the bait, patrolling up and down the trade routes. After a considerable period, Fighter Command were induced to accept this principle and its success was instantaneous.

(8) You will not expect me here to enter into discus-
sion on convoy protection. I will merely record my disagreement.

9. A further point on which, in my view and that of others, our methods want changing, is in the areas used for interception. The principle, as I understand it, so far applied, has been to try interception on the lanes of approach or departure of the enemy aircraft. In my view, if this method had succeeded one would have nothing to say against it but it has not succeeded and I think other methods should consequently be tried.

(9) This paragraph is a little confusing. It starts by recommending a change of area and finishes by recommending a change of method.

10. If the bomber is to do real damage he must, sometime or other, arrive over his objective, which at the moment is London, and consequently interception at or close to this objective must be much easier that interception elsewhere. In view of the full moonlight of the last few nights I cannot believe that a number of interceptions would not have been achieved if our fighters had been flying about over London waiting for enemy aircraft who would have to come to them in a steady stream.

(10) Recommends a change of area and method; or rather a change of area and abandonment of method.

11. This, of course, would mean having fighter nights and gun nights over the London area but I see no disadvantage in this and certainly if on the fighter nights enemy aircraft were brought tumbling down on the housetops, the population of London would willingly do without noise of the guns which they only welcome at present because they believe it to be their only means of defence. A further point, of course, is that the fighter nights would provide some relief to the expenditure of AA ammunition which is proving a serious matter in view of the reduced quantities now being obtained from production.

(11) We must also consider what would happen in the much more probable contingency of enemy aircraft not being brought tumbling down on the housetops. [And the defending fighter pilots might not be best pleased at having to fly amidst the defending AA fire!]

12. To sum up, the two things which I should propose should be tried at once are that a minimum of three eight-gun fighter squadrons should be specialised in night fighting and be taken off all day work. We cannot expect to have AI at present but I believe they might achieve a considerable measure of success especially if used as recommended in (2) below. In any case as we hope to have AI in single-seat fighters early next year [?] it would be of the greatest value to have certain fighter squadrons already trained in night work.

(12) I should very much like to know where Admiral Phillips got his authority for this statement. It would probably disclose the source of his inspiration.

(2). I consider that we should try having fighter nights over London when the weather is suitable, as I believe that there is a far better chance of intercepting over the objective than on the lanes of approach.

T. S. V. Phillips
16 Oct 1940

Dowding added his own comments to his letter:

The fact of the matter is that from the beginning of this war we have been trying to carry on, on the assumption that night fighting could be taken up smoothly where it left off at the end of the last war.

This expectation has been entirely falsified, although a great deal of latitude has been given to various Commanders to develop theories and variations in conjunction with searchlights.

Illumination by searchlights was the basis of successful interception during the last war; and, if this were still generally possible, successful night interceptions would be extremely common. (As was the case one night before the Germans recognised the danger of flying below 10,000 feet.)

The fact is that the speed of modern bombers combined with the great altitudes at which German aircraft operate in clear weather make the combination of searchlights and sound locators quite ineffective. Illuminations of a target are comparatively rare and are seldom held long enough to enable a fighter to be brought to the spot.

Flying about on patrol lines and hoping to pick up un-illuminated targets against a luminous background or by means of exhaust flames, results in an occasional interception, but if the whole airforce were relegated to night duty on these lines, the number of interceptions would not suffice to check the night bombing menace. Furthermore, such methods are totally ineffective on moonless and cloudy nights.

In my considered opinion, the only method of approaching the problem is to devise a methodical system of utilising the two new aids which are coming forward to our assistance, viz: AI for the fighter and radio aids for the searchlights which will enable them not only to follow the target with approximate accuracy, but also to give the fighter the height of his target.

You will note that Admiral Phillips suggests no method of employment of fighters, but would merely revert to a Micawber-like method of ordering them to fly about and wait for something to turn up.

H. C. T. Dowding, Air Chief Marshal

In 1941 Sir Tom Phillips became C-in-C Eastern Fleet. On 10 December 1941 he went down with the battleship *Prince of Wales*, when she and HMS *Repulse* were sunk by Japanese bombers off the Malayan coast.

One wonders where Phillips heard about single-seat fighters with AI. How a pilot was supposed to fly and study a radar contact on a screen at the same time cannot be imagined. It was tried in India in 1943 with Hurricanes but was not a success.

CHAPTER 13

From Defence to Offence

THE BATTLE OF Britain and the fighting during November and December 1940 had cost Fighter Command dear in both men and machines. It had taken quite a beating but had remained unbowed. The severe winter weather curtailed a good deal of operational flying but it gave time for the Command to rebuild its strength.

What would the New Year bring? There was no real reason to suppose the Germans would not continue to pound Britain from the air by day once the spring weather came. The British Government knew that the planned invasion of England had been postponed indefinitely, but if a renewed assault on RAF fighter airfields started again, who could say that the invasion plan might not be reactivated?

We now know that Hitler had other plans for 1941 – Russia – but that was still some months into the future. Meantime, Fighter Command had gone some way in regrouping; it had replaced much of its lost equipment through Lord Beaverbrook's endeavours[1] and pilots continued to be produced through the training schools and OTUs. Help in numbers had also come from abroad. In 1940 there had been a steady stream of foreign nationals making their various ways to England. Airmen from Poland, Czechoslovakia, France and Norway were still arriving and even the American volunteers who joined the RAF via the Eagle squadrons were helping to swell the number of operational fighter pilots.

M. A. 'Tony' Liskutin was a Czech pilot who had escaped to Britain, via the French Air Force in 1940,

to fight on. Just like the Poles and the French who found their way into the RAF, the Czech experience was very similar. Tony Liskutin recalls what it was like for the foreign pilots who came to Britain:

When we arrived we were in rather poor shape. Hungry, dirty and despondent – it was a sad picture. The anxiety over Hitler's quick victory in France had prompted repeated questions: 'Is Britain still willing to go on fighting?' The answer came soon after landing in various places on the south coast.

Here was a calm country with self confident people and a determined Government under Winston Churchill, to fight until the end. Furthermore, there were visible signs that the RAF would accept the Czechoslovak Air Force personnel for service in the RAFVR. This friendly welcome and the speedy action formed the root from which grew new admiration for Britain, the RAF and especially the Fighter Command.

With the exception of a few communists among the Czechoslovak personnel, all applied to join the RAF almost immediately. Some of the pilots were accepted into the RAFVR within days of arrival and flying Hurricanes on operational duties a few weeks later. The efficient organisation was a real eye-opener to everybody. A remarkably friendly start, without a trace of red tape or administrative hindrance was truly astonishing. The hopes of Czech pilots had been quickly realised.

As can be expected the new arrivals were struggling with the language and only a very few were above the fundamental basic English, but they were all accepted for service, not only in Czech units but also given the opportunities to fly as fighter pilots in RAF squadrons. This new chance to participate in air battles was particularly appreciated by fighter pilots who took part in the air battle over France. Clearly, they all wanted to continue the fight.

The pre-war Czechoslovak Air Force was well trained and well equipped, but its standard fighter, the Avia

[1] Beaverbrook was the Minister of Aircraft Production. Dowding was once asked about his own victorious role in the Battle of Britain but he told the questioner that if it hadn't been for Lord Beaverbrook's energy in maintaining fighter aircraft production during this critical phase of British history, Fighter Command and its pilots would not have had the equipment with which to win. It is typical of Dowding that he should not be seen as the victor of the Battle, but to give credit to another whose achievements as far as he was concerned, outweighed his own.

B-534, was still a biplane with the performance of a Gloster Gladiator. During 1939-1940 in France, nearly 100 Czechoslovak pilots were converted onto French front-line fighters – Morane 406, Dewoitine 520 and Curtiss 75s. Despite Czech losses in France, about 80 of these pilots were made immediately available to RAF Fighter Command. Others had to undergo various degrees of retraining before entering operational service with the RAF.

It is important to note that to the Czech pilots in 1940 Fighter Command looked far more impressive than was expected. In their eyes the Command was an extraordinarily superior organisation. They quickly realised they had much to learn but this had led to the strengthening of earlier feelings of genuine admiration.

The reasons for this admiration were numerous. First of all, Fighter Command aircraft were well up to the Messerschmitt 109's performance; they carried eight guns and were equipped with a very practical gun-sight. All Hurricanes and Spitfires were equipped with full panel for instrument flying and night flying. All aircraft carried radios for a high quality R/T communication. There was a reliable system of D/F for homing and fixes and its radar system enabled the Control Rooms to control interceptions. All this was far ahead of the Luftwaffe, the French Air Force, or anybody else! Also, the practical result of this advanced aviation technology appeared to be faultless.

On the human side, the Czechoslovak pilots found Fighter Command personnel exceptionally friendly and helpful. The easy-going, friendly relationship among pilots, regardless of rank, was an entirely new experience, even though this may be difficult to explain. The organisation at squadron and flight level was also much admired. Everything looked so sensible and logical; the practical duty rostering deserves a special mention.

Last, but not least, came the feeling of complete confidence in leadership. The commanding officers were universally held in the highest respect and were much admired. Squadron Leaders Stan Turner, Tony Lovell, Wing Commander H. Bird-Wilson and Wing Commander G. D. M. Blackwood remain in my own memory as outstanding examples.

All the favourable impressions from early experiences were confirmed in the remaining years of the war. Fighter Command remained as an excellent example to Czechoslovak pilots in every way. In fact, it was inspiration on which to base the formation of the post-war Czechoslovak Air Force between 1945 and 47, which, unhappily, the communist putsch swept away in 1948.

Taking the Offensive

Having survived the onslaught of 1940, even the most humble of RAF fighter pilots began to think it was time to start 'dishing some out' to the Luftwaffe. While the

Pilots of 312 Czech Squadron, March 1942, at readiness. L to R: J. Novotny, V. Kaslik, V. Slouf, J. Soder and M. Liskutin.

future was still very uncertain, perhaps during this supposed lull, the RAF could have a go at hitting back.
Not that there was much to hit back with. Bomber Command was stepping up its night bombing of Germany
but still on a very limited scale and not with any great
effect. Coastal Command was busy trying to organise
itself for a war in which German occupation of French
coastal bases had not been envisaged, so what could be
done? Well, if nothing else perhaps Fighter Command
could begin by taking some of the war to the enemy.

The nearest enemy was in France – the Luftwaffe,
which had given Fighter Command so much trouble in
1940. With the best form of defence still being attack,
why not seek out the enemy over its own – even if
occupied – territory? Nobody envisaged this would last
for long. Once the spring weather came along the
Germans would probably be back but meantime . . . .

It began with just a small showing of bravado by
sending out a couple of Spitfires of 66 Squadron flown
by Flight Lieutenant G. P. Christie and Pilot Officer
C. A. W. Bodie, on what was no more than a nuisance
mission. They flew out on 20 December 1940 at low
level, shot up the airfield at Le Touquet and returned.
They had met no opposition and had done very little
damage, merely shooting up some buildings, but it had
been a start.

These sorts of sorties would later be known as
'Rhubarbs' although in the beginning they were code-
named as 'Mosquito' raids. Like the bite of a mosquito,
they could be irritating and sometimes deadly! In the
beginning there was a good deal of excitement in flying
these missions. It was a chance to hit back; it had all
the elements of fun, especially to the exuberant character of the fighter pilot. Here they were, like errant school-
boys, sitting in a powerful weapon of war, being allowed
to shoot up almost anything they saw which looked
German or that might be helping the German war effort.
Later, as the reality of it became clear, it became less
funny, very costly, and the results questionable.

But for the time being, almost any squadron based
in southern England, who felt they'd like to nip over
to France and have a crack at road or rail transport,
perhaps surprise soldiers on a road or an unsuspecting
German pilot flying from one base to another, were
usually allowed to do so. The weather had to be right,
however. Group HQ would only sanction such an operation if there was plenty of low cloud about into which
the two fighters could quickly hide if they ran into

trouble from Me109s. The fighters had of course to fly
at low level both to avoid detection by enemy radar, and
to be low enough to surprise a would-be target and be
away before any ground fire got them.

Fighter Command, however, while not discouraging
this sort of operation knew full well that if it was to
hurt the Luftwaffe, it had to bring it into combat. In
many ways it was brave thinking in early 1941 after
taking such a hammering just a few months earlier, even
to contemplate engaging enemy aircraft over their own
territory. It seemed just like the doctrines of WW1 all
over again, only this time for the trenches, read the
English Channel.

Throughout the First War in France, the Royal
Flying Corps and then in 1918, the RAF, had followed
a course of offensive action, of always taking the war
to the enemy. The Germans, for their part, took on a
purely defensive role in that war, being quite content
in letting the British and French flyers come to them.
This was about to happen all over again but on a much
larger scale.

Still with the thought of a continuation of the Battle
of Britain, Fighter Command agreed to send out RAF
fighters across the Channel to do battle with the Luftwaffe. On 9 January 1941, five squadrons of RAF
fighters boldly flew to France, penetrated 30 miles inland
then flew back again. They had seen nothing of the
enemy. If it seems surprising that the Germans took no
apparent notice of 60 fighters flying above northern
France, it shouldn't. As Fighter Command itself, and
especially 11 Group's commander, Keith Park, had
found, enemy fighters on their own constituted no danger
in themselves, so it was best to leave them alone. Only
if they escorted bombers or carried bombs themselves
was there a need to engage the deadly Me109s, or the
less deadly Me110s.

Fighter Command, therefore, had to entice the enemy
into the air with some form of bait, so that its own Spitfires and Hurricanes could get to grips with the German
fighters. They termed these operations as 'Circuses', a
small group of bombers, generally Blenheims from 2
Group, escorted to a target with the sole object of bringing the enemy into a combat situation. Circus No.1 was
mounted on 10 January.

The First Circus Operation

Originally this sort of operation was planned for late
December, but bad weather had prevented it until now.
On this Friday, haze over the Channel prevented its com-
mencement till just before noon. Three squadrons of
Hurricanes took off from RAF North Weald, led by
Wing Commander Victor Beamish DSO DFC AFC, the
37-year-old station commander of North Weald, meet-
ing six Blenheims over Southend. Here they were met

Top left: *Among the first chosen wing leaders
in 1941 were Douglas Bader . . .*

Far left: *. . . Bob Stanford Tuck . . .*

Left: *. . . and A. G. 'Sailor' Malan.*

by three Spitfire squadrons from Hornchurch and then headed for France.

The target was the Forêt de Guines airfield. Some Me109s did make an appearance, Beamish and a Polish pilot each shooting down one, the latter then shooting up some Heinkel bombers he spotted on the airfield. Three Spitfire squadrons from Biggin Hill became part of the operation when they took off to patrol the French coast to assist in the formation's withdrawal, but they did not engage the enemy. They left it rather late to return home, losing a pilot when fuel ran short.

The official report on this operation read as follows:

1. An Offensive Sweep was carried out over NW France by three Hurricane squadrons, 46, 242, 249, three Spitfire squadrons, 41, 64, 611, and six Blenheims of 114 Squadron. In addition, three Spitfire squadrons, 66, 74, and 92, patrolled the Channel and acted as cover for the return of the main body.

2. The Blenheim bombers flew at 10,000 feet and were closely escorted by 56 Squadron, with 242 Squadron 1,000 feet below and to the right, while 249 Squadron were stepped up at about 100 feet and to the right and 'up-sun' of 242 Squadron. The three Spitfire squadrons were stepped up above the bombers and to the left, with the top squadron – 41 – at about 16,000 feet.

3. The formation left Southend at 1219 hours and made landfall just East of Calais at 1240. The bombers lost height and approached their target at 7,000 feet from the SE. Dispersal pens and huts in the wood SW of Guines landing ground were bombed from 6,800 feet, at 1249 with 16x250 lb and 48x40 lb bombs. The bombs straddled the wood and black smoke from the fires was observed. The Blenheims crossed the French coast on the return journey, west of Calais at 7,000 feet and made landfall at Folkestone at 3,000 feet, landing at Hornchurch at 1329. The weather was clear and cloudless during the entire patrol and visibility was excellent.

4. 249 Squadron reports having accurate AA just inland after first crossing the French coast and very accurate AA from Bofors guns on four boats off Calais on the way home. Our pilots remark on the complete absence of life on the roads, countryside and coast. Gun posts were seen 'deserted' and aerodromes and fields near them which were covered with snow, quite unmarked.

5. Wing Commander Beamish machine-gunned the four AA boats and saw his bullets raking their decks and this causing AA fire to cease. One pilot saw an aircraft blown to bits by the AA shells and since all of our aircraft are accounted for this must be assumed to be an enemy aircraft. No balloons and no other shipping were seen.

6. On the way back across the Channel Wing Commander Beamish saw a Hurricane being attacked by a yellow-nosed Me109. The Hurricane was streaming

glycol and eventually crashed into the cliffs near Dover. Pilot Officer McConnell baled out and is in hospital with a broken leg. Wing Commander Beamish shot this 109 into the sea.

7. Sergeant Maciejowski, Polish, got separated from his section and attacked two Me109s. They were at the same height as himself so he climbed a thousand feet and attacked the rear one. It turned steeply and dived vertically towards the ground, as though the pilot had been hit, and crashed into some trees.

8. 41 Squadron reports that when the Blenheims were leaving the French coast on the return journey, Sergeants Baker and Beardsley, who were acting as rear guards at 19,000 feet, attacked five Me109 with yellow noses, who were at 17,000 feet and climbing steeply behind the Squadron into the sun. One of these 109s was probably destroyed by Sergeant Baker and was seen diving vertically from 15,000 to 1,000 feet haze over the sea near Gravelines by two other pilots.

9. The organisation laid down in 11 Group operation Order No.17 appears to work perfectly but it is considered that with so many squadrons working at such a distance apart, communications on the Group Command frequency are unsatisfactory.

This operation set a pattern for the year, sending small formations of bombers into France escorted by large numbers of fighters. It became the fighter pilot's summer, or as they sportingly called it – 'The Shooting Season'.

Operations Over France

As the spring came, and with it better flying weather, so Fighter Command with 2 Group light bombers, began to step up its new offensive actions. It developed, too, a number of distinct operations by code names, with which to carry out its assigned task of, as Leigh-Mallory liked to put it, 'leaning into Europe'.

Circus. A bomber or fighter bomber operation heavily escorted by fighters. Designed primarily to draw enemy fighters into the air.

Sweep. General term for fighters flying an offensive mission over enemy territory or sea. Could be flown in conjunction with but not in direct support of a force of bombers.

Rodeo. Fighter sweep over enemy territory without bombers.

Ramrod. A similar operation to a Circus but where the objective is the destruction of a specific target.

Rhubarb. Small scale freelance fighter operation to attack targets of opportunity, usually in bad weather.

Once these operations had been devised and laid down, they changed little over the next couple of years. They did become more sophisticated, the Group or Command planners increasingly trying to devise more ways of

Hurricanes of 601 Squadron flew early Ops in 1941 before the Spitfire began to dominate day offensive operations.

Sergeant Frank Mares DFM, a Czech pilot with 601 Squadron, 1941.

ensuring the enemy would (a) come up, and (b) be caught in the net of fighter operations which either escorted or supported the main operation.

Thus eventually, the following types of tasks could be assigned to one or any number of squadrons or wings:

Close Escort	Surrounding and keeping with the bombers at all time.
Escort Cover	Protecting the close escort fighters.
High Cover	Preventing enemy fighters positioning themselves above the close escort and cover escort wings.
Top Cover	Tied to the bomber route on Circus and Ramrod missions but having a roving commission to sweep the sky in the immediate area of the bombers' route.
Target Support	Independently routed fighters flying directly to and then to cover the target area.
Withdrawal Cover	Fighters supporting the return journey when escorting fighters would be running short of fuel and ammunition.
Fighter Diversion	A wing or wings creating a diversionary sweep to keep hostile aircraft from the main target area on Ramrod operations.

The Wing Leaders

To ensure the smooth running of any of these operations men were needed who could oversee the operations in the air. Planning was all very well but it would need the air fighter leaders to achieve success. It was now that Leigh-Mallory's ideas from his 12 Group days began to be realised. The days of single squadrons operating independently were largely over as far as major operations were concerned. Fighter squadrons were now being grouped in fighter wings under a wing leader, a man of proven ability in air combat and leadership. These leaders (based at sector stations) and their wings were known by the station name: e.g. Kenley Wing, Biggin Hill Wing, and so on.

A list of the first men suggested for such tasks was put together as early as 7 December 1940, by Leigh-Mallory when he was still AOC 12 Group. He wrote to Sholto Douglas confirming that in his Big Wing operations they had so far used five squadrons together, i.e. 60 aircraft. He also considered operating on offensive actions with up to three wings of three squadrons: 108 aircraft.

The main objective, as already mentioned, was to have enemy fighters engage the wings. At this early stage it was envisaged that only Hurricanes would give bomber cover while Spitfires covered both. There would not be any Hurricane-only fighter wings. Leigh-Mallory thought the following men suitable for leading the new wings:

Wing Commander F. V. Beamish DSO DFC AFC, commanding North Weald.

Wing Commander H. Broadhurst DFC AFC, commanding Hornchurch.

Wing Commander J. H. Edwardes-Jones DFC, formerly CO of 213 Squadron.

Wing Commander H. W. Mermagen AFC, formerly CO of 222 and 226 Squadrons.

Wing Commander R. B. Lees DFC, commanding Coltishall, and formerly 72 Squadron.

Wing Commander H. A. V. Hogan DFC, formerly CO of 501 Squadron.

Wing Commander S. F. Godden, formerly CO of 3 Squadron.

Wing Commander H. S. Darley DSO, commanding Exeter and formerly 609 Squadron.

Wing Commander R. H. A. Leigh, HQ 12 Group, former CO of 66 Squadron.

Wing Commander H. D. McGregor DSO, formerly CO of 213 Squadron.

Wing Commander J. Worrall DFC, Senior Controller Biggin Hill and former CO of 32 Squadron.

Wing Commander J. W. C. More DFC, 9 Group and former CO of 73 Squadron

Squadron Leader D. R. S. Bader DSO DFC, CO 242 Squadron and the 12 Group Big Wing.

Squadron Leader R. G. Kellett DSO DFC, CO 303 Polish Squadron.

Squadron Leader W. M. Churchill DSO DFC, CO of 71 Eagle Squadron.

Squadron Leader J. R. A. Peel DFC, CO 145 Squadron.

Each had merit in the eyes of Leigh-Mallory; a number of them were very much Leigh-Mallory men. Looking at Fighter Command as a whole, as obviously Dowding did, there were some names missing. Squadron Leader A. G. Malan DSO DFC, CO of 74 Squadron, Squadron Leader R. R. S. Tuck DFC, who commanded 257 Squadron, Squadron Leader M. L. Robinson DFC, CO 609 Squadron, Squadron Leader I. R. Gleed DFC, CO 87 Squadron and Squadron Leader J. A. Kent DFC, CO of 92 Squadron, must all have been contenders as their later records show.

In the event, some of the first wing leaders were Harry Broadhurst (Hornchurch), Victor Beamish followed by Ronald Kellett (North Weald), Johnnie Peel (Kenley), Sailor Malan (Biggin Hill), Douglas Bader (Tangmere). It was these men, and others like them, who truly began to take the war to the enemy and paved the way for all future offensive actions and tactics.

At the Sharp End

The impression shouldn't be taken that the Luftwaffe was now dormant, far from it. The night-time blitz was in full swing, so with the bombers now occupied in this way, there was nothing for the German fighters to escort. The Me109 pilots, however, were still offensive in that they were keen, and were encouraged, to fly hunting sorties over southern England in the spring of 1941 – almost like the RAF Rhubarb sorties.

This forced Fighter Command to fly standing patrols of fighters off the coast in order to be in the air and ready for when these *Freie-Jagd* 109s headed in, usually low and fast.

The airfield at Manston was often hit by strafing 109s during this period so the base continued to be just as dangerous a place as it had been in 1940.

No.601 Squadron was based at Northolt in the first months of 1941, then moved to Manston in May. Through the recollections of one of its Czechoslovak pilots, Sergeant Frantisek Mares, we can see the growing dangers of a Rhubarb sortie and the drama of a standing patrol, watching for Me109s. He too had come to England to fight via the French Air Force:

On 12 April 1941 came the first Rhubarb operation flown by our Squadron. Naturally every pilot wanted to be chosen to be the first to go, everyone begging the CO, Squadron Leader O'Neill for the honour, so he eventually had to put all the names into a hat. To my and Flight Lieutenant Whitney Straight's delight, we were the two who won the draw. After briefing, the two of us flew from Northolt to Manston where we had the fuel tanks of our Hurricanes topped up and the aircraft checked.

Wasting no time and in good visibility, we took off and at 900 feet climbed into a dense, moisture-laden 10/10ths cloud. This was excellent weather for Rhubarb Ops, but I found the visibility so poor I had to keep myself tucked well in behind my leader's starboard wing. We headed on our previously agreed and timed course, aiming to emerge below the clouds close to the German fighter base at St Omer.

Maintaining my position and strict radio silence, we finally emerged from the clouds, opened out our formation to begin the search for suitable targets. Within a couple of minutes Straight began a steep left diving turn onto a reciprocal course, which was the last I saw of him until I got back to base.

My opportunity for action came near Hazebrouck when I spotted an oil/gas storage tank among some trees to my right. I immediately dived, fired, but when no flames or explosion ensued, attacked again. In the second

Flight Sergeant Frank Jensen, 601 Squadron, 1941, later Group Captain DFC* AFC.

dive I was hit from behind by a cannon shell which hit the outside edge of the behind-the-seat armour plate, sending shell fragments smashing into the cockpit and instrument panel. Powdered glass and cordite made my eyes sting and then I became aware that my right arm had also been hit. I sustained more damage to my fighter, and quickly became aware of four Me109s trying their best to shoot me down. With my engine at full power I went into a very tight loop, the Hurricane shuddering as I came close to a high speed stall. I levelled out at no more than 100 feet above the earth and there in front of me, dead ahead and just begging to be shot down, sat one of the Messerschmitts. I was still firing when at no more than 50 feet above some trees, the 109 turned onto its back spewing smoke.

A quick glance into my rear-view mirror almost led to disaster and I thought for certain I was going to die. When I looked ahead again, blades of grass were being mowed down by the tips of my propeller. I yanked back on the stick to prevent imminent disaster, which resulted in my tail wheel hitting the ground – hard! The Hurricane lurched, the engine died and I watched petrified as the prop began to mill round silently. Then I was going through some high voltage electricity cables, a steel pylon flashing by. Protectively, my hands and feet came off the controls and I prayed!

Suddenly and miraculously the engine then burst into life. I was still on the deck with the 109s behind, their shells still ripping into my fighter. In sheer desperation I decided to hug the ground and began weaving around trees, scattered buildings and other such obstacles. With no sun to guide me, my homing instincts took over and then I was over the coast, bullets still hitting the Hurricane, churning up the sea ahead of me. Now, with nowhere to hide except the clouds above, I pulled the emergency boost lever, went into a steep climb and prayed I could reach them before the 109s got me. I made it, only to fall out of their safety as none of my blind flying instruments worked. Back in the clouds I 'switched on the seat of my pants', in which mode I flew on for 15 minutes.

When I eventually emerged below the clouds, the English coast was just ahead and I quickly looked for a place to land. I came down on Gatwick airfield and despite having no 'green lights' when I selected wheels down (although I heard the wheels lock), and no flap control, landed safely after a couple of attempts. As I climbed down I was amazed at the damage to my Hurricane (Z2803).

A section of 601 Squadron standing patrol.

Apart from 240 plus holes, a 50-foot length of finger-thick HT cable was hooked around the radiator and I had no tail wheel! When Sergeant Frank Jensen later came to collect me in the squadron 'Maggie' he asked me if I'd forgotten my parachute. As I sat in the two-seater, he went to my Hurricane and with the help of an airman took it from the bucket seat. They found that five bullets had penetrated the bottom of the fuselage, gone through the seat and into the parachute pack, the folds of silk saving me from serious – and embarrassing – injury!

Then, flying from RAF Manston:

Shortly after 3 pm on 16 May 1941, Sergeant T. A. McCann and I took off to carry out a 'Channel patrol' designed to combat hit and run raids by German fighters over the south-east and southern coasts of England. Our patrol line was between Ramsgate and Dungeness and we reached 4,000 feet in clear, cloudless weather. I took station some distance behind McCann's Hurricane, doing 'S' turns, which we called 'weaving'. Then, low over the sea, I spotted a monoplane heading for the English coast but at my height I could not positively identify it. Suddenly the machine went into a steep climb and headed for McCann, who was about half a mile ahead, heading west.

I had a suspicion that it was a 109 and now this confirmed it. I finally recognised its shape and saw the black cross on the fuselage. I reduced speed slightly and by retaining my altitude let the 109 pilot set himself up in front of me and it was then that I called McCann to break. McCann abruptly went into steep diving right hand turn and the 109, like a 'sitting duck', about 100 yards in front, took a long burst of steady fire from my guns. The enemy pilot reacted by turning left towards the French coast and foolishly went into a steep climb. I pulled the boost control and with my Hurricane 'hanging on the prop', I opened fire again from 50 feet right into the 109's belly. Bits started to come off, then black smoke poured from its engine as the fighter went into a steep dive which ended in the sea not far off Folkestone.

I had fired 480 rounds of ball and 960 of armour-piercing bullets and from the time I first sighted the 109 until it went into the sea it was just as if the pilot had wanted to commit suicide.

I was on another Channel patrol just short of a month later, 13 June, this time with Sergeant Norman Taylor, although on this occasion I had a Mark IIC with 20mm cannon. Unfortunately I had no chance to fire them. I was again weaving behind my leader when we were suddenly confronted by four Me109s, two coming at us head-on! Taylor immediately began to fire, but I could not do so in case I hit his Hurricane. It all happened very fast and one 109 was already streaming smoke. When Taylor dived after the second 109 he was again right in front of me so again I couldn't fire. This 109 was hit as it went into some haze and when I went through it, saw a large white patch in the sea where presumably the 109 had gone in.

Flight Sergeant Frank Jensen, who had collected Mares from Gatwick, was himself subjected to an attack by Me109s as he landed at RAF Manston, by some free-ranging Me109 fighters on 4 May, 1941. Manston had been nick-named 'Hell Fire Corner' in 1940 and had not lost its famous name:

I was completing a dusk patrol, flying on finals with my No.2 covering above, when twelve Me109s came in from the sea at low level and beat up the airfield – and me!

They dropped four bombs and put bullets or shells through *both* my mainplanes, setting the Hurricane on fire. When I had got it on the ground and slowed a bit, I jumped out of the cockpit. However, I was landing uphill and so the aircraft stopped and the fire went out. I got back in and taxied in to Manston's dispersal area.

Looking at the damage to my wings afterwards, I often wondered whether or not the attacking 109 was before or beyond its harmonisation point of its guns! It was not very comfortable sitting in the middle of it all. At the same time, I suppose it could have been two 109s, going for the same target!

CHAPTER 14

1941: Build-up for Supremacy

FIGHTER COMMAND ENDED 1940 with a strength of 1,243 pilots plus a further 281 non-operational or non-effective pilots. Of the latter, 45 non-operational men would be available in seven days, while 86 non-effective men would also be available in seven days. Thus by early 1941, total pilots was estimated at 1,655.

Pilot casualties for December 1940 alone had been 57 and with a further 111 men posted away, the end of the year figure was down 168. There was then an immediate increase in squadron establishment by a further six squadrons and an Operational Training Unit which creamed off a further 130 pilots. OTU output in December had been 111 (the same figure as those posted to other duties) so there was a net deficiency of 187 pilots as January began.

By 31 March 1941 numbers had risen slightly to 1,759, made up from 1,414 operational, 264 non-effective, but with 81 available within seven days. On the same date, the Command had 82 squadrons with 1,702 pilots (20.7 per squadron). Between the end of 1940 and the end of

Feeding ·303 ammunition (left) into the wing bays of a Hurricane. And (right) keep it coming lads! More ·303 ammo for a 249 Squadron Hurricane. Note patches over the gun ports to protect them from dust and dirt during take-off.

March, the Command had lost 414 pilots made up as follows:

Posted overseas	52
Wastage from squadrons	189
Posted to OTUs as instructors	80
Posted to Training Command	93

Sholto Douglas wrote to Sir Charles Portal, Chief of the Air Staff on 16 April 1941, reporting on the enormous amount of operational flying being carried out by his pilots. This was largely made up of shipping protection sorties. The fighter pilots might have been busy in 1940, but now the flying seemed even more intense even if they were not often engaging the enemy.

Between November 1940 and February 1941 Fighter Command was flying an average of 424 operational flying hours per month, which increased to 2,103 hours in March. In the first two weeks of April the figure topped 2,708 hours with an expected ceiling of 5,000 by the end of that month.

Added to the daily workload was the Command's commitment to help night fighter operations. For the first three months of 1941, day fighters had flown the following hours on night sorties:

Month	Hours flown	EA destroyed
Jan	295	1
Feb	453	–
Mar	740	4
Totals:	1,488	5

Douglas's problem was that he now only had 66 front line day fighter squadrons and six had just been ordered overseas. The war in the Middle East was beginning to drain Fighter Command's resources just at a time when it was regaining its lost strength after the Battle of Britain and was expecting a renewal of active operations against Britain.

Portal, in response to Sholto Douglas's concern over numbers in case of a renewal of activity over southern England, was that Air Ministry Intelligence estimated that the Luftwaffe was no larger than it had been in 1940 and that it too had commitments in the Middle East and was having to support the Italians in the North Africa and in Greece. If, however, another assault on Britain began, the RAF would once again take experienced pilots from other Commands and put them through quick conversion courses at OTUs. For instance, the Fleet Air Arm had supplied 22 pilots who had fought with RAF squadrons in the Battle of Britain, nine of whom had been killed.

Douglas had to be content with this and a week later his Command reported that his total of operational pilots in his 66 squadrons numbered 1,148 with another 314

non-operational. His hard-pressed night fighter squadrons totalled just 16 with 251 operational pilots and another 20 non-operational. He lost another squadron before April.

The only glimmer of hope was that at the OTUs the present capacity of pilots was 556 with a pupil strength of 453. Despite Portal's optimism, Fighter Command was estimating that Germany still had a strength of 2,500 aircraft to operate against Britain.

What all these figures meant was that by April 1941, Fighter Command strength was only 20% stronger than it had been at the start of August 1940. The following list shows the figures clearly:

	Day Sqdns	Op pilots	Non-op pilots	Total
1 August 1940	53	909	213	1,122
14 April 1941	65	1,129	191	1,320

When he lost the six squadrons to the Middle East the figures read:

1 May 1941	59	991	191	1,182

What was also exercising the C-in-C's mind was that the proportion of experienced pilots in the Command was less than it had been in the summer of 1940, because of losses; not just casualties but men and experience 'lost' to Training Command and to overseas units. And he knew too, that the advantage in fighter performance at high altitude still lay with the enemy, despite promised new performance fighters.

Tools of the Trade

Fighter Command's two main fighters were still the Spitfire and Hurricane, although the Spitfire squadrons now exceeded the number flying Hurricanes. With the offensive against the Luftwaffe over northern France starting in earnest, the Spitfire was taking the major share in these sorties.

The improved Spitfire Mark II with the Merlin XII engine (1,175 hp) began arriving on the squadrons in late 1940. The Mark IIB carried four ·303 machine guns and two 20mm cannon. The cannon armament problems had largely been solved by this time, and although there was a strong debate going on not only at Command but at squadron level as to whether cannon or machine guns were the best armament, the 20mm gun was here to stay.

Then in March came the first deliveries of the Spitfire Mark V with its 1,440 hp Merlin 45 series engine. The VA still carried eight machine guns but the VB again had two cannons and four machine guns. Later came the Mark VC which had a 'universal' wing capable of taking either machine guns, machine guns and cannons or four 20mm cannons.

Enter the cannon Hurricane IIC. 20mm ammunition being fed into the gun bays.

The Spitfire Mark V enters service in 1941. 222 Squadron, with two 20mm cannons.

No.92 Squadron was the first unit to receive the Mark V Spitfire and this variant gradually equipped all front-line Spitfire squadrons during the year.

Some reluctance to use cannon armament was because of the previously bad reputation the cannon had received when first introduced during 1940. There was also the problem that each of the two cannons only carried 60 rounds, whereas the eight machine guns each carried 350 rounds of ·303. There is often talk of the rate of fire of RAF fighter armament, such as 1,100 rounds per minute for the ·303, or 750 rpm for the cannon. Whatever the published rpm's were, because of the rounds carried, it only gave the pilot some 16-18 seconds of fire for his ·303 or just 8-9 seconds of fire from the 20mm guns.

The seasoned fighter pilots had begun to find, especially in the latter stages of the Battle of Britain, that German bombers were becoming more heavily protected by armour plating, and that the ·303 ammunition was not causing the damage it had earlier. With the cannon, however, even if its capacity was less, it needed far less rounds to do the damage necessary to bring down an opponent.

Meantime, the Hurricane had also been improved. The Mark IIA began arriving at squadrons in the summer of 1940, followed by the IIB in the new year. The Mark II also had an improved engine; the IIB also being fitted with 12 x ·303 machine guns. However, it had already been decided that the cannon was to be the RAF's main fighter armament by this time and so the IIC began to arrive, carrying four cannons, two in each wing. By then, however, the Spitfire was flying most of the day operations over France, so the IIC-equipped Hurricane units began to be used for anti-shipping sorties or for attacking specific targets in northern France.

The Hurricane had still a lot of useful life left in it, but by the late spring of 1941, in Europe it was taking less of a day fighter role and was more of a ground attack aircraft. In the Middle East, and later the Far East, it would continue to be the backbone of day fighter Ops until Spitfires too went into those theatres.

Controlling the Fighters

With Fighter Command now beginning to go on the offensive, there were two elements which went together in order to bring off a successful operation. One was a competent wing leader flying on the 'show' the other was the equally capable fighter controller.

As the war progressed, the fighter controller really came into his own, aided by ever increasing improvements in radar. The lions share of the kudos did go to the leader and his pilots, but if it had not been for the controller, the build-up to an air battle or interception would have been very haphazard. Indeed, if the controll-

ing side of the air war hadn't been able to do the job, there probably wouldn't have been an 'offensive' as we know it.

It didn't happen overnight, but built up steadily over 1941 to become almost an art form by 1942-43. In the beginning it was very different. In 1940 the controllers had gradually built up a reasonable reputation for putting the defending fighters in the right place at the right time, but not always. It was not an exact science by any means and although radar gave an enemy's position, the number of aircraft could vary widely, and the height was always difficult to ascertain with any accuracy.

When operating over northern France, it became more difficult but fortunately the radar accuracy improved and so too did the controlling. In the beginning, however, it wasn't always a success. On 5 March 1941, for instance, the RAF fighters came off second best during a fighter sweep to Boulogne. Wing Commander Gerald Maxwell DSO MC DFC, a first war fighter pilot, and now Wing Commander Tactics at 11 Group, had to make a report on this operation for the AOC, Leigh-Mallory. It read:

No.610 Squadron under Flight Lieutenant S. C. Norris DFC led the formation and was told to fly at 25,000 feet with 616 Squadron at 28,000 and 145 Squadron at 30,000. Formation circled Hastings at the right time and the proper heights but failed to find the bomber formation or its escort fighters. After circling for 10 minutes, leader asked Controller for instructions, saying he was unable to contact the 'friends'. The Controller took the friends to mean the other two squadrons, ie: 610 and 145, whereas, of course, the leader meant the bomber formation.

At about 1330 hours the formation had been in the air for one hour, Controller vectored the three squadrons on 100 degrees which took them out to sea towards Boulogne. About mid-Channel they were told by Control that bandits were approaching from the south in their vicinity. Immediately after, leader sighted four yellow-nosed Me109s which attacked from about 500 feet higher, apparently with great determination. A dog-fight ensued and the whole squadron – 610 – broke up and eventually eight pilots returned to their base singly, landing between 1410 and 1430. Neither leader nor anyone else knew what had happened to the four missing pilots who were inexperienced and the only information I was able to obtain from one of the 610 pilots was that six more 109s approached from the south after the dog-fight had been going on for some time.

In the meantime, the two higher squadrons, 616 and 145, had lost touch with 610, and 616 did not see any enemy aircraft and they eventually returned to its base. 145 ran short of oxygen and returned to base at 1340 without having anything to report.

The whole operation seems to have been unfortunate and it was incredible that four 109s with only 500 feet advantage in height should have been able to break up completely a squadron of twelve Spitfire IIs and presumably bring down four of them.

Leigh-Mallory came to the conclusion that the problem was the controllers who failed to realise the bombers had not linked up. When the airfield controllers gave the vector towards Boulogne without any reference to the Group Controller, it was considered a very improper action.

The Me109s were obviously up because bombers were known to be in on the main operation, but as Johnnie Johnson recalls, it was different in the early days. In early 1941 Johnson was just an ordinary squadron pilot, flying with 616 Squadron. His days as Fighter Command's highest scoring pilot were still in the future:

Apart from trying to be offensive over France there was little else we could do in 1941. In the early days, when we used to fly over at 25,000 feet, they used to take no notice of us at all. Then Leigh-Mallory persuaded 2 Group to put a few bombers up and the Germans reacted quite violently. Before the Germans opened the Russian front, there were quite a few fighters in France.

Of course, we thought we were bloody marvellous. We didn't know the claims were over-optimistic, bombing claims were over-optimistic; Leigh-Mallory would come down and say we were all doing bloody well, so we all thought we *were* doing well. But other than Bomber Command, there was no other force fighting the enemy in Europe. At least we were carrying the fight to them and Leigh-Mallory was eager to 'reach out' and 'get over to the Hun.'

We thought really that this was just an extension of the Battle of Britain and we were making a big contribution. We expected, of course, for the battle fought in 1940, to be continued in 1941 which was why Wing Commanders Flying were appointed and we would now be fighting in wing strength. All the talk was about – 'when they come back in the spring . . . .'

New Aircraft and New Ideas

In 1941 there were a couple of new aeroplane types coming forward to take their place in Fighter Command's arsenal. One was the Westland Whirlwind.

The Whirlwind was the result of the pre-war thinking of having a twin-engined bomber destroyer. It was also to be the first RAF twin-engined single-seater to see service. The Whirlwind did not appear until July 1940, going to 263 Squadron at Drem, but owing to problems with the Rolls Royce Peregrine engines the squadron retained its Hurricanes until late in the year. 263's first claim against a German aircraft with the new

type was in January 1941 off the Scillies. As its primary role had been to destroy bombers, the Whirlwind had a heavy armament of four 20mm cannons in the nose.

John Wray, after his period on night fighters, later flew the Whirlwind, and remembers:

It was designed as a fighter – a bomber destroyer – and was the only aircraft at that time to carry four 20mm cannons. Again it was the classic example of an aeroplane that was built with defensive thinking and purposes because there was no cross-feed between the two fuel tanks. So if you lost an engine, you couldn't use the fuel out of its tank which in almost all multi-engined aircraft is the normal requirement. But the aircraft was only expected to go up over the UK, do what it had to do and come down again. There was no question that if you lost an engine, instead of using the fuel, you just came down and landed. It was only much later when we started using it on offensive operations over the other side, that while two engines were a godsend, it was a damn nuisance about the tanks. How absurd to have a tank of petrol you couldn't use with an engine knocked-out, with the other running out of petrol!

Unfortunately it had such a stop-start development, that by the time it got into service, the Hurricane IIC with its four 20mm cannon and the Spit V with two cannon, had arrived and so the Whirlwind didn't have a place. There was no sense in building three aircraft so the Whirlwind was stopped.

Only 112 were built and formed 263 Squadron. They toyed with the idea of using them for night fighting and gave 25 Squadron one to try, but then they formed a second squadron, 137, and tried to use them as long-range fighters, which was clearly not on because it just didn't have the range necessary. But it did carry out one or two operations in an escorting role to fairly nearby targets such as Antwerp and so on, and the famous one to Cologne in August 1941 but that was all.

However, in the hands of an experienced Whirlwind pilot, it could hold its own against an Me109 or FW190 provided he wasn't up against Adolf Galland or someone like that. The Whirlwind really was a remarkable little aeroplane, particularly at low level.

Fighter Command began to look round for another role for the Whirlwind and came up with the idea of using it as a fighter bomber. It adapted to this role very well, but it had other problems as John also remembers:

The other trouble was that the Whirlwind had an exactor system for operating the throttles and the airspeed controls: i.e., oil under pressure rather than linkage. So as soon as one started getting up to altitude and different changes in air pressure the engines started getting out of synchronisation. The way we dealt with that was with the throttles. We pushed them hard forward against the stops and with the airspeed controls you pulled them back into fully coarse in order to prime them. Can you imagine doing that in the middle of a combat situation? We began having that trouble a lot of the time at altitude, so once 263 Squadron put bombs on their aircraft it breathed new life into the aircraft.

It had enormous advantages as a fighter bomber. It was able to carry 2x250lb or 2x500lb bombs, although we rarely carried the 500-pounders. It had four cannon stuck in the nose – right down the line of sight – ideal for attacking ground targets. But here again we go back to its original development as a defensive fighter for we only had 60 rounds per gun (drum fed).

It was very fast and in fact at low level, without bombs, it could outstrip a FW190. It also had a big teardrop hood which other fighters hadn't got at that time which gave the pilot enormous visibility all round.

Another aircraft that made its appearance in 1941 was Hawkers' replacement for the Hurricane, the Typhoon. Again it was an aircraft designed primarily to carry 20mm cannons, and although promised for 1940, did not arrive on a squadron (56) until September 1941. This new fighter, too, suffered from many engine problems (the Napier Sabre), plus a number of other unfortunate happenings like tails falling off and fumes coming into the cockpit!

For a while it was touch and go whether the Typhoon would survive these problems but it did eventually, although then it was found that as a pure fighter it did not match up to the latest Spitfires. However, it was, like the Whirlwind, found to be extremely good at lower altitudes and so was developed as a fighter-bomber and ground attack aircraft, in which role it was devastating later in the war.

With the Lease-Lend scheme now firmly established with America (still neutral) the RAF had purchased some American aircraft in an attempt to fill the void. Two fighters which appeared in RAF units in 1941 were the Bell Airacobra (601 Squadron) and the Curtiss P.40 Tomahawk (No.2 Army Co-operation Squadron). Neither was good enough for the European theatre, although the P.40 did see some operations in the Army Co-operation role. It found its niche in North Africa, while the Airacobra saw no action with the RAF.

Whatever the aircraft or the role, Fighter Command's new offensive stance needed range to achieve its goal. Thus by April 1941 the use of external long range tanks was under active discussion and consideration.

One place Fighter Command needed to go was to Brest, to escort bombers trying to hit the two German battlecruisers *Gneisenau* and *Scharnhorst*. 234 Squadron at Warmwell was sent what were described as 'Bastard Mark IIC Spitfires' which carried a single 30 gallon fuel tank fixed (and non jettisonable) to the port wing. Each time a pilot took off with one of these machines the control column had to be placed hard over to the right in

20mm shells for a Spitfire V.

order to counter the drag the tank induced. If the pilot got into a dog-fight and had to make a tight turn, he invariably went into an immediate spin. The tanks did not last long and soon disappeared from the scene.

Later, long range external tanks, jettisonable, became available, usually fitted under the belly of the Spitfire. With these the ranges were increased and depending on the duration needed, either a 45 or 90-gallon tank was being carried by the mid-war years.

Germany Invades Russia

When Hitler invaded Russia on 22 June 1941, the reason why the Luftwaffe had not continued its daylight assault on Britain became clear. It also explained why the night blitz had eased since the middle of May. This immediately took the pressure off Fighter Command, but to what extent German fighter forces had been withdrawn from France to the East was not known for certain.

We now know that the Luftwaffe left just two fighter *Gruppen* in the West in order to contain any RAF daylight offensive actions. JG2 covered the area from Cherbourg to the Seine Estuary and JG26 from the Seine to the coast of Holland. These two *Jagdgruppen*, plus the occasional unit which 'passed through' from time to time, were to be the main antagonists of Fighter Command for the rest of the war.

Above: *Westland Whirlwind. Designed as a bomber destroyer it became a fighter bomber with 137 and 263 Squadrons. It carried four 20mm cannons in the nose and 250lb bombs.*

Right: *Initially designed as a fighter to replace the Hurricane, the Hawker Typhoon had a poor performance at medium and high level but excelled at lower altitudes. With four 20mm cannons and later adding bombs and rockets to its arsenal, it became the RAF's foremost ground attack aeroplane.*

Below: *The Whirlwind.*

Churchill, of course, saw the attack on Russia not so much a problem as the gaining of an ally, however distrustful of the Russians he might have been. Any enemy of Germany was a friend of Britain and, even though Churchill had little to offer in the way of help or support, what there was he felt obliged to give.

Initially, there were two ways of helping. One was by providing what military support could be spared, the other was to ensure Britain kept pressure on the Germans from the West. While not a complete surprise, the attack on Russia was a complete success, the invaders pushing back what resistance there was with comparative ease. In the air, the Luftwaffe, far from despondent at their lack of a major decision over southern England, again became successful at what it had been designed for: Blitzkrieg in support of the German army.

As early as July 1941, Churchill offered to send two squadrons of Hurricane aircraft to Russia, both as protection to the northern ports of Archangel and Murmansk, into which British supplies were sent, and to train Russian pilots on the Hurricane fighter, as numbers of these would in due course be sent for their use. As to the pressure in the West, it is interesting to note that at a conference at Fighter Command HQ on the 19 June: i.e., three days before the invasion, the situation on the Russian border was so serious that the delegates met to consider ways of keeping enemy fighters in the West and stop their transfer to the East. Points made were:

1. Enemy very sensitive about [recent] attacks in Béthune-Lens area – so plan and develop day ops here.
2. Continue attacks on shipping in the Channel.
3. Dummy preparations for invasion.

Targets in the Pas de Calais area would include transport and rail centres at Hazebrouck, Armentières, Lille, and Abbeville, and power stations at Commines, Sequedin, Pont-à-Vendin, Bully, Beuvry, Chocques, Lomme, Mazingarbe and Bruay. The Blenheims of 2 Group would be used almost exclusively in these tasks, not only against land targets but also against shipping in the Channel.

The English Channel has always been a sensitive spot for the British, especially in war. Now, in 1941, it was essential to try to make it impossible for any enemy ships to use it without incurring the wrath of either the Royal Navy or Royal Air Force.

In line with this, and in line with British pressure on the enemy forces in Northern France, Operation Channel Stop was also designed during 1941. As the name implies, the objective was to stop any enemy vessels using the Channel and the Channel ports. To this end, not only Blenheims of 2 Group, plus some Fleet Air Arm aircraft and the Navy's fast MTB and MGB flotillas, would be involved, but also Fighter Command Hurricanes. For certain periods, two squadrons of Hurricanes would be based at Manston specifically for low level Channel operations. These would be supported by a Jim Crow squadron, a unit whose job it would be to seek

The bait! Blenheims of 2 Group Bomber Command were used to help entice Luftwaffe fighters up over France so that Spitfires could bring them to battle. This Blenheim IV of 21 Squadron failed to return on 12 July 1941.

out any signs of hostile shipping and report their presence in order that they should be attacked at the earliest opportunity. 91 Squadron was to be the Jim Crow squadron and very effective it proved over the next year or two, while in mid to late 1941, 607 and 615 Squadrons got Channel Stop down to a fine art.

All these activities covered the first two points of the 19 June Conference but the third, a dummy invasion of France, would have to wait until a more opportune moment.

Luftwaffe Strength in the West

As Fighter Command and 2 Group began to operate with renewed vigour following the Russian invasion, the Command estimated that enemy fighter strength opposing them was as follows:

Twin-engined Fighters		Single-engined Fighters	
Denmark	10	Norway	20
Schleswig/Holstein	30	Sylt	10
NW Germany	90	Pas de Calais	160
Holland	130	Cherbourg	30
		Holland	20
	260		240

To an extent the actual numbers are not relevant in that the above numbers represented what the Command believed it was up against. To oppose them, Sholto Douglas now had some 80 squadrons although, of course, they were spread throughout Britain, not all 'down south' where the main operations were being flown. Leigh-Mallory's 11 Group had perhaps two dozen or so squadrons, 10 Group another ten to a dozen. Some of these were night fighter units and others were flying Hurricanes, which by the high summer of 1941, were not generally used on major Circus operations.

The German fighters, too, were spread out as can be seen, and the RAF would not expect to meet twin-engined fighters over France in daylight. So the expected number of approximately 210 Me109s in France and Holland would probably be reduced to about 150 with serviceability problems. Therefore, any full scale operations should at least have an equal number of Spitfires in the air. Thus the major circus operations in the summer of 1941 became a fighter versus fighter conflict.

CHAPTER 15

Fighter Pilot's Summer

AT THE BEGINNING of July 1941 a German airman who was taken prisoner by the British said that the Luftwaffe were using the same tactics that Fighter Command used towards the end of the Battle of Britain. This was by flying a special high level recce fighter aircraft to examine the RAF formation as it reached the French coast and report to its Control whether or not there were bombers present.

If bombers were in the formation then Me109 fighters were instructed to engage but if no bombers were present the fighters were ordered to avoid combat. This is exactly the order Keith Park issued during the later stages of the 1940 Battle, knowing that fighters alone gave no problem unless they carried bombs. In late 1940, 421 Flight were flying the 'observation' sorties.

Fighter Command knew, therefore, that in order to bring the 109 pilots up to fight, bombers had to be present, and be known to be present. To ensure a fight, they might consider flying bombers just to the French coast and then retire them, leaving the Spitfires to take on the 109s who appeared on the scene. But this was rather hit-and-miss and in any event, if the bombers had got that far they might as well go for a target and do some damage. Better still, make the bait even more attractive.

To this end, a decision was made to use some of the new four-engined Short Stirling bombers on day Ops, whose primary aim was to destroy certain important targets with their heavier bomb loads. As this Ramrod tactic developed, engaging enemy fighters became incidental to the actual bombing operation, but initially the sight of three or four large bombers was a tempting target for the 109 pilots.

Whatever ruse was used to entice the German pilots into a combat situation, it was still not easy to bring them down. Just as the RAF found over England in 1940, they could often choose the moment to engage and so now could the 109 pilots, flying over their 'own' territory. It was now the Spitfire pilots who would have

one eye on their fuel gauges and not the Messerschmitt boys. The German pilots would climb up to well above 25,000 feet, and place themselves above the British formation and choose the best moment to pounce. There would rarely be any question of a dog-fight, just a high speed dive through the escort, a quick squirt at the bombers, then continue the dive out and away before climbing back for perhaps another go.

If the Spitfires managed to see them in time, something might be attempted, but the Spitfire pilot still had the problem of not having fuel injection carburettors, making it difficult to dive after a 109.

Fighter versus Fighter Tactics

Victor Beamish, who was now at 11 Group HQ, sent out a memorandum to all fighter stations in July, suggesting methods of keeping in range of the Me109 diving to evade:

1. The favourite method of evasion for a Me109 when pursued by one of our fighters is to dive suddenly and steeply. The Merlin engine will cut at present with negative 'G'. This applies and, as a consequence, much distance is lost initially when endeavouring to keep in range of the steeply diving enemy fighter aircraft. It often happens that a pilot who is just beginning to reach the range where he can open fire on a 109, has his final attack thwarted by his inability to cope with this sudden dive on account of his engine cutting.

2. Some pilots push their control columns forward and follow the 109 down but they at once lose about 300 yards in the initial dive. Other pilots endeavour to keep their engines running and at the same time they try to keep the enemy in view. Both the above methods result in the enemy aircraft getting out of range. On several recent occasions, an ex-squadron commander has found that by anticipating the sudden dive of the enemy aircraft and by pulling out a little to one side, then roll-

Six Spitfire Vs in line abreast.

A bigger 'lure'. Short Stirlings were also used to make Luftwaffe pilots react over France. Here a Stirling of 15 Squadron heads for Lille, escorted by Hurricanes.

Three successful pilots of 92 Squadron who saw action with this unit 1940-41. L to R: Tony Bartley DFC, Allan Wright DFC and Brian Kingcome DFC.

ing deliberately onto his back as he came into range, he could both see and fire at the enemy. As soon as the enemy aircraft started his dive the squadron leader eases his control column back and continued to follow the enemy aircraft in the dive and was able to fire at him. As there is no negative 'G' applied in this manoeuvre the engine did not cut and during the dive the squadron leader completed a roll and on each occasion found he had gained about 200 yards on the enemy aircraft very quickly.

Myles Duke-Woolley:

If you applied any negative 'G' at all to the Spitfire or Hurricane the engine would cut as fuel would be drained from the carburettor. The answer was, therefore, to arrange things so that you never got any negative 'G'. When I commanded 124 Squadron in 1941, I used to practise going into a steep dive by rolling the aircraft and then rolling it back again. In this way you always kept positive 'G'. I couldn't simulate a German doing a nose-down dive because it couldn't be done but I told my chaps that what I will do is to do a half roll and pull through and out and put on the same profile as a 109. So we eventually got quite expert at flicking onto our back, pulling through, then flick back. I made them produce camera gun film in practice to see how they progressed with this manoeuvre. First of all they produced nothing at all. I used to watch them in my mirror as they tried to line up, so I'd push the stick gently forward, gently forward, then a bit more and there

is no more difficult way of shooting than when your target is going down from you and you're going down, down, down. You can't do it because as soon as you put the stick really forward the engine would cut, but it was the only way to teach people the problems they might encounter in actual combat.

When I did my rolls through, I taught them to do a bit more, so when I rolled out I was slightly above them and as I went down the advantage was with them. They would let the target come down into their sights and they'd be under my tail where they couldn't be seen. They quickly learnt that a German in a similar position had to swish his tail about in order to see behind and below, which of course, cut his forward speed down. So you had all the advantages provided you used every trick to help yourself.

I never found too much trouble with the negative 'G' because of this training – it became instinctive. If I was following a 109 and it put his nose down, I'd half roll. We didn't have to think about it, you just did it automatically.

The new wing leaders had now improved their almost daily routines and, unless something went disastrously wrong, most 'shows' were termed a success. Pilots would be lost, of course, for the Me109 pilots were becoming just as adept at picking off stragglers or bouncing the unsuspecting. Everyone was still learning. Allan Wright:

It surprised me how terribly difficult it was to shoot things down when I was with 92 Squadron. I tried to

Ten Rules for Air Fighting

1 Wait until you see the whites of his EYES. Fire short bursts of 1–2 seconds, and only when your sights are definitely ON.

2. Whilst shooting think of nothing else, brace the whole of the body, concentrate on your ring site.

3 Always keep a sharp lookout. "Keep your finger out."

4 Height gives you the initiative.

5 Always turn and face the attack.

6. Make your decision promptly. It is better to act quickly even though your tactics are not the best.

7 Never fly straight and level for more than 30 seconds in the combat area.

8 When diving to attack always leave a proportion of your formation above to act as top guard.

9. Initiative, aggression, air discipline, and teamwork, are words that mean something in air fighting.

10 Go in quickly. — punch hard. — get out. !

Above: *Air Marshal Sholto Douglas, C-in-C Fighter Command in 1941-42.*

Left: *Sailor Malan's 'Ten Commandments' went up in every fighter squadron crew room in several forms. Printed copies went to every Command unit.*

work out how much one pulled through; the enemy aircraft was under the nose anyway. It's difficult, too, to get up close. Sailor Malan, leading the Biggin Hill Wing, was the type of man who got his results by sheer determination. He had decided that you couldn't shoot anything unless you got really close, and there was nothing against getting close. Our guns were now harmonised at 250 yards as that was the range at which we were expected to fire. His reaction was to get closer and he constantly rammed that home to us. I remember once flying on his wing and we saw some 109s. They must have seen us and they turned. He was ahead of me by a few hundred yards just by being quicker. As soon as he saw them he was there. I was flying full bore and just couldn't close up. Anyway, he shot one down while I was still way back.

I recall his Wing briefings, instilling in us that we had to get at them and this was what he had to do. He was older than us, of course, but was full of confidence and we had equal confidence in him when he was leading; knew he'd see the enemy first and be in the right position.

Trafford Leigh-Mallory, AOC of 11 Group, 1941-42, later C-in-C of Fighter Command.

Another thing I remember was that if suddenly we saw some 109s, we'd immediately go. We wouldn't ask permission, you'd just go. Report them, of course, but you'd not ask permission. The leader would get you there but didn't necessarily lead us into combat because there wasn't always time. It wasn't often that the leader would allocate an attack or to wait, it really was a matter of getting in quickly.

Of course, it was the No.2 who had to keep his No.1 out of trouble. If he saw something, he should report it to his No.1 who went down covered by the wingman. His job was to look after his No.1's tail and watch out for other aircraft or ensure it wasn't a trap.

Sailor Malan was a great influence on the many pilots who came into contact with him through his Wing or later the gunnery schools. His 'Ten Commandments' on fighter tactics was read by almost every pilot as he went through the various OTUs in 1941-42. Ending up with between 32 and 35 combat victories, the would-be fighter pilot was in no doubt that the writer of these 'Rules' knew what he was talking about.

Fighter squadrons were still flying their individual formations but this was soon to end. Most fighter leaders had acknowledged the German tactic of flying in fours and then in pairs. Some still flew in a sort of 'snaking

four in line astern' but at Tangmere, Douglas Bader and his pilots had begun to develop what eventually became the standard fighter formation for the rest of the war. This was the 'finger four' formation, as in plan view it looked like the position of the finger tips of an outstretched hand. Oddly, the one leader who did not adopt this tactic was Malan, who continued his proven line astern formations.

Anthony Bartley flew with 92 Squadron too, from Dunkirk, through the Battle of Britain and then became a flight commander with 74 Squadron in 1941. He remembers the developing tactics:

The tactics practised at Dunkirk were the standard vic of three aircraft following one after the other and named in colour sections. These were ordered to perform functions according to the squadron commander's orders which depended on the enemy formations. Most attacks were finally from dead astern but some head-on if the positioning happened to warrant this. In a stern attack on Dorniers one came in from below on account of their top firepower. Beam attacks were also favoured to avoid enemy return fire.

During the Battle, height and attack from out of the sun were top priority but we stuck to the vic formation with two aircraft trailing, acting as 'look outs'. They weaved from side to side to get full view behind. This formation was practised by 92 and 74 Squadrons at Biggin Hill.

However, Duggie Bader started and practised the famous 'finger four' formation which became very popular. Four aircraft sections patrolled spread out laterally and at slightly different levels. Later when I flew in North Africa, due to the inferior performance of our Mark V tropical Spits to the Me109 and FW190s which could always have the height on us, I evolved a new tactic and formation which was sections flying at different levels spread laterally fairly wide apart and following an undulating flight path. This created, in effect, a formation in depth which confused and trapped many attacks from above.

[As a matter of interest, having sections known by colours had been put forward back in March 1938 by Leigh-Mallory (at least, he sent in the suggestion to Dowding). The main sections would be Red and Yellow for A Flights, Blue and Green for B.]

Nevertheless, the finger-four formation became the main fighter tactic, each four breaking down into a pair, leader and wingman, once a fight started. As Allan Wright says, it then became the leader's job to engage the enemy, while his No.2 protected the leader's tail. There were any number of excellent No.2's during the war, and many of the top scoring fighter pilots have reason to thank their wingman for both their success and survival.

Members of the Air Council in 1941: Captain Harold Balfour мс мр, Under Secretary of State for Air; Sir Archibald Sinclair, Secretary of State for Air; Air Chief Marshal Sir Charles Portal кcв dso мс, Chief of the Air Staff.

Even so, there were always the individuals, the men who did it their way. Douglas Bader may have helped to develop the 'finger four' formation but he led his wing in his own inimitable style, as Johnnie Johnson recalls:

When I flew with Douglas Bader in 1941, he always went after the Germans himself, wherever he or they were placed. You could say, therefore, that he was a very gallant man, but there were very many times when, say, a squadron above or to one side, was better placed to attack.

Finally, of course, the day was lost on 9 August 1941. Bader's R/T wasn't working very well and Huns were reported down below him, time after time, by Ken Holden, but he couldn't see them. We began to lose valuable time and Ken actually asked, 'Shall I attack and you cover me?', but Douglas said, 'No, I've got them.' But what nobody had seen was another bunch of 109s up to our left. So by the time we went down, we were being badly bounced, and Douglas was shot down and taken prisoner.

Sergeant Jeff West, a New Zealander, often flew as No.2 to Bader when a member of 616 Squadron at Tangmere, and recalls the roll of a wingman in the summer of 1941:

In March 1941 when I joined the squadron from OTU, with 189 flying hours total – 22hr 10min on Spits! The usual formation was 12 aircraft in two sections of vic from A Flight and a similar number from B Flight. We had a variation of three sections of four aircraft, three in three vics with the 4th aircraft flying in the box: i.e., behind and below each leader to be clear of the leading aircraft's slip-stream.

It was found on operations it was impossible to attack in either formation and we finished up with either three or four line astern of the section leaders. Naturally the leader got in the first shot and the remainder could not engage for fear of clobbering their own leader unless the enemy were 'spread' or the leader broke away. In the latter event it was the understood thing for the No.2 to not lose touch with his No.1.

After we had done a few sweeps, Douglas came down early in his car when the officers were still in their Mess, and we sergeants had been on readiness for a dawn sweep and had not been advised of its cancellation the night before! 'Dogsbody' (Bader's well-known call sign)

The American Eagle Squadrons became operational in 1941. Two of their pilots were Flight Lieutenant C. W. 'Red' McColpin DFC . . .

. . . and Flying Officer E. Q. 'Red' Tobin, who was killed in action over France, 7 September 1941.

Two successful pilots over France in 1941 were Squadron Leader Jamie Rankin DSO DFC, CO of 92 Squadron (later Wing Leader Biggin Hill)...

...and Flight Sergeant Don Kingaby of the same squadron. He was the first and only RAF pilot to win three DFMs.

fixed that. But he complained, in a nice way, that he could spend much more time over France looking for the Hun, if he did not have to return to England early because we were running short of fuel. He had plenty left with a similar tank capacity.

I said that if he flew at the rear and had to weave furiously from side to side to see behind and below, he would find his aviation fuel evaporating more quickly with all the throttle juggling! This was one of the reasons we experimented and designed the 'finger four' formation, universally adopted by Tangmere in mid-1941.

I was quite happy to drop in behind Bader, but on 25 June, on our way home, Douglas stall-turned off after climbing after a 109, and I gave the 109 an extra squirt for luck. On landing, Douglas asked me if I saw the pilot bale out. I said no, I was too busy catching up with him. He made me share half with him.

A week later he called the wing together at 610 Squadron's dispersal at Westhampnett and said he had just learned that the No.2s had been wet-nursing the No.1s. His job was to lead us to the enemy and our job was to shoot them down but never hang around on our own but re-join the nearest Spitfire. That is why we had our own aircraft and marking so we knew who was in what!

Later we had a chap named E. P. P. Gibbs who'd come down in rank to supernumerary flight lieutenant to join 616 from Training Command. He needed operational experience before taking command of a squadron. On a morning Sweep he and his No.2 were shot up, and that afternoon he was 'spelled' by our CO, Billy Burton. Gibbs, who I was told had over 10,000 flying hours, objected, but the CO said he had done a trip already and could do with a spell after his 'hurry-up' in the morning. Gibbs still wanted to go, and as we only had ten machines serviceable, the CO scrubbed off the section of two machines detailed as Red Section, put Gibbs down to lead and then looked round dispersal for a No.2. I saw my name go up.

Gibbs was sitting next to Johnnie Johnson and he asked, 'Which one is West?' When Johnnie pointed at me I heard Gibbs ask, 'What's he done?' I heard Johnnie truthfully say, 'Nothing, he's new from OTU.' Gibbs threw his hands up to his head, and said he'd already been shot-up that day. But he couldn't withdraw now.

When he recovered his aplomb he came across to me and said, 'All you have to do, laddie, is stick with me', which he repeated several times. When take-off time arrived he came over to me and said again, to 'just stick with me, laddie.'

We were flying on the extreme port, me on the outside. Roy Marples in B Flight called up Red Section to report two EA at six o'clock above. I kicked the tail round to hear Roy say they were coming down, when my leader started a Rate One turn to starboard. With needles upright, tracer passed over my right wing. I yanked the stick back and into the left-hand corner, kicking full left rudder. Looking down my right side, the two 109s were fifty feet below and opposite me. By centralising rudders I had a perfect shot at both. I aimed in front of both who dived away emitting black smoke. It was 21 June and one of them could have been Adolf Galland who was hit twice this day.

I caught Gibbs up and he was happy to have me!! In fact, he used to ask for me thereafter. He was difficult to fly with because he played with the throttle, and on the way home, often over the Channel, would dive into the beehive [formation]. I'm sure this was to try to shake me off, but I was determined not to lose him and I never did. He nicknamed me 'The Human Limpet'. But we lost him with engine failure over France. He escaped and eventually got back to UK with the American Whitney Straight.

Fighter Escort Tactics

By mid-August 1941, there was a definite policy concerning the tactics employed by Fighter Command during escort missions. Everything was becoming geared not only to bring the enemy into a combat situation but to ensure that if this was achieved, both bombers and fighters got back.

Losses were rising which was a worrying feature of the summer campaign. Losses had been bad in 1940 but at least a percentage of the pilots managed to bale out or crash-land their fighters over England. Flying and fighting over northern France or the Channel, a downed fighter usually meant a lost pilot, who would then begin a long term as a guest of the Germans.

Between June and July 1941, in just 46 Fighter Command operations, 123 fighter pilots had been posted as

Above right: *Winston Churchill often visited the fighter squadrons, here with 609 Squadron at Biggin Hill in the summer of 1941, with Sholto Douglas (left) and Biggin's station commander, Dickie Barwell DFC.*

Right: *Churchill was also Commodore of 615 County of Surrey Squadron. Here he is with 'his' Squadron, with its CO, Squadron Leader Denys Gillam DFC AFC, during their Channel Stop operations from RAF Manston. Among the pilots are those from South Africa, Belgium, France, and Poland as well as Britain and the Commonwealth.*

missing, which was the equivalent of seven fully manned squadrons. The RAF claimed over 300 German aircraft shot down during the same period, a figure greatly overestimated as it turned out. Indeed, if it had been true it would have meant the whole of the German fighter arm in France had been knocked out!

To some extent, as one fighter pilot told this author, the RAF seems to have remained a victim of the offensive spirit from WW1 days, together with the fatalistic attitude of pioneer aviators. The way that senior officers pressed on with dubious overall effect must be called into question: e.g., the sweeps over France in 1941-42. The RAF's aggressive policy was unquestionably correct with surprise being the great virtue in air operations, so 'he who dares wins', but the pounding Battle of the Somme approach (see who quits first) often produced more losses than gains.

Because of the losses, serious consideration to tactics had to be given. Directives laid down that August stipulated:

Target Support Wings' role is to clear the road to the target and the target area, also to cover the withdrawal of the bombers and escort wings. There are usually two Target Support Wings of three squadrons each. One wing is routed the same way as the bombers, to arrive over the target three minutes earlier and the other is given a different route, also to arrive three minutes before the bombers.

Close Escort Wing role. Direct Protection of the bombers. These fighters must not be drawn away from the bombers. Of the fighter escort only the escort wing and top cover squadrons are not free to seek out the enemy. One reason for the failure of the German bomber offensive last year [1940] was that their fighters were easily drawn off. The first close escort squadron is divided into three sections of four aircraft; one section is positioned above and 1,000 yards to each flank and the third section over the bomber formation. The aircraft of this squadron operate in force if required. These aircraft do not weave so freely as the other two squadrons. The first close escort squadron is positioned 1,000 feet above and just astern of the second close escort squadron. The aircraft of this squadron again formate loosely and weave freely.

Above left: *Last briefing for a sortie: 222 Squadron at North Weald, summer 1941. The CO with back to camera is Squadron Leader R. C. Love DFC.*

Left: *Fighter pilots operating over France and the Channel were often to be thankful for the services of the Air Sea Rescue Squadrons, whose crews in their Walrus amphibians did valiant work picking up downed pilots.*

Escort Cover Wing. The role, to cover the bombers and close escort wing. [And] to cover the withdrawal of the remainder of the force. There are generally two rear support wings of three squadrons each. They start later than the remainder of the force and one patrols ten miles off the English coast between sea level and 10,000 feet and the other patrols just inside the French coast between 12,000 and 20,000 feet. Thus between them they form a fighter screen to sea level to 20,000 feet. The reason for extending the screen to sea level is because German fighters have approached the English coast at sea level then climbed to medium height and dived back towards the French coast attacking our returning aircraft *en route*. Also there is:

Very High Cover Wing and Freelance Squadrons, Diversion Squadrons. Diversion squadrons are those usually detailed to attack fighter aerodromes a short time before the main attack.

Despite all the planning and tactical thinking, losses in men and aircraft continued and by August, Sholto Douglas himself was having serious doubts as to the advisability of continuing Fighter Command's daylight operations. In a letter to Air Chief Marshal Sir Wilfred Freeman KCB DSO MC, the Vice Chief of the Air Staff at Air Ministry, Douglas wrote of his doubts on the effectiveness of all the sweeps and circuses. He continued:

The good start did not continue and has certainly changed in the last month to six weeks. Either the enemy has increased in numbers which the Intelligence people say has not happened, although the fighter boys think that it has, or the Germans are getting more experienced in fighting and have improved RDF systems.

It is strange to note that Douglas and his Command were finding exactly the same situation over northern France, that Göering and his Luftwaffe had found during the summer of 1940. That despite claims by the fighter pilots made in good faith the opposing fighters were not diminishing. The truth in both cases, of course, was that the numbers of enemy fighters being claimed as shot down were not in any way related to the true figures.

In early September, Leigh-Mallory produced figures of known losses by RAF squadrons during operations, and claims of EA shot down, in which his 11 Group had been involved but they did not include operations by 10 Group over the Brest/Cherbourg areas. His figures showed:

RAF fighters lost	218
RAF bombers lost	15 (five shot down by fighters)
GAF losses	444 destroyed
	192 probably destroyed
	240 damaged

Fighter Command's figures, including all groups' operations, were:

RAF fighters lost   273
RAF bombers lost   39
GAF losses   460 destroyed

Actual German losses, from all causes, for the whole of 1941 were less than 200! The final year's figure for the RAF was also much higher than the figures admitted by early September.

By September, the concensus was that the operations should continue only when the weather was favourable. The overall conclusions were that during the summer Fighter Command had forced the enemy fighters in the Pas de Calais area to a high degree of readiness and if they continued both there and further west, around Cherbourg, the Luftwaffe would soon feel the added strain, especially if heavier bombers were used.

While it was still necessary to keep the Luftwaffe 'stirred up' and have them at a disadvantage, it was admitted that the 109 pilots had become skilled at picking off stragglers rather than engage the main formations. Sholto Douglas therefore proposed to scale down the offensive slightly in the Pas de Calais area, and instead undertake more widespread attacks on a broader front between Texel and Brest, in the hope of dispersing the Pas de Calais fighters. What bombers were used must produce heavier and more accurate attacks so as to compel the enemy fighters to make more determined efforts to engage them, and thus be destroyed by the Spitfire escort.

However, whatever plan was proposed, another problem reared its head in September 1941. The previous month, a pilot in 609 Squadron had reported seeing a 109 with a radial engine, but this had been discounted by RAF Intelligence. It was even suggested that the Germans were using captured Hawk 75 fighters from the French. In September came more reports and finally in October a camera gun film definitely confirmed a new radial-engined fighter being used against the RAF.

The fighter was the Focke Wulf 190, a machine superior in many ways to the Spitfire V which now equipped the majority of front-line squadrons in 10 and 11 Groups. This new fighter was about to give the RAF over France a bad time and start once more the race for air superiority.

CHAPTER 16

The RAF at Bay

THE ARRIVAL OF the FW190 on the scene heralded a bad time for Fighter Command. It didn't look such a menacing aeroplane but its big 1,700 hp BMW 801D-2 14 cylinder radial engine gave it a maximum speed of 312 mph at 19,500 feet. With a one-minute override boost it could get to over 400. Its ceiling was nearly 35,000 feet, it could climb to 26,000 feet in 12 minutes and was very manoeuvrable.

Its armament comprised two 7·9mm MG17 machine guns housed atop of the engine cowling, each with 1,000 rounds, two 20mm MG151 guns in the wing roots with 200 rounds each and two 20mm MG FF cannons in the wings with 55rpg. Its sliding bubble hood gave good all-round vision which the pilots of JG26, who were the first to receive the new fighter, liked very much.

By October 1941, over 100 FW190s had been delivered to the Luftwaffe and the pilots of II Gruppe JG26 soon found it could out-perform their main opponent, the Spitfire VB on almost every count, save that of the turning circle. The German pilots liked its rate of roll and diving acceleration and despite some early teething troubles with the aeroplane it was a fighter that was here to stay. So too was the Me109F (and later 109G), which still equipped I/JG26 and the JG2 *Gruppen* and would do so for some time to come.

Once the RAF became fully aware of the FW190's

The Focke Wulf 190 was to give Fighter Command serious problems from the end of 1941 until well into 1943. These 190s are of the 8th Staffel of JG2, in 1942.

combat potential, it put a whole new concept on the combat scene, for they would now be trying to entice a vastly superior fighter up to fight, and if not careful, would be left 'holding the tiger by the tail'.

With the FW190's high combat ceiling, the fighter battles tended to go higher than ever before. The pilots were still, rightly, following the First War doctrines of he who has the height controls the battle, but now that control had passed conclusively to the Luftwaffe and its FW190, Fighter Command was in for a grim time.

The Fighter Pilot's Lot

Every pilot will have a very different story to tell of his experiences while on operations. George Mason might be described as a typical squadron fighter pilot during the period 1941-43, before, that is, he was shot down and taken prisoner, of which more later.

George had joined 122 Squadron in mid-1941, at Turnhouse, when the unit formed part of the defence of the *Prince of Wales*. A sergeant pilot, he had just 70 hours on Spitfires but felt he had pretty well mastered the aeroplane by that time. He felt his formation flying and manoeuvring were quite reasonable, but as yet had not fired his guns – at anything. He recalls:

We'd done a lot of cine work but none of the output from my OTU, which was about 50 people, had fired their guns at a drogue or anything like that. My whole experience during the war was that gunnery received the least attention, thus the general standard of gunnery was low. People fired out of range, their understanding of deflection was not all it might have been and in fact, when I left 122 Squadron after about three months, not having sighted the enemy at all during that time, despite several scrambles and so on, the advice given to me by my leader, Flying Officer W. G. G. Duncan-Smith DFC, was: 'If you fire at something turning, I usually aim at the wing tip which usually gives about the right deflection.' And it wasn't until a booklet came out in early

Above left: *The Me109F, the Luftwaffe's main day fighter over France until the arrival of the FW190.*

Far left: *Leader of the Biggin Hill Wing in 1941 was Wing Commander A. G. 'Sailor' Malan DSO* DFC*, who would score 35 victories. Like most wing leaders he used the prerogative of having his own initials painted on the side of his fighter: AGM.*

Left: *Leader of the Ibsley Wing was Wing Commander Ian Gleed DSO DFC; he too carried his personal initials on his Spitfire V.*

Fine aerial view of the Spitfire V, this one from 92 Squadron. It was no match for the FW190 except in the turn.

1943 called *Bag the Hun*, that I learnt more about shooting than any other way.

It was a presentation I personally could relate to. I used to spend hours studying it and it wasn't really till then that I knew how to recognise the angle-off of an enemy aeroplane from any sort of angle.

I did improve my tactical flying with 122 Squadron and developed an understanding of flying with other people which meant you learnt how to know who were the more reliable, less reliable, who had good eyesight; to know if you were with a leader who would throw a particularly hard turn on you so that you had to react quickly to stay with him. And I did some section leading which also helped.

Then I went to join 611 Squadron at Hornchurch where I was frankly horrified at what I thought was very low morale, amongst the sergeant pilots anyway. There was none of the enthusiasm I'd expected, which I found rather unsettling. I think the loss rate was quite high in 1941, but then I only took part in one operation because I was shot down and put into hospital.

I had done something I should not have done on my first operation. I chased something I really had no right to chase, suddenly finding myself in combat with about ten Me109s and not a Spitfire in sight! I got shot up, ran out of fuel just as I was coasting over Cap Gris Nez and began to glide back.

I planned to land on the tidal part of a beach to avoid any mines but my Spitfire was rather badly hit in the cannon magazine – which was fortunately empty, the 60 rounds having gone God knows where! I must have lost control during the turn for I remember absolutely nothing until I found myself on my side in the cockpit and not much else. As it was I was in a minefield, having blown up two I think, but was rescued by two chaps from the Royal West Kent Regiment. I was off flying for about six months, then found myself back at Hornchurch and went to 64 Squadron. I was happy to join them for Duncan-Smith by this time was its CO.

The whole situation had changed. Morale was high because the loss rate was much lower, probably because the leaders had now learnt how to conduct these offensive operations which were done at limited range, partly outside or at least partly on the fringes of our radar cover, with the enemy having all the tactical advantages. The fact was we were stretched for fuel and they were not and they had radar coverage and could be vectored onto us. The Me109 could fly higher than the Spitfire, so they were always above us. When the FW190 came along, they were even better!

Circus 110

In case any reader thinks operations over France in 1941 were fairly straightforward, with bombers and escort just swanning over to France and hoping to engage German fighters, reading the report of Circus No.110, flown in three parts on 8 November, might help to understand the difficulties, especially if the operation did not go off too well. It also demonstrates how complex some operations had become. The report on this Circus, prepared by Leigh-Mallory, reads:

These operations were carried out in two phases. First phase consisted of an attack by eight Hurribombers assisted by four Hurricanes for anti-flak work. This force was covered by two Spitfire squadrons from Tangmere which acted as escort and the Biggin Hill Wing which acted as High Cover.

The squadrons for this attack made rendezvous at Dungeness and approached the French coast between Berck and Le Touquet. At the same time as this attack, a Diversionary Op was carried out by the North Weald Wing which made RV at Manston and approached the French coast east of Dunkirk and then flew back towards England again. These two Ops were intended partially to get German fighters into the air before the main attack which was to take place 30 minutes after the first operation.

The main operation was directed against the locomo-

tive works at Lille and was to be undertaken by 12 Blenheims [from 21 and 82 Sqdns] with three wings in immediate attendance and two other wings located to cover the withdrawal.

The first two Ops worked out very well with the exception of the Biggin Hill Wing which suffered four casualties for one enemy aircraft destroyed. The attack of the Hurribombers, covered by the anti-flak aircraft – 615 Squadron – was particularly successful. It was the first time we had attempted a diving attack from the coast into the target. They crossed the coast at 10,000 feet and dived right down to ground level into the target area accompanied by the two Tangmere squadrons. The attack on the target was entirely successful. Only a few EA were encountered on the way out and these did not press home their attack. One Sergeant Pilot of the Tangmere Wing is missing.

Meanwhile, the Biggin Hill Wing had crossed the coast at Hesdin where it orbited twice. There is evidence to show the Wing got split up during this process which indicates a lack of judgement on the part of the wing leader. As to the speed and size of the circuits which were carried out, this resulted in the loss of four of our pilots for only one EA destroyed. It is unfortunate that the normal Wing Leader, Wing Commander Rankin, had been given 48 hours leave owing to indisposition and was not leading the Wing. The Operation of the North Weald Wing passed off without incident.

It is estimated that these two actions brought up 60 EA which was exactly the kind of reaction hoped for when the operation was planned.

The main operation, 12 Blenheims, made RV at Manston at 1130 with the Northolt Wing as close escort. A 10 Group Polish Wing as escort cover and the Kenley Wing as high cover. The Northolt Polish Wing arrived at the RV about 5 minutes before the time laid down. This was apparent at the time, in the plotting which appeared on the table. The Kenley Wing arrived at the RV one minute before the RV time when they could see no trace of the bombers, the escort or the escort cover. They orbited for three minutes, then set course.

In the meantime, the flight commander of one of the Flights of Blenheims experienced trouble with his aircraft and turned back. This upset the Escort Wing, as it took place just after they had set course for the French coast and one of the Northolt squadrons accompanied the box of six. The squadron later realised its mistake, went back over France and eventually picked up the bombers in the Béthune area, when the bombers were on their homeward journey. Thus six Blenheims started off at the French coast, accompanied by two squadrons of the Escort Wing and the Escort Wing Cover. The High Cover Wing was not in contact.

The bombers were due to cross the French coast five miles east of Dunkirk – they actually crossed the French coast between Calais and Gravelines. Instead of going to Lille they went to Arras, turned over Arras and consider they bombed Gosnay on the homeward journey. As the bombers turned over Arras, the 10 Group Wing turned inside them and got in front of them and at this time caused some confusion to the two Close Escort squadrons. The 10 Group Wing continued in front of the bombers throughout the journey home. From this time onwards, the two Polish squadrons of the Close Escort Wing were engaged frequently.

In the meantime, the Kenley Wing had made straight for the target, then wheeled westwards as they saw AA bursts some way to the SW of them. They picked up the bombers and the escort somewhere in the Béthune area and from that time followed their role as High Cover. Their top squadron was continuously engaged and owing to this some of their pilots ran short of petrol, three of them actually landing in the Channel, being subsequently picked up. Altogether in this part of the operation, we had four casualties, which considering the penetration and the fact that our forces were incomplete, most of the time, can only be regarded as extremely fortunate. In this phase, three EA were destroyed, two probables and three damaged.

At 1140 a 12 Group Wing were due to RV at Manston and proceed to patrol five miles SE of Dunkirk. This Wing was ordered to patrol at 24-27,000 feet. They did in fact patrol at 20-23,000 feet. It must be pointed out that this was the original height they were ordered to patrol when the complete Wing was available to patrol above them. Owing to fog at Hornchurch, this arrangement had to be altered when it appeared it would not be possible to supply any High Cover to this Wing. The height was accordingly altered and telephoned by Wing Commander Beamish to Wing Commander Scott. The Wing reports it was broken up by flak in the Dunkirk area. It would appear the Wing did not get together again as they lost the Wing Commander, one squadron commander and two pilots. No definite engagement is reported and only one EA was claimed as damaged.

As the weather at Hornchurch improved slightly one squadron was dispatched rapidly to fly above the 12 Group Wing at 28-30,000 feet. This squadron finally escorted the bombers out and reports seeing diving attacks on the tail of the main formation, They dived and drove off the EA but made no claims.

In conclusion, it appears that on the main penetration, the casualties were not high but the Germans evidently carried out their attacks with much fewer casualties to them than if the High Wings had been in position to exploit the tactical advantage which the High Escorting Wing usually has. Still, it could not be regarded as one of the more successful operations as we lost four aircraft for only three EA destroyed. The casualties which appear justifiable are those in the Biggin

Hill and 12 Group Wing – and in the Biggin Hill Wing, I consider this was in no small measure due to poor judgement on the part of the leader. In the case of the 12 Group Wing, it would appear that the Wing flew out at lower height than ordered to, thereby giving the EA a tactical advantage. They flew over the enemy flak area, which was not necessary in the carrying out of their role and by doing so, got split up, enabling the enemy to make use of his height advantage by diving on stragglers. During the second operation, the enemy fighter reaction appeared to be on a moderate scale only but it is difficult to judge their numbers owing to the lack of enemy plots during the operation. The weather was fairly good but there was some haze.

The Kenley Wing Commander reports that he could see St Omer from the coast and had no difficulty in finding his way to Lille.

The missing 12 Group wing leader was Wing Commander D. S. Scott, who had been appointed Kirton-in-Lindsay wing leader the previous month. A pre-war auxiliary pilot he does not seem to have been able to gain much experience of leading a wing, although he had been a flight commander on 605 Squadron and commanded 306 Polish Squadron at the end of 1940. One wonders how certain pilots were appointed as wing leaders without first having been able to gain the very real experience essential for such an important post.

Scott was picked off by a FW190, the first of the type seen by the unit he was leading, 616 Squadron.

Another problem the layman reader might not realise was the weather. During the operation it transpired that while the wind strength at ground level only recorded 5 mph, it was blowing at 75 mph from the north-west at 35,000 feet. This would have meant that formations returning to England would take an appreciably longer time to get away from flak and fighters. The wind undoubtedly caused pilots to run short of fuel after being heavily engaged at full throttle, which is why some pilots ended up in the Channel.

Now, however, Sholto Douglas ordered the scaling down of offensive sweeps and Ramrods, proposing to carry out not more than two or three a month. It had been a long summer.

Winter and Channel Dash

Most pilots were glad of the break the approaching winter gave them. They had been hard at it since April and May, many pilots flying on as many as 50 to 60 sweeps and Circuses. It had cost Fighter Command dear, and several successful pilots had been lost, or were being rested. Others would not survive till the next spring offensive.

Among the first successful wing leaders, Douglas

The infamous Spitfire IIC with the 'fixed' 30-gallon fuel tank to its port wing. It was not difficult to get into a spin during a tight turn.

Bader was a prisoner, Sailor Malan, having brought his score to 32/35, had almost burned himself out and was now off operational flying. Johnny Peel had been shot down twice in 1941, but had been rescued both times and was now being rested. Early in 1942, Bob Stanford Tuck would be brought down by ground fire on a Rhubarb operation and taken prisoner and in March the indomitable Victor Beamish would be shot down into the Channel by a FW190 and lost.

All the while, the German pilots flying the new FW190 were gaining experience and with the aeroplane's early problems largely solved, they were looking forward to a renewed fight when the weather improved.

Before that, however, came the famous Channel Dash operation. The Germans had three capital ships in Brest and needed to sail them to Norway. The RAF bombers and 10 Group's fighters had been trying to bomb them on and off for most of 1941 without much success. Those in the know felt certain the Germans would attempt to get them away from the immediate danger; meantime, the Navy and Coastal Command kept an ever watchful eye on them. Operation Fuller had been devised, should the ships (the *Scharnhorst*, *Gneisenau* and *Prinz Eugen*) try to slip out and make a dash to the north. When they

finally did just that, after dark on 11 February 1942, they also had the temerity to sail up the English Channel rather than go round Britain the long way.

Luck was on their side, and despite the watch on them, they slipped out without being noticed and when first sighted at around 10.45 am, on the 12th, they were off Boulogne! They were spotted by Beamish and Wing Commander R. F. Boyd who had flown out to investigate aircraft activity over a possible convoy off the French coast. Having seen the ships, Beamish kept radio silence as per standing instructions, so again it took some time for the sighting report to be made.

Meantime, Squadron Leader R. W. Oxspring DFC and a wingman, from the Jim Crow Squadron (91), had been sent out, and broke radio silence to report seeing a large force of warships. On their return his wingman told him he was sure one was the *Scharnhorst*. Despite this information higher authority needed a lot of convincing that the ships were in the Channel. It is not the intention here to describe the events of the Channel Dash in detail as these have been adequately covered elsewhere. Suffice it to say that the sacrifice of Commander Eugene Esmonde and his six Fleet Air Arm Swordfish crews, which were all shot down in an attack on the ships, resulted in the award of the Victoria Cross for that gallant officer. It was all a bit of a fiasco, as Myles Duke-Woolley remembers. He was still commanding 124 Squadron based at Biggin Hill:

We had been released that day because the weather was so bad but I had decided to spend the morning with my pilots in the Intelligence Section, in order to catch up on the reading we hadn't done. I'd been chatting to the other squadron CO so he and his pilots were doing the same thing.

The station commander and wing commander were off the station when the telephone rang, and with the I/O also absent I answered it. A panic-stricken voice yelled squeakily, 'Scramble – scramble!' followed by a word, then click, the phone was hung up. I thought I'd heard the word somewhere but couldn't place it, so I walked back into the Intelligence Section and told the boys there seemed to be some sort of panic on, so ordered them down to dispersal, while one of them telephoned them to get the aircraft ready. In the mean-

time, I would try to find out what was happening.

I rang back 11 Group HQ and the same voice answered. Before I could calm him down he yelled Scramble again and once more the telephone went click.

I rang back again and before he could say anything, I cut in and asked, 'Scramble where?' He shouted back, 'North Foreland, 12.30!' – click.

It was now ten minutes to midday, but we quickly got airborne and once in the air I suddenly remembered the word the man had used. 'Fuller' – it was the signal that the German warships were out of Brest. I quickly briefed the chaps over the R/T – in clear – but said that was all I knew. So here we were, flying to give cover to a handful of Fairey Swordfish who would endeavour to attack three large German warships at 12.30 in bad weather, yet just half an hour or so earlier I and my pilots had been sitting in the I/O's office with the other squadron pilots. We too could easily have been off Station.

As I recall it, we'd taken off about ten past twelve,

Mechanics often had to work long into the night to have aircraft ready for operations the next day. This Spitfire V, with its cowlings off, shows clearly the vulnerable coolant tank behind the propeller and oil tank beneath the engine. Note the black-out curtains over the hangar windows.

which, considering we'd been released for the day, was pretty good. But now we had to get to North Foreland and I seem to remember we arrived at about two minutes past the half hour. In between times, I'd got hold of our third squadron at Redhill and they made rendezvous with us: I saw them arrive a couple of miles ahead of me. By now, of course, the Swordfish had gone on. I had no idea where the ships were, nobody had bothered to tell me that, probably they didn't know for sure.

We headed out to sea, with visibility down to three or four miles, cloud base down to perhaps 1,200 feet. I just didn't know what else to do. Then some miles out, I suddenly saw off to my right, that area between the cloud base and the sea, was black with flak fire. And in the middle was what I took to be the six Swordfish, right in the middle of the biggest concentration of gunfire I'd ever seen in my life.

I cut round the front of this lot, went up into the cloud, on the basis that we might be able to find the odd German aircraft above. There was certainly no future in going into that wall of flak with my Spitfires.

Left: *Wilf Goold, from Australia served with 607 Squadron at Manston 1941-42. He later won the DFC flying fighters in Burma.*

Below: *Bomb-carrying Hurricane of 607 Squadron at Manston, winter 1941.*

Coming out, we flew around, saw a couple of Me109s but they smartly disappeared when they saw us. Then, finally I let down and breaking through below, found myself slap on top of the funnel of the *Scharnhorst*! I very quickly turned towards France thinking it safer to fly south than north at that precise moment. Soon after that bit of excitement, with fuel beginning to run low, we had to return to base.

It was then that I called the Controller – again in clear – and told him it was definitely the three big warships. When I got back I telephoned my old friend Bobby Oxspring who said he'd been out earlier, seen some shipping but the weather, flak and fighters had prevented him from seeing exactly what was going on except that there seemed to be a lot of small craft buzzing around.

Pilot Officer Wilf Goold, an Australian on 607 Squadron, had flown out with the other Hurricane pilots to attack the escort ships. When he arrived on 607 at the end of 1941, the Channel Stop operations had been scaled down due to the winter. He recalls:

Manston was right in the thick of the Channel offensive in 1941 and our continuous low-level bombing attacks on Flushing, coastal shipping and harbours kept us busy. Manston was a grass airfield in those days and we used to take off twelve abreast, which was a bit hairraising. Weather was very dicey and the winter was approaching rapidly.

It turned out to be an extremely cold winter which impeded flying quite a lot. I think that saved the bacon of quite a few of us because with the weather closing in, operations were heavily curtailed.

The experience we got at Manston was extremely good. It had been heavily strafed during the previous summer and had received a lot of hit-and-run raids by the Luftwaffe. One of the things that struck me was both alarming and amazing. Near to Dispersal there was a large pile of long spikes and stakes that stood up in one corner. After a while I had enough gall to ask what they were for and was told, for aerodrome defence! At that stage arms were in short supply and the threat of invasion still being rife, the idea was that if paratroops attacked the aerodrome we were to grab a spike, run out and attack them!!

One of the incidents before 607 and 615 left for the Far East was the Channel Dash operation. Our squadron was heavily engaged in attacking the flak ships which escorted the big ships. The thing that sticks out in my mind was that before this happened we had six

Some of 607 Squadron at Manston. L to R: Johnny Stark, Stan Paris, W. D. 'Jimmy' James, Squadron Leader Noel Mowat, Joe Davis, and Robin Hedderwick.

Hurricane IIC with four 20mm cannon. These machines of 247 Squadron were used for night intruder sorties over the winter of 1941-42.

Swordfish of the FAA stationed at our Dispersal. The chaps lived in our Mess. None of us knew what they were there for, and nor did they – at least that is what they told us. Apparently the Navy and RAF Intelligence people had some idea that the German ships in Brest would try to make a run for it and they were stationed at Manston in case they came up the Channel. As history relates, when they attacked the ships all of them were shot out of the sky by flak and fighters, with great loss of life.

The three ships and their escort got through the Channel and reached Norway with almost no serious damage.

It was a blow to Britain's and the Navy's pride, but on the German side it had been a success. In truth it was a well-planned and well-executed operation, covered by Luftwaffe fighters who did a good job defending their charges.

Leigh-Mallory's 11 Group had a total of 25 squadrons on the morning of the 12th, all but four equipped with Spitfires. He was able to increase that number to 34 squadrons if he called on help from 10 and 12 Groups: a possible 550-600 fighters. But the time delays, weather and enemy fighters frustrated the whole episode. It wasn't a good day for anyone on the British side of the Channel.

CHAPTER 17

Pressure on the Western Front

IN 1942 THE Air Ministry was having increasing demands placed upon it to reinforce units not only in the Middle East, but also now in the Far East. The North African battles were draining the Middle East Air Force of men and machines as Rommel tried to defeat the Allied forces defending Egypt, the Arabian oilfields and the Suez Canal.

In the Mediterranean, the island fortress of Malta needed Spitfires in addition to its small force of Hurricanes to fight off the Italian and German air assaults, so as to enable its bombers and naval forces to harass Axis shipping supplying Rommel. And now, with the Japanese war exploding in Malaya and Burma, reinforcements were desperately needed to try to stem the Jap advances towards the Indian border.

All the while, the Russians, themselves being hardpressed on their massive battle front, were urging Churchill to begin a second front in the West in order to take German pressure off them. Britain and her new ally, America (who had finally come into the war on Germany following the Japanese attack on Pearl Harbour), were still in no position to open a second front by invading France. Apart from the futility of such an action, doomed to failure at this early stage if tried, it would only throw away valuable men and equipment needed for the real invasion when it could eventually be mounted. The U-boat successes in the Atlantic also ensured that only a percentage of supplies from America, Canada and other parts of the Empire, arrived.

All Churchill could do was to ensure his air force continued to bomb Germany by night and hope to inflict at least some damage on its industrial might, and have 2 Group and Fighter Command continue the pressure with daylight Ops. Thus the summer of 1942 was really a continuation of 1941, although this time the Germans had the FW190.

There was to be a Combined Operation in mid-1942,

a large scale commando-style raid on the French coast which would, it was hoped, achieve two objectives: first, maintain the pressure on the German forces in the west, forcing the Germans to continue to keep men and machines in France in case an invasion was mounted; second, gain knowledge and experience for such an eventual landing. For its part, Fighter Command – Sholto Douglas – welcomed the chance of bringing the Luftwaffe to battle during such an operation, thereby inflicting heavy losses upon its forces.

This major operation, code named 'Jubilee' was originally planned for late June 1942 but was delayed until August. Spitfire aircraft were by now in high demand, not just to replace Fighter Command losses but to support the Middle East, the coming invasion of French North Africa, and for Australia for the defence of Darwin. (The Far East would have to wait a further 18 months, but Hurricane squadrons were being sent to India in the interim.)

In consequence, Sholto Douglas was informed that he was going to have his monthly allocation of Spitfires cut to 225. Obviously he was far from happy at this. During the first seven months of 1942 his actual allocations had been:

January	146	*May*	194
February	152	*June*	413
March	363	*July*	269
April	288		
		Total:	1,825

The average figure, therefore, was 271, but as he had had to give 160 Spitfires to the USAAF, Fighter Command itself averaged only 238 per month. There was also a strong suggestion that five Spitfire squadrons would have to be transferred to Army Air Support, but fortunately this was later resolved by forming two new

The FW190 which landed intact at RAF Pembrey in June 1942 was a gift for the RAF 'boffins'. Suddenly all the 190's secrets were unfolded.

The answer to the Focke Wulf 190: the Spitfire Mark IX. A section of four from 611 Squadron AAF.

Pilots of 602 Squadron at Kenley in 1942. The CO, Paddy Finucane DSO DFC, seated centre row, with pipe.

Typhoon squadrons and initially the two Whirlwind squadrons, 137 and 263, would also be assigned to Army Support. Personnel for the Typhoons would come from Hurricane squadrons. Later of course, Army Support would be predominantly made up of Typhoon squadrons as they became available, although initially the Hurricane-equipped units soldiered on, carrying bombs, rockets and even 40mm cannons (Hurricane IVs).

It did not help that the Luftwaffe was becoming more active in hit-and-run raids along the south coast. Bomb-carrying Me109s and FW190s of the Jabo Staffels were making these lightning strikes almost at will. The only way to combat them was by flying standing patrols, which was time-consuming and costly in fuel, but it had to be done.

While a final role was still being sought for the Typhoon, because of its performance at low level, it was given the major task of combating the hit-and-run raiders, a task it excelled at. In this way its performance showed its capability and by the end of the year it was being hailed as the main type for Army Support. In some ways it was to become as deadly in this role as the German Stuka dive-bomber had been during the *Blitz-krieg* days.

Meantime, Fighter Command had still to maintain its offensive role against targets and the Luftwaffe in France, still with its Spitfire Vs and was finding it hard

going. Casualties inflicted by the Focke Wulfs were high, but just like Trenchard's doctrine of World War One, the RAF continued to take the war to the enemy.

A major problem, of course, was that nobody knew anything about the FW190. It will be remembered that a Me109 had fallen into Allied hands early in the war, but although the RAF had seen many 190s – too many – nothing was known of it technically. Then, on 23 June 1942, quite fortuitously, a lost German fighter pilot put down his 190 at RAF Pembrey in South Wales. To have a damaged one would have been a help but to have one undamaged and in perfect condition was the answer to the back-room boys' prayers. Suddenly all the Focke Wulf's secrets were secrets no longer. Help was also on the way from Supermarines – the Spitfire IX.

The Spitfire Mark IX

The Spitfire IX was basically a Spitfire VC but with the new Merlin 61 engine and a four-bladed propeller. Jeffrey Quill, Supermarine's test pilot, took the first example down to his old Battle of Britain stamping ground at Hornchurch, to show it to the station commander, Harry Broadhurst. He not only tested it, he promptly took it out over France, flying high above a wing operation, much to the consternation of Quill, who had visions of this invaluable prototype not coming back.

Above: *Dieppe from 10,000 feet, showing the jetties and harbours.*

Left: *The front at Dieppe and the harbour. Machine-gun fire from the cliff either side of the town pinned down the assault force.*

Luckily Broadhurst found no difficulty in getting up to 35,000 feet, so was way above any trouble.

Broadhurst was impressed by the IX's performance and very soon the first production models were on stream, the new type going to 64 Squadron at Hornchurch in June. The captured FW190 was immediately tested against the new Mark IX and, although the difference in performance was not so marked as had been hoped, it did have some advantages.

Between 15,000 and 23,000 feet the 190's rate of climb was superior and the 190's excellent lateral manoeuvrability was confirmed. However, overall the Spitfire IX was superior to the 190 in speed at most altitudes except that vital 15-23,000 feet band. However, the main advantage of the IX was that it looked exactly like the Mark V and would thus give the German pilots a nasty shock when taking it on in combat.

George Mason, now flying with 64 Squadron at Hornchurch, soon had his hands on a Mark IX:

Our main problem in those days was that if you had a combat, it was disengaging that was the dangerous period. Our losses should have been a lot higher than they were under the circumstances.

Duncan-Smith, our CO, had us fly as a squadron and fight as a squadron. We flew in line astern in flights and weaved our way around the sky; the first pair going one way, the next the other way, scissoring along, the Red – leading – section, weaving a bit less violently than the rest. He could in this way manoeuvre the squadron very quickly. I don't think we expected to shoot down a lot of enemy aircraft, what we were much more concerned about was cohesion and survival.

Nevertheless we did manage to shoot down a few. Duncan-Smith was a very good shot and we had Don Kingaby as a flight commander who was also a good shot. So was Tommy Thomas, on whose wing I usually flew.

When we got the Spitfire IX, which we had first because of the record of Duncan-Smith as a leader [perhaps influenced by Harry Broadhurst too], we reckoned we were no longer so concerned with survival because we very soon discovered that we could out-climb FW190s, so knew we could save ourselves if we got in a spot. So we began to fly a little bit more aggressively, in that we would go after things. Tommy Thomas was always very good. He'd always tell me, you have that one and I'll have this one and so on. We also began to be a little more fluid in the way we flew but we still kept as a squadron. We were probably the only squadron in Fighter Command that used to return from battle as a unit. In fact we took pride in it.

After Duncan-Smith left us we had Tony Gaze, then Colin Gray, but then Crawford-Compton arrived. He was an aggressive leader. He was out to shoot down the enemy and to get us all involved in doing the same thing. We continued to fly in our line astern way and as aggressively as we could. The restriction to being aggressive was in flying close escort to the American B.17s when they started to operate. You had to stay close to them so couldn't go after things. We much preferred flying fighter echelon where you had more freedom to chase things.

Dieppe

For Fighter Command, the Dieppe Raid was the biggest thing since the Battle of Britain. It was finally launched on 19 August 1942, starting with commando troops attacking gun positions on the flanks of the harbour town, followed by a seaborne assault by two brigades of the 2nd Canadian Army and a Canadian Tank Regiment. In all the force comprised just over 6,000 men, 5,000 of whom were Canadian.

The objectives were strictly limited. The intention was merely to see if a harbour on the French coast could be taken and held for a day, and while there, the troops would destroy such installations as a power station, local defences, aerodrome installations on the nearby airfield and any craft in the harbour. At the end of the raid the troops would withdraw in good order.

On the air side, 11 Group would front the battle, giving protection to the raiding force, the ships taking them and bringing them home, also attacks on gun positions defending the beach and harbour from cliffs on either side of the entrance. Leigh-Mallory, however, wanted his pilots to inflict a crushing blow on the Luftwaffe who were bound to react to this assault.

Leigh-Mallory in fact had no fewer than 48 Spitfire squadrons on this day, four of which were equipped with the new Mark IX. He also had eight cannon-equipped Hurricanes for flak and gun suppression, two being fitted as fighter-bombers. They were not all 11 Group fighters, of course, other units having been drafted in for the operation. 2 Group also provided three Boston squadrons, the Douglas Boston now taking over from the Blenheims as the group's main light day bomber; Fighter Command also provided a handful of intruder Bostons while Army Co-Operation Command added some Blenheim IVs. In addition, Army Co-Op provided four squadrons of Mustang 1s to be used on rear area observation work: i.e., keeping an eye on possible heavy German ground reinforcements which might be brought up to make a counter-attack.

Ralph Sampson shot down his first enemy aircraft over Dieppe. In 1945 he was leading a French Spitfire wing in France.

A great deal has been written about the ill-fated Dieppe Raid, both at the time and since. Propaganda at the time tended to minimise the massive losses inflicted on the Canadian troops, and emphasise the great victory Fighter Command achieved over the Luftwaffe. Certainly 11 Group believed it had inflicted tremendous damage both on German fighters, and on bombers which had tried to attack the convoy of ships. When the scores were counted, it looked as if RAF fighters had accounted for nearly 100 enemy aircraft with another 170 probably destroyed or damaged. We now know that actual losses were just 48 (23 fighters and 25 bombers), with 24 more (8 fighters and 16 bombers) damaged.

Considering the losses to the RAF, which amounted to something like 97 to enemy action plus three more in accidents, with another 66 damaged to all causes, really made it a victory for the Luftwaffe and flak gunners. Of the losses, 59 were Spitfires, 20 Hurricanes and ten Mustangs, so the fighters suffered heavily. A number of pilots were saved, coming down in the sea off Dieppe and being rescued by the myriad of ships taking part, but in all 47 fighter pilots were lost, as against just 13 from the two major *Jagdgruppen* (JG2 and JG26) with seven more wounded.

In all on this day the RAF flew over 2,900 sorties, the Luftwaffe 945, so the enemy had reacted, but the hoped for results, while they appeared good, were in actual fact very poor.

It has been said that the Dieppe raid paved the way in helping the military planners decide that when a real invasion was made, it would not be with the capture of a port in mind. In 1944, the D-Day planners made their own harbour off the Normandy beaches. Undoubtedly a great many lessons were learnt at Dieppe, but many, including many Canadians, felt that the attack should never have taken place. The raiding force lost some 1,000 men killed, 600 wounded, plus 1,900 taken prisoner. There was little material damage to the port itself, the men and tanks hardly got off the beach, most being pinned down by murderous gunfire throughout the period. Half the men never did get off.

Of the fighter pilots who got back from Dieppe, most felt that it had been a terrific day. Indeed, few had seen so much action in a long time, and it had been far better than stooging around over France on a sweep or Circus operation. With the number of enemy aircraft believed shot down, they were cock-a-hoop! One pilot who saw his first real action over Dieppe, flying on four sorties that day, was Pilot Officer Ralph Sampson, of 602 Squadron:

Dieppe to me was a very, very exciting operation. This

Tony Liskutin also saw action over Dieppe, shooting down a Dornier 217, flying with 312 Czech Squadron.

This page: *The Dornier shot down by Tony Liskutin off Dieppe, 19 August 1942.*

was the fighter pilot's dream. We had Pete Brothers commanding 602 at the time, who was a very good chap and one of the best leaders I ever came across. He had what can only be described as 'the feel' for the battle. His briefings were always very good.

He took us over Dieppe and on three occasions we ran into Huns. It was due to his briefings and sticking to what our job was that we did so well. It wasn't too much of a fighter pilot's dream for me because I should have shot down four aircraft during the day but being comparatively inexperienced I only shot down one and only hit three more. I should have got two Dornier 217s but failed due to over-excitement. I generally opened fire at far too long a range.

There is no doubt the Navy shot down a number of our aircraft and I suppose one can't blame them. FW190s attacking ships with bombs and their pilots were very daring, very daring indeed. I saw one 190 go right down and put his bomb on the deck of a ship and he couldn't have been more than 200-300 feet when he dropped it. The flak was coming up in every direction but didn't hit him.

In our original briefing, I think we were told not to go below 6,000 feet or we'd be shot at, but as soon as the 190s and 109s began dive-bombing, the Navy shot at everything and some of our chaps, trying to engage these aircraft, did fly below the set height.

Johnnie Johnson, by August 1942 commanding 610 Squadron, flew over Dieppe claiming a FW190 and sharing a Me109F. He says:

I went over to Dieppe in 1990 with a bunch of Canadians and we stood on those cliffs with the narrow beach below us. How men could be sent there, heaven knows. It was absolutely disgraceful. Bad security too. We were all briefed in the July, 610 flying down to West Malling, then it was called off. Louis Mountbatten brought it on again for mid-August.

I flew over Dieppe four times on 19 August 1942, but I didn't realise what an impossible tactical situation it was.

Tony Liskutin, flying with 312 Czech Squadron, shot down a Dornier over Dieppe and damaged a Focke Wulf. He was to record:

To think of 19 August just as 'another day' would be completely unrealistic. As far as I am concerned, that day has to be regarded as something quite out of the ordinary. It was a day of feverish activity, a day full of dangers, a day of some extraordinary memories.

Writing as one who was there, not knowing the intentions, or the strategy, or the intended tactics of our chiefs, for me it was just the expected activity within the frame of my duty.

My memories do not hold criticism of anybody, as

All nationalities were represented over Dieppe. Major Helge Mehre, who commanded 331 Norwegian Squadron, shot down two FW190s.

I assume we all tried to do our best. For me, personally, it was a time to get on with the job and achieve maximum results. A time for me to try hard; to die, if need be. It was one of those times when 'England expects every man to do his duty.'

Tony had attacked a FW190 on his second sortie of the day but was quickly engaged by others. Despite a 190 trying to position itself on his tail he went for the second of two 190s ahead of him. He scored hits on his target but his own Spitfire was also hit and he relates:

My short burst from my guns caught the 190's right wing, producing a spray of silvery sparks. At the same moment I saw two glowing white rods appearing just above my head, accompanied by a rattling sound throughout my aircraft with the smell of cordite filling my cockpit.

I had a sudden sensation of acute danger. My reaction was quick, and I think completely instinctive – to get out of his gun-sight! I stepped on the rudder, applied full ailerons, throttled back the engine and pulled back on the elevators. My Spitfire performed a violent flick roll. Never before had I experienced a violence like it. Keeping the controls in extreme positions I continued deliberately with a spin. Obviously my aircraft was in bad shape and there was a possibility that one of the FW190s might follow me to deliver the coup-de-grâce.

I continued spinning down to 4,000 feet in cloud, then

Above: *Wing Commander M. V. Blake's Spitfire V (with personal initials) when leader of the Exeter Wing.*

Left: *Wing Commander M. V. Blake DSO DFC, shot down over Dieppe to become a POW.*

as I centralised the controls, fell out of the cloud and recovered level flight without difficulty, to find myself alone.

He got his damaged Spitfire home, despite a huge hole through the starboard wing and other damage. In another Spitfire he flew a third patrol to Dieppe, this time engaging a Do217 which he shot into the sea, although it gave the combat evaluation team cause for some unflattering remarks concerning his gunnery:

I opened fire at a longish distance but saw no visible strikes, but the bomber's astro-dome flew off. Closing nearer for the second burst I saw the starboard engine start burning, but at that moment I nearly collided with another Spitfire which flew right under the nose of my aircraft. Pressing on with my attack although I had been shaken, a final long burst from all guns then sent the Dornier into the waves. Without hesitation I made an extra pass to take a cine-shot of the burning wreck in the sea.

The film showed my attack on the Dornier starting

at 700 yards and ending at 150 yards. There was also a clear picture of the burning wreckage on the sea. It provided a complete proof of the destruction of a Do217. However, it also gave evidence of my inaccurate shooting. The evaluation team made remarks about wasting ammunition and shooting at longer than optimum range as well as careless and unsteady aim.

I had to admit my shooting was below acceptable standard and I resolved to make sure of doing better in the future.

Hit and Run

For the rest of the summer of 1942, Fighter Command and 2 Group, with its new Bostons, continued to carry the offensive war to the enemy over France, Belgium and Holland. Not only 10 and 11 Groups were continuing this action but 12 Group too, with its wings from Coltishall, Duxford and Wittering. 12 Group found, as 10 Group had found, that they had a vast expanse of water to cover before reaching the hostile coast. 10 Group often operated around Cherbourg and Brest, even the Channel Islands, while 12 Group needed to cross the North Sea to operate over Holland or the Dutch Islands. Long range tanks were starting to arrive to give the Spitfires added range.

Throughout the latter half of 1942 and into 1943, the bomb-carrying FW190s and Me109s continued their sneak raids along the southern coast of England, keeping the Typhoon pilots up on their standing patrols. But they achieved success, managing to bring down a number of these hit and run raiders. The Germans mainly used two tactics, either a very low level approach to avoid radar detection, or a high level approach and dive, using their high speed to escape back across the sea.

Occasionally the Luftwaffe mounted a larger scale operation, using a number of aircraft, the target being more specific than the usual random lobbing of bombs into seaside towns. One such operation was a raid on Canterbury on 31 October 1942 with not only FW190s but some Ju88s as well. It caused casualties and damage to buildings, but, as we shall see, Fighter Command was always at a disadvantage to counter this sort of sudden attack.

To begin with the Germans began to jam British radar and also managed to confuse the issue because some attention had quite naturally been drawn to a large convoy sailing in the Channel, heading for the Port of

Wing Commander Blake's Spitfire in August 1942. He was shot down in this machine while experimenting with his own design of a gyro gun-sight. He got a FW190, but another got him.

London. As was usual, Spitfires were providing air cover for the ships, on this occasion, a section of 453 Squadron from Hornchurch.

The first indication of trouble was when one of the pilots yelled over the radio, 'There are hundreds of the bastards coming. For Christ's sake send somebody out!' It was natural to assume the aircraft might be going for the convoy but they were not. The three Spitfires were soon to be relieved by three more, so six fighters were in the vicinity. They got stuck into the raiders and quite a battle developed which did manage to break up the Germans somewhat. One pilot, Flying Officer G. G. Galway, was shot down and spent 12 hours in his dinghy, ending up on a buoy until rescued by a launch. The subsequent report of the raid is therefore of interest, although surprisingly there is no mention of Ju88s present. Perhaps they had departed after 453 engaged them:

Area of Attack

The main attack consisted of a fighter-bomber attack on Canterbury in which 28 bombers were reported by the Observer Corps. Subsidiary attacks were made by Me109s which machine-gunned Deal, Manston and Whitstable areas. It is estimated that the raid that attacked Canterbury consisted of about 30 aircraft and that the subsidiary attacks consisted of about 20 aircraft, the total force being estimated at between 60 and 80.

RDF Information

The first plot was at 1659 hours about 6 miles west of Gris Nez – Raid 68, shown as 1 aircraft at 2,000 feet. At 1703 hours this raid was about 5 miles south of Hythe and still showing as 1+ at 2,000 feet. At this time the Observer Corps reported that the raid consisted of at least 20 aircraft with more behind. RDF plotting became confused and no tracks of formations which attacked Deal and Manston were recorded.

Observer Corps Information

Due to the low height of the raid Observer Corps information was also confused and although Canterbury was bombed, the nearest plot was 5 miles away.

Weather

The weather over the area of combat was cloud 9/10ths at 2,000 feet, visibility fair with some haze below cloud. At inland aerodromes, however, visibility was very much less and the Biggin Hill squadrons were grounded. Kenley found difficulty in forming up.

Action by the Group Controller

At 1700 hours the Group Controller ordered the section which was on standing patrol to intercept Raid 68. Subsequently a total of 48 aircraft took off for the attack, including six which were on standing patrols or airborne for relief.

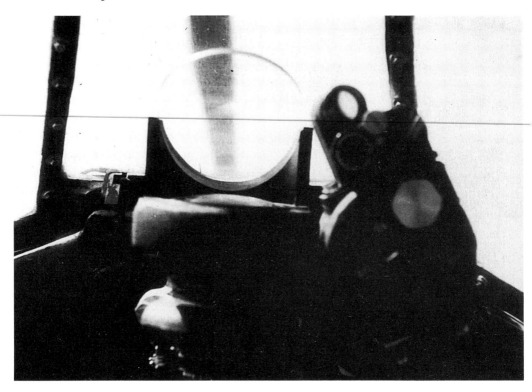

Action by Fighter Squadrons

Nineteen pilots in all engaged the enemy, and the following results were claimed:

5 – 0 – 4 by 91 Squadron
0 – 0 – 1 by 453 Squadron
1 – 0 – 0 by 122 Squadron

11 Group total: 6 – 0 – 5

Left: *Close up of the experimental gyro gunsight. It helped claim a 190 but moments later it and the Spitfire were at the bottom of the Channel.*

Right: *One answer to the Luftwaffe's 'hit-and-run' tactics was the Typhoon. It was excellent at low level although it did have the appearance of a 190 itself. Two large white stripes were painted on the wings to help identification from 'friends'! Narrow black and white stripes were also painted under the wings for British AA gunners.*

Below: *Flight Sergeant Frank Murphy and Flying Officer Allan Smith of 486 (NZ) Squadron who shot down two Me109s on a 'hit-and-run' raid, 29 April 1943.*

plus: 1 – 0 – 0 by Balloons
                       4 – 0 – 1 by AA
                       _____
                       11 – 0 – 6

Our casualties – two pilots missing.

Conclusions

The raid attained a certain measure of surprise in that the first plot had no more than 1 aircraft. The CHL Stations were jammed at 1647 and this was not reported to the Group Controller till 1705. Had this been reported at once it would have been clear advance warning to the Controller that an enemy attack was likely. On checking the extent of the reported jamming subsequently, it was found that the area affected very clearly indicated the possibilities of Canterbury being the target for an attack. The Filter Room at Stanmore was thus in early possession of the information of most vital value to the Group Controller but this information was not notified to No.11 Group until the enemy attack had in fact developed. In view of the density of the raid in the small area – Whitstable-Hawkinge-N. Foreland – Control interception was impracticable and there was a certain waste of effort due to pilots giving chase to friendly aircraft. It appears advisable in similar raids in the future to restrict the number of our own fighters patrolling in the area and if possible to use aircraft with special camouflage for identification. It is suggested that squadrons should be moved to forward aerodromes daily.

The Stanmore Filter Room later reported that Dover CHL reported the serious interference started at 1642 and that no entry was recorded at that time. At about the same time, three other CHLs – Foreness, Fairlight and Truleigh Hill – reported interference on certain bearings only. Beachy Head reported that interference started at 1657. It was not, however, until 1657/8 that North Foreland reported serious interference. The Controller was therefore not in a position to state that normal CHL jamming was in progress until that time. The Controller, in view of the numerous occasions when such interference had taken place and had appeared only to be a test carried out by the enemy, did not report the fact to the DAC. It is, however, questionable that he was in a position to do so until 1658 when he came into possession of the information from North Foreland that they were also seriously jammed. This information gave him all the necessary facts for reporting normal CHL jamming.

The North Foreland CHL Station was tuned to 193 Mcs. On the tube the trace depressed and the amplitude modulated, lashing up and down with complete blanket effect above, saturating the tube. The appearance on the PPI was a complete flooding of the tube due to greatly increased brilliance.

A similar attack on Bromley on 20 January 1943 also caught the Command's fighters on the wrong foot, although Spitfires were again to get in amongst the raiders. Some 20 FW190s came inland, skirting the base at Biggin Hill, much to the indignation of the pilots and especially the station commander, Group Captain Sailor Malan.

Lunch was being served when the alarm was sounded with a call for a Scramble! 'Of all the bloody nerve,' was Malan's own comment when he saw for himself enemy fighters flying low past the northern boundary of the airfield. The 190s overshot Biggin to drop their bombs on nearby Bromley. One bomb hit a school, killing 45 children and four teachers. The 190s flew over Croydon, then south towards Beachy Head, the Biggin Spitfires heading them off; in the chase they shot down six, but again the damage had been done. Fortunately, the Luftwaffe only occasionally made these sneak attacks, but used on a larger scale could have caused havoc with the defences.

By this time, of course, Fighter Command had a new C-in-C. Sir Trafford Leigh-Mallory was given command in November 1942. He had finally dragged himself to the pinnacle he had desired for so long.

Counter Measures

Obviously counter-measures against the hit and run attacks needed to be formulated, and by early 1943 the following policy was adopted:

Standing patrols are maintained along the south coast whenever weather conditions permit. These patrols fly low, 2-3 miles out to sea and whenever possible are controlled by a forward station, at which information for one or more Type 13 or Type 14 Station is received. The forward station used for such control of Foreness, Swingate, Beachy Head and Kingswear CHL stations and the GCI Station at Blackgang, which possesses unusual low-looking characteristics.

At the same time the Controller at the Sector supplying the patrol is able to pass to the pilots the first reports from the ROC [Observer Corps] of courses of EA that have penetrated the RDF network without detection. Steps have been taken to ensure that the report of low-flying EA passed by the ROC observer is relayed to the Sector Controller with the minimum of delay.

During the month of March, Germans made 128 tip-and-run sorties of which 21 [EA] were destroyed by fighters and AA ($7\frac{1}{2}$ AA – $13\frac{1}{2}$ RAF) which is roughly one out of every six raiders. All were 109s or 190s except for a couple of Ju88s, one of which was shared by AA/RAF.

The attacked places were Eastbourne, Worthing/Hove, Falmouth, Hastings, E. Essex/Romford and Ilford,

Salcombe, Kellerton, Frinton, Walton, Kingswear, Start Bay, Ashford, Dimchurch, Brighton and Bolt Head.

The Type 13 RDF covers were at Fairlight (Hastings) and North Foreland, the Type 14 at Beachy Head and Capel. The set at Capel proved its value at once on 24th March, when a $17\frac{1}{2}$ mile warning was given of the enemy raid which attacked Ashford. This enabled fighters to destroy one FW190 and damage another, and AA guns to destroy one and also allowed the Air Raid warning to be issued in time to save many lives in Ashford.

There is, however, a substantial gap in the Brighton/Worthing area, shown up on 24 March when four aircraft approached and bombed Brighton and Hove without being detected at all! It is hoped in due course that this gap will be covered by Beachy Head and the one being installed at Truleigh Hill. A site has also been found on the Isle of Sheppey which should give some degree of cover against Estuary attacks.

Leigh-Mallory recorded on 3 May 1943:

A survey of the tip-and-run raids made in March indicates that the Type 14 stations are capable of giving operationally useful warnings. An outstanding example is on 13 March when the Station at Ventnor IOW gave a 40-mile warning on two FW190s, as a result of which they were both destroyed by fighters.

On 1 April, three FW190s succeeded in reaching Ventnor without being detected at all. This occurrence illustrates the extent to which Type 14 Stations can be adversely affected by reflections off the surface of a rough sea. On this occasion, Ventnor Station was ineffective out to 25 miles, and until a greater number of Stations are in action, we must expect disappointments of this kind.

In the Ashford attack on the morning of 24 March, 12 FW190s were involved. In April 1943 there were seven attacks totalling 34 sorties, three were destroyed by AA and four by RAF fighters – all either 190s or 109s, the largest being on 3 April when Eastbourne was hit by 12 190s, with AA fire destroying one. In fact April 1943 was the lowest enemy effort since November 1942.

Late afternoon of 29 April, off IOW, two low-flying EA approached this country and were attacked and destroyed by two Typhoons which were on standby at Tangmere and were not airborne when the track of the enemy was first read. I regard this as the most important incident as it proves that when our very low RDF system is working efficiently I may well be able to avoid the use of standing patrols and still achieve success against tip-and-run raiders.

No. 486 (RNZAF) Squadron shot the two Me109s down on 29 April, the victorious pilots being Flying Officer Allan Smith and Pilot Officer Frank Murphy. The 109s came from 4(F)/123.

There were 11 raids in May 1943, 224 sorties, AA shot down 21, RAF 10 and other causes one. (Included in the RAF fighters was one by Mustang of Army Co-OP). Altogether 32 EA were shot down. These raids were as far afield as Yarmouth and Lowestoft, down to Bournemouth and Torquay.

In June only five raids were recorded during the first six days; IOW, Margate, Felixstowe, Ipswich and Eastbourne. 65 enemy sorties but three EA were shot down by the guns, seven by RAF fighters and one by another cause, total 11. By July it seemed as if the raids were beginning to be scaled down by the Germans.

CHAPTER 18

Towards Invasion

AMONG THE MANY problems Leigh-Mallory had at the end of 1942 was the question of fighter types. In December he wrote to Air Ministry about their forecast for 1943 which indicated that by September, half of Fighter Command fighter force was likely to consist of Sabre-engined aircraft: 38 squadrons of Typhoons, two of Tempests and just 50 of Spitfires.

In the anti hit-and-run battles, and on some day intruder sorties, the Typhoon had proved itself as a bomber destroyer but its inferior rate of climb and limited manoeuvrability made its effective use in sorties against enemy fighters suspect. Added to the fact that there was as yet no end in sight to the aircraft's prolonged teething troubles, especially the Sabre engine, one can see Leigh-Mallory's problem. He wrote:

If I am to undertake offensive operations in the coming year, I shall be severely hampered by so large a proportion of Sabre-engined aircraft in my fighter force, so I urge that [every effort] should be made to provide squadrons of Merlin 61 Spitfires in place of Typhoons. The qualities of the Spitfire are now fit to be used in any fighter role and with the improved Merlin 61 engine it should be able to hold its own against contemporary enemy fighters and bomber types, as well as being used in an army support role.

The Hawker Typhoon started to pave the way for invasion during 1943-44. This machine is from 486 New Zealand Squadron.

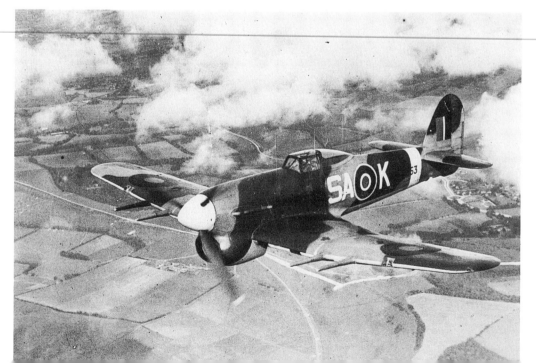

I understand there is a possibility of some of my squadrons being re-equipped with Merlin 61 Mustangs. Although I have no official intimation of the performance or qualities of this mark of Mustang I have no doubt that it will prove much superior to the Typhoon as a general purpose fighter and I shall welcome re-equipment of my Typhoon squadrons with this type of Mustang with Merlin 61s, if Spitfires should not be available.

Clearly, Leigh-Mallory didn't want the Typhoon as his primary day fighter, and of course he was right. Air Ministry was obviously still concerned with the Spitfire's problems in combating the FW190, even though this was slowly being overcome with the Spitfire IXs. It is interesting too, that Leigh-Mallory was happy to accept a new mark of Mustang, which he did not know, rather than have the Typhoon.

Allison-engined Mustangs (Mark Is) had been with the RAF for some time flying with Army Co-operation units, but the promised performance of the Merlin-engined Mustang IIIs was encouraging. In the event it was to be another year (February 1944) before the first RAF squadron began to receive them. Quite correctly, the USAAF had first priority.

At the end of 1942 there was still grave concern with the problems confronting the Typhoon. This included the cost for one thing, which was much higher than the Spitfire took to produce in terms of raw materials, finance and manpower; maintenance and service for instance, meant that the average squadron had to have 20 Typhoons rather than the 18 aircraft on Spitfire squadrons, in order to retain operational commitments.

The main strength of the Typhoon, of course, was its superiority in speed at selected low and medium altitudes. Its use, therefore, was being confined to specialised operations such as bomber interceptions or low altitude attack in the army support role.

This latter role was soon to become the niche of the Typhoon and once the invasion of Europe had taken place, it became the most deadly close support weapon ever. It was this role that men such as Roland Beamont, who commanded 609 Squadron in 1942-43, and Wing Commander Denys Gillam DSO DFC AFC, who had commanded the first Typhoon Wing in mid-1942 began to develop. Gillam would emerge as the most aggressive Typhoon pilot of the war and his exploits really put the machine on the map. The Typhoon would be totally at home with cannon, bombs or rockets.

Year of Escorts

In retrospect, the year of 1943, for Fighter Command, was one of continuous escort duty, not only for 2 Group's medium bombers, but also for the American 8th Air Force heavies – the B.17 Fortresses and B.24 Liberators.

The war in the west had stagnated somewhat. 1942 had seen the continuing daylight offensive Circus and sweep operations and the battle between the Spitfire V and FW190 eased only slightly by the Spitfire IX's gradual arrival on front-line squadrons. With America now in the war and her industrial and material might now starting to pour into Britain, the obvious thought now was of an invasion of France, certainly of Europe somewhere.

The American 8th Air Force started operating in the summer of 1942, gently at first, just going for targets near the French coast, etc, but by the new year the Forts and Libs were beginning deeper penetrations. The problem, of course, was that they could only be escorted so far before the Spitfires and American P47 Thunderbolts had to turn for home. It was like the Battle of Britain in reverse; this time it was the Allied fighter pilots who were watching their fuel gauges.

The Americans, of course, wanting to go deeper into Germany, adopted the policy long rejected by RAF Bomber Command of unescorted daylight raids. They were resurrecting the doctrine of the bomber fighting its way through. It was true the American heavies bristled with ·50 machine guns, but as they were soon to learn, the German fighter pilots knew how to fight an air war over their homeland.

In North Africa, Rommel was in retreat and the campaign would end with the fall of Tunisia in mid-1943, thereby opening up the 'soft under belly of Europe' as Churchill liked to put it. The Atlantic war, while far from over, was being fought with increasing versatility by both the Navy and Coastal Command, while Bomber Command continued its nightly pounding of German towns and industry.

Fighter Command now had its wing organisations down to a fine art, and while the Luftwaffe often seemed more and more elusive, occasionally they would be met in combat, and brief but hectic air battles would be fought over France and the Low Countries. Meantime, other fighters, Typhoons and Hurricane fighter bombers would harass German military targets in France from low level while long range fighters would mount both day and night intruder missions, showing up almost anywhere to wreak havoc amongst both air and ground targets far from the accepted battle front.

Rhubarb sorties were beginning to be phased out, having proved too costly for the return in damage to the enemy. Daylight and night intruder sorties by long range Mosquito aircraft would soon be proving a much more effective way of surprising the Germans. By the war's end, the RAF would have flown over 11,000 intruder sorties, resulting in claims for the destruction of 513 enemy aircraft destroyed, 56 probables and 401

damaged, plus no end of ground targets and trains.

The Spitfire Mark V still predominated in Fighter Command squadrons by the spring of 1943, which was a source of weakness. It really was completely out-classed by the FW190 but the new Mark IX was showing a claim to loss ratio of three to one in its favour. The Mark V was now being used solely for defensive escort duty, and really only close escort at that. As a fighter on defensive operations it was practically useless. Out of over one hundred attempts at interceptions, Spitfire Vs only destroyed three German raiders. The brunt of day operations was being borne by the ten Spitfire IX squadrons although these ten were seriously handicapped by reduced strength. In order to maintain 10 squadrons the average per unit was 13 aircraft instead of the usual 18.

Strangely, in April 1943 the Spitfire IX had been around for nine months but supply was not sufficient for the demand. Stranger too was that the Spitfire V was still being built, some of which would eventually see service in the Far East by the end of the year.

At least the demand for pilots was largely being met. The training schools at both home and abroad, and the OTU's were now turning out sufficient numbers to accommodate both increases in the number of squadrons being established and to replace losses. At the beginning of 1943 Fighter Command reached a peak of 102 squadrons of all types.

Fighter pilots could now expect to finish a tour after a laid down number of flying hours which in May 1943, for instance, was normally 200 operational hours, although any pilots spending time on convoy protection or interception work out of range of enemy fighters would only count half the hours flown on these types of sorties. Night fighter pilots had tours of 100 night operational hours or 18 months on a squadron, whichever came first.

As for new fighter types being considered in early 1943, the new Hawker Tempest was being scheduled as the replacement for the Typhoon for ground attack

Top left: *When the US 8th Air Force's B.17 bombers began to attack Germany, RAF fighters would escort them as far as the Dutch border. From there, until the American long range fighters arrived, they were on their own!*

Far left: *Wing Commander J. E. 'Johnnie' Johnson, wing leader of the Kenley Wing in 1943.*

Left: *Wing Commander W. V. 'Bill' Crawford-Compton (New Zealand), commanding the Hornchurch Wing in 1943. He would end the war with 22 victories.*

sorties. The Tempest, which was now being test flown, was due in squadron service by the end of the year and although its performance looked promising, was, at this stage, only being considered as a replacement for the Typhoon and not the Spitfire IX.

There was a new Spitfire now with two squadrons (41 and 91) the Mark XII which had the Griffon engine as opposed to the Merlin. This type and these two squadrons were being used to help combat the hit and run raiders along the south coast; both squadrons were based at Hawkinge. Unlike any previous mark of Spitfire, the XII had clipped wings to improve its lateral manoeuvrability at speed. Later this clipping of wings extended to some variants of the Mark IX when used at low and medium altitudes.

Meantime, the Spitfire IXs tended to take on the major escort roles and long distance escort sorties with the Americans, while the Mark Vs (some also with clipped wings) escorted the RAF mediums.

The Air War over France

Johnnie Johnson took over the Kenley Wing in March 1943, comprising two Canadian squadrons, 403 and 416. More important from his point of view was that the wing had Spitfire IXs.

At this stage, Johnson, although an experienced air fighter with two years of operations behind him, was still fairly unknown outside his usual circle of friends and comrades. When he took over the wing he had but eight victories, but that number was soon to increase rapidly. He wasn't long in his new job when he began to arrange things to advantage. He had learnt his trade and watched other leaders such as Douglas Bader, and Pat Jameson. He was now ready to make his impact on the Kenley Wing and Fighter Command. Of this period he recalls:

When I became Wing Leader at Kenley we had a better Spitfire, the Mark IX, which was better than the 190 or 109F, I always tried to control the air battle and not necessarily go down myself. Unlike Bader, I would send down the best placed section or squadron and cover them myself. I'd always had a reforming point too. Before we set off I'd say that if we got into a fight we'd reform over St Omer, or some such point, so that we could form up and go on once more as a cohesive unit.

In 1941-42, we all went 'balls out' into the middle of everything and nobody ever formed up again, all coming home singly or in pairs. I seem to remember someone once saying to me that I must rather fancy myself as an Admiral deploying his forces, bringing in the destroyers and corvettes etc. I agreed it might be a good parallel but at least I did try to retain some cohesion and leadership over the thing. My Canadians, contrary to popular belief, were first class disciplinarians in the air – very good indeed.

In 1943 we began to see large gaggles of FW190s and Me109s, sometimes up to 50 or 60. My Kenley Wing was only a two squadron wing, 24 Spitfires, so I got onto our AOC, Air Vice Marshal Hugh Saunders, and said, I think that now that the Germans are reacting strongly, especially when the American Forts were out and that sort of thing, I could do with more aeroplanes, so could I try two wings? He agreed to let me have a go with the Hornchurch Wing, led by Bill Crawford-Compton.

My idea was to try to get the whole wing stuck into one of these gaggles, but it didn't work. The trouble was, the minute that Bill saw anything and I'd say OK, will you cover me, while we attack he'd bring his wing right through us! So it never really worked although we tried it half a dozen times, so finally I rang up Hugh Saunders and said it was too cumbersome. But basically it was Bill, who was of equal rank to me, of course, just wanting to get at them. In fact it got quite dangerous once or twice.

I always tried to be rather meticulous in the air and not have everybody funnel-in, always leaving top-cover,

which I'd learned from Douglas Bader. I sent sections or squadrons down but always left something up top, but then Bill Compton would come whistling through the bloody lot of us!

Johnnie Johnson was also coming to terms with another problem which faced him and other 'thinking' wing leaders, as he explains:

The greatest drawback to me in those days was when the American Fortresses started going out and were taking some terrible losses. For our part, we would fly down to Manston or Bradwell Bay to refuel before flying out to rendezvous with them over the Dutch coast as they went out. We then flew back, refuelled again, had a cup of tea, and then went out again to meet them coming back. We just hadn't the range to escort them all the way and it was terrible to see them struggling back, engines knocked out, huge holes in wings and fuselages, trailing smoke, and knowing there wasn't a thing we could do to help them. I think that was a great error of Fighter Command's fighting in not having the radius of action.

This even got up to Churchill. He asked Portal, the Chief of the Air Staff, why couldn't the range of the

Pilots of 122 Squadron, part of the Hornchurch Wing 1942-43. The CO is Don Kingaby (6th from left). 5th from left is Flight Lieutenant C. Haw DFM, who had won the Order of Lenin in North Russia in 1941. The Spitfire is a Mark IX.

Spitfire be increased? Churchill, of course, was under pressure from the politicians because there were something like 60 Spitfire squadrons sitting around in England when the Yanks were taking a lot of punishment.

Portal wrote back and said the Spitfire as a long-range fighter would never have the performance of the short-range fighter and he got away with it. So we ended up with about the same radius of action as we'd had in 1940, which was a disgrace really, because we were not able to help the Americans.

The most significant fighter of the whole war was the Mustang, not the Spitfire. The Spitfire was only a defensive fighter, designed for defensive work. We pressed for as long as we could for longer range and we got the 90-gallon tank, which meant that we then actually held more fuel externally than internally. This would take us to the German border, but that was all.

So in many ways I think Fighter Command was a 'busted flush'. Even over the Normandy beaches around D-Day we could only remain there 40 minutes or so before having to fly home. No, Fighter Command never had a good long-range fighter which we wanted. That, I believe, reflects very badly on Portal and the Air Staff at that time. So when I was a wing leader in 1943-44, we were doing almost exactly what Douggie Bader was doing as a wing leader in 1941. We could have achieved so much more with just a little more engineering on the Spitfire.

One of the pilots in the Hornchurch Wing, supporting Johnson's wing on occasion, was George Mason, back for a second tour of duty. He remembers:

I went back to Hornchurch to join 222 Squadron, having rung up Bill Compton who was now commanding the wing there. 222 hadn't yet discovered the art of flying the Spitfire IX and used to get strung out on the climb.

The climb on the IX was very very steep and we'd been advised by Jeffrey Quill that the way to climb to

Pilots and senior staff of 64 Squadron, Hornchurch, when still commanded by Bill Compton (sitting astride propeller). Standing on wing: –?–, Flight Lieutenant Mike Donnet, Sergeant Coupland, Jack Batchelor; Sitting: Sergeant Bilsland, Sergeant Byrne, Flying Officer Hank Harris, Bob Poulton, George Mason, Lieutenant Thorvald Johnsen (KIA 1944), Junior Harder, Flying Officer Curd, Pilot Officer Dalziel, –?–, Flying Officer Pat Patterson (usually flew as Don Kingaby's No.2) Killer Kelly, Rocky Ledington (later Lt-Colonel with USAF), Sergeant Ian Burge; Front: –?–, –?–, Flight Sergeant Lowe, Flying Officer Mellersh (IO), Doc Dewell, Flying Officer Farries (EO), Flight Sergeant Moon, –?–, –?–, Flight Sergeant Rose.

610 Squadron, Part of 13 Group's Exeter Wing, 1943. L to R: Flying Officer F. Crewe, Flying Officer P. Small, Flight Lieutenant P. Pound, Flying Officer Tex Donahue, Squadron Leader W. A. Laurie, Flight Sergeant D. Jones, Flight Lieutenant W. Lightbourn, Flight Sergeant W. McFetridge, Pilot Officer J. Campbell, Flight Sergeant W. A. Nichols, Sergeant T. Higgs. Far right is Wing Commander Cam Malfroy DFC, wing leader and former NZ Davis Cup Tennis player. On wing: Flight Sergeant M. Pain, Captain A. Hoinden, Flying Officer S. Venesoen.

make it easier for the chaps at the back, was to get into a slight echelon so that you got the attitude right. If you weren't very careful, because of the steepness of the climb, you could get your aircraft into a bad attitude with the nose too high and you had to pour on more and more 'coal' to keep it in position. I had a little trouble convincing the CO to get into echelon, not taking kindly to me telling him how to run his squadron.

However, I am one of those guys who is blessed with very good eyesight, so I proved to be quite an asset, and they began to listen to me after a bit. Then we had Ray Hesslyn posted in, back from Malta, and he was a natural fighter pilot – quick, very good eyesight and a good R/T voice that you could hear (which wasn't always the case). It wasn't long before I was given a Flight in 129 Squadron with whom I ended my days.

It was while we were on 129 that we got the Spitfire IX with the Merlin 66 engine. Its second stage cut in at 13,000 feet so its combat height was medium altitude really. This was super as I'd been starting to get the bends slightly, flying HF's at 35-36,000 feet. The Germans by this time had decided to concede us the sky above 20,000 feet actually, so there weren't many of them up there. The place to find them was down below. You were more likely to get an engagement there, for higher up it was very easy to avoid combat if the enemy wanted

to avoid it – they had no problem in doing so. By the time we'd got round into a satisfactory position they could be gone, but at lower level it wasn't so easy. We got in quite a lot of combats during this 1943 period.

I remember meeting Jack Charles whom I'd first met in 1941 before he went to Biggin to command 611 Squadron. He said to me that we were now going through a period when we should engage the enemy on every conceivable occasion because it wouldn't last long. We had superiority now, just as we had it with the Spitfire IXs before the Germans discovered there was no future for them at high altitude. Now we had it back again, at lower level. The answer was to be very much more aggressive than before.

On tactics as a whole, I don't think we were ever as aggressive as the Americans. We had learnt a lot more caution in the early days of 1941. Fighter Command became more aggressive after the invasion when there was more purpose to it. But in 1942/43 we always tempered our aggression with a fair amount of moderation.

The exception perhaps was Johnnie Johnson's wing. In the beginning we had been told to jettison our long-range tanks when we reached the French coast in order not to upset the French, so we didn't get the full value of them. Johnnie took no notice of this and carried his all the way and only jettisoned his if they were about to join combat. He was also one of the only wing leaders I ever flew with who actually could control an air battle after the initial stage.

He could also see and visualise the whole air picture. He used to give even his sub-sections colours, so instead of being Red 3 and 4, they would be Gold, Silver and so on. I could hear him on the R/T actually saying, 'Gold, get into that lot over there.' 'Silver what the hell are you doing hanging around?' and so on.

He could actually control a battle down to that sort of level even into the first 60 seconds, which was quite a lot. Broadhurst used to control his wing with an iron discipline but he controlled it as just a wing and didn't really see the picture sufficiently in detail, but Johnnie really could.

Johnnie also wanted his withdrawal cover, so we at Hornchurch for a while flew on the same frequency with him. We used to deploy to Biggin Hill and would act as rear cover but we didn't think much of that, especially as Johnnie and his boys were getting all the Huns.

Long Range Tanks

The Spitfire's main fuel tank took 85 gallons, the larger drop tank 90 gallons. Cruising at an economical speed of 170 IAS with a drop tank, the Spitfire could cover six air miles per gallon at 6,000 feet. This improved to $6\frac{1}{2}$-7 with the 'cleaner' lines with no drop tank; formation work probably five miles per gallon with a tank, six without. After take-off the main tank was already down to 82 gallons, with 88 in the drop tank. Increasing speed to 240 mph reduced the miles per gallon to $3\frac{1}{2}$-4 miles.

In contrast, the American P.51 Mustang had two wing tanks each with 92 gallons. With two 110-gallon drop tanks and a fuselage tank with 85 gallons, the machine's endurance was seven hours – with combat! That could, and did, take the pilots to Berlin and back.

By 1944 the radii of action for the main RAF fighters were as follows:

	45-gallon tank	90-gallon tank
Spitfire V	225 miles	not used
Spitfire VII	290 miles	360 miles
Spitfire IX	240 miles	270 miles
Spitfire XII & XIV	190 miles	240 miles
Tempest V	With 2x30-gallon nose tanks plus two 45-gallon drop tanks: – 300 miles.	
Mustang III	With 2x62-gallon drop tanks: – 450 miles on escort work; 500 miles on freelance patrols.	

This page: *The destruction of a Messerschmitt 109F as recorded on a camera gun film.*

Griffon-engined Spitfire XII with clipped wings, 41 Squadron, early 1943.

While Squadron Leader H. Russell DFC, receives his 164 Squadron badge from the Duke of Gloucester, a future C-in-C Fighter Command, Roderic Hill, stands far right. To the right of the Duke is Air Vice Marshal Sir Hugh Saunders, SASO of 11 Group.

George Mason DFC, had considerable experience as a fighter pilot. The Americans also gave him their DFC for flying escort missions to their bombers.

Generally the 90-gallon drop tank could run for 1 hour 20 minutes before the pilot had to switch to main tanks. However, pilots often tended to switch to main tanks before this, preferring to waste some fuel rather than have their engines suddenly cut out. When enemy aircraft were spotted external tanks were dropped. It was not unknown for enemy fighters to make an appearance, force the Allied fighters to drop their tanks, then fly off. They had thus effectively cut down the combat radius of the fighters without even engaging them.

Ralph Sampson, who had been with 602 Squadron over Dieppe, was, by 1943, a flight commander with 131 Squadron. He states:

We carried out a tremendous number of escorts to daylight Marauder missions during 1943, before the build-up to the invasion and we used to carry, depending on the distance to the target, either 45-gallon or 90-gallon slipper tanks.

The 45-gallon tank was the better of the two because it meant you were not going all that far in and, if you dropped it early on (and you did drop it as soon as enemy aircraft were sighted), it did tend to cut the time in the air as escort. If we carried the 90-gallon tank and had to jettison that early on, it was very much more seri-

ous. If for example, the target was on the fringes of Germany or northern Belgium and we had to drop tanks before we had used it, then we might well have to abandon the bombers.

Fighter Command was still doing a great job and flying in a very aggressive way. Many of the early sweeps were purely to entice the Luftwaffe up from Abbeville, St Omer, etc. These operations gave you $1\frac{1}{2}$ hours in the air, so we could get to where we wanted to go in 30-40 minutes, have half an hour in the combat area, then back to England. So I think, by 1943, although those of us doing these escorts still flying Spitfire Vbs, which was no match for the FW190, we were doing an important job.

Virtually all close escorts were flown by Spitfire Vb squadrons and wings, and the few units which were getting the Spitfire IX, flew high cover or rear cover to take on the Germans before they could get to the bombers. The Vbs would stick to the bombers and do nothing else.

No.131 Squadron was part of the Exeter Wing but in addition to Ops over Cherbourg, we continually moved into 11 Group airfields for particular shows. We often had to escort the American heavies partway to Germany and bring them back. We hadn't got the distance to do more and the long-range Mustangs hadn't come in yet. On 11 Group shows we could fly twice, but escorting heavies over Brest or beyond Cherbourg, the distances were too far to do more than either take them out or bring them back.

Influencing Factors on Combat Tactics

George Mason received both the British DFC and American DFC for his fighter pilot service during the war. The latter decoration was for flying many escort missions to American heavies. He continues:

I think the ground environment and the communications were as important as personalities. Originally we had few radio frequencies available; we didn't have very well defined radar coverage over France, so we tended to fly much more defensively. Later when we got an aircraft that could match the enemy, we still flew fairly defensively – we could have been more aggressive, looking back on it. We probably would have had losses, but we would have shot down more of the enemy. In fact, given the circumstances of the time, building up for the invasion, gaining experience, etc., I think we did it right. And I think it was a policy decision, but I wouldn't know about that.

In 1943 we got better radar, better communications and we learnt more how to use them. There was a radar station on the south coast which was a higher resolution than most of them so that they could actually control interceptions over France which none of the others really could; they could only give you a general picture. We used to fly fighter echelon, spaced at about ten minute intervals over an area and you would be allocated time with this Controller and he would take one wing, get it into combat, then take another wing and try to get that into combat. That was much more satisfactory. You had a very much better chance of engaging under those circumstances, and engaging from a favourable tactical position – up sun and above – which we made use of.

Johnnie Johnson flew what he called a 'Wolfpack' formation, which was much looser, more open, more aggressive and, although he did command the battle, he did give freedom of action where he felt it helped. If somebody saw something they were free to go; and he would know they'd gone – he would be keeping an eye on them. Otherwise he'd have detailed them to go.

In all my fights, I only had one 'ding-dong' and that was with a Me109 in early September 1943. We got into the classic turning engagement and much to my surprise I found myself continually overrunning him. About 15 feet over the top of him trying to get back into a firing position without having to turn away and leave myself in a vulnerable position. We started at 20,000 feet, went right down to the deck, climbed back up to 20,000 and finally went down to the deck again. Then I got into a firing position and a bloody cannon jammed! It was the only time in all my missions that I had a gun stoppage and it had to be then. The cannon jamming immediately caused a yaw and it was extremely difficult to shoot with one cannon only, so I just fired the machine guns at him.

I did actually stalk two Me109s once in a very confused situation for about two minutes before getting into a firing position and that was quite exciting. I was in about 52 actual engagements with the enemy but these were the only two occasions when I got in more than a fleeting engagement where you could actually say you were fighting each other.

Shot down!

I was finally shot down myself on 24 September 1943. We'd been to Amiens on an escort and were coming out when we got a plot of enemy aircraft behind us so turned to engage them. I reckoned I was about to get into range on one of them, and looking up to my right, there was a 190 at about 80 degrees deflection. I then made the stupidest decision of my life, saying to myself, well you're not going to hit me from there! I went back to my gun sight and continued lining up on my target, when there was an almighty 'clang'. I was hit in the engine, hit in the radiator – and in a trice, the whole sky was obscured by black smoke. I couldn't see a thing out of the canopy, the radio didn't work so I couldn't talk to anybody. I

turned round and thought at least I could get out to sea.

The drill in those days was that if you had anything wrong with your engine, use it while you've still got it; put it on to full power and climb. This I did but the gyro had toppled so I didn't know which way I was going. Suddenly everything got very hot indeed and I had to go. I did my trick of winding the trim forward, jettisoned the hood, let the stick go and I shot my way out. It was not the standard procedure, but had decided upon it when I'd been in hospital in 1941.

I landed not far from Amiens very close to the aeroplane. I was a bit worried because we hadn't had our latest Merlin engines for long and I thought perhaps the Germans didn't know about them, but the engine was way down in the mud somewhere so I don't expect they found much of it.

Charlton 'Wag' Haw was also at Hornchurch in 1943, firstly with 122 Squadron under Don Kingaby, before taking command of 611 Squadron at Biggin Hill. He had fought in the Battle of Britain and then in Russia where he had received both the DFM and the Russian Order of Lenin:

I was a flight commander in 122 under Don Kingaby where we were engaged in a lot of sweeps and a lot of escorts to US Marauders and Mitchells.

When I went to Biggin Hill with 611 Squadron we began to receive the Spitfire IXBs. They were better low down than the IXA had been. The IXAs were fine above 20,000 feet but the IXBs were a match for the FW190 at all heights, but especially lower down. This was good because the air battles were beginning to come down by then.

Don Kingaby was a great chap. I confirmed his last Hun he shot down with us. We were over Cap Gris Nez and it was a lovely climbing shot. We were at 25,000 feet when Don chased this fighter which then began a gentle climbing turn to the right. Don pulled round after it, cut inside and fired and that was that!

All Fighter Command was really doing in 1942-3 was pinning a lot of fighters down in France by our sweeps etc., although the Germans didn't like to mix it much. I remember I was chasing a FW190 and was slowly catching it up, when out of the blue this Spitfire arrived between me and the 190. It rolled upside down, shot the 190 down, then rolled right way up. As he regained level flight I could see it was our wing leader. When we got back I said I'd been amazed at his manoeuvre to which he replied, 'Well I had to lose some speed, didn't I?' Of course, it was common sense when one thinks about it, you start rolling and it puts a bit of brake on. He was certainly going like the clappers but I'm sure I'd have got the 190 myself for I'm sure he hadn't spotted me. But it was brilliant shooting.

I remember, too, flying on a sweep one day, quite

late and it was almost dark. Six squadrons of Spitfires, all flying along heading for home, when suddenly towards us out of a layer of cloud just below us came a lone FW190. The pilot must have looked up, seen this mass of Spitfires and thought, 'Christ!' I've never seen any aeroplane flick over so fast and disappear!

Composition of the Fighter Force

The requirements of Fighter Command were constantly under review, as we have seen in earlier chapters, many factors necessitating revisions. In April 1943, Group Captain Theodore McEvoy OBE, at HQ Fighter Command, maintained that they required 62 day-fighter squadrons, eight army support squadrons and four dive-bomber squadrons. It had been suggested that the latter be equipped with the new Brewster Bermuda (the American Navy called it the SBD2 Helldiver) much to McEvoy's dismay, and whose reaction can be imagined. He was certainly very disparaging in his comments on the type.

In April 1943, Fighter Command's strength was 47 Spitfire squadrons and 13 Typhoon squadrons, total: 60. In addition it had five bomb-carrying Typhoon units (Bombphoons), two equipped with 40mm cannon Hurricane IVs and the two Whirlwind squadrons, making a grand total of 69. Although production of the Whirlwind had now ceased, it was thought 137 and 263 Squadrons could be kept for army support; therefore they would need to be replaced by forming two new day fighter units. One of these would be a Belgian squadron that was due home from Africa. (349 Squadron had been flying Tomahawks since being formed in January 1943 but had not seen active service. It reformed in England in June 1943 with Spitfires.) The second squadron had still to be formed.

In the event, with numbers of Whirlwinds now limited and reducing, 137 handed over its machines to 263 in June 1943, and although hoping to equip with Typhoons, had to soldier on with Hurricane IVs until the new year. 263 would eventually have Typhoons too by the new year.

Within Fighter Command, of course, by this time, there were a large number of 'foreign' squadrons. Since the start of the war, an increasing number of squadrons had been formed or made up of men from all corners of the Empire and from occupied Europe. There were now New Zealand, Australian and Canadian squadrons, daily taking the war to the enemy, plus Free French, Dutch, Belgian, Czech, Polish and Norwegian units.

Demands for squadrons and aircraft still came to Air Ministry's door on a regular basis. With the battles in North Africa almost over, there was obviously going to be a build-up in order to invade the 'soft under-belly of Europe'. However, the Americans were also building their forces up in the Middle East, so demand could be tempered, although some squadrons of the US 12th Air Force were flying Spitfires, thus limiting RAF replacements.

In the Far East, the demand now was for Spitfires to replace the long-suffering workhorse, the Hurricane. For eighteen months or so, the army and air forces in India/Burma had fought a largely containing war, but with signs now of an impending attack by the Japanese, designed to punch through to India, the RAF in that theatre needed better fighter aircraft. Spitfires began to arrive in India in October 1943, and by the end of the year, two operational Spitfire squadrons were moved from the Middle East to India.

With plans now well-advanced for an assault on France in 1944, the fighter force really needed to be shaped to fit the known or believed requirements. There would be two basic needs, air cover and ground support. As far as day fighters were concerned this would really mean Spitfires, Typhoons and possibly Tempests.

In September 1943, Leigh-Mallory, in writing to the Under Secretary of State at the Air Ministry (Sir Archibald Sinclair), said that he would have a total of 85 squadrons in 1944, made up of 59 day fighters, 18 fighter-bombers and eight reconnaissance squadrons. At this stage he assumed all his fighter bomber units would be equipped with Typhoons although there was some discussion as to whether some of these would in fact be replaced by Merlin-engined Mustangs in early 1944. The recce squadrons would be flying Allison-engined Mustangs until the supply of these ran out when Merlin Mustangs would replace them.

Even at this time, Leigh-Mallory was assuming the Tempest would be the replacement for the Typhoon and one squadron might be re-equipped with the Westland Welkin – it wasn't! Leigh-Mallory's policy was to have 25% of his force as high altitude squadrons and 75% as medium altitude. Thus of his 59 day fighter units, 14 would be high and 45 medium altitude. (He regarded the Welkin to be high altitude.)

The new year of 1944 would see some changes in attitude to the force composition in the light of several changing circumstances, but then Fighter Command would have two challenges to face. One was the greatest invasion in history, the second was an entirely new enemy. One which would put the Command back on the defensive.

CHAPTER 19

Night Fighters and Intruders

BY THE END of the night blitz of 1941, Britain's night defences were just starting to get to grips with the German night raiders. With the coming of the shorter nights, the Luftwaffe's effort eased off, combined with the assault upon Russia. However, the Beaufighter with airborne radar had now become established and training and expansion continued over the summer of 1941 in readiness for the winter, when the next round of night attacks was expected.

While this training was in progress, there were several novel schemes devised to augment the night fighter force. One was the Turbinlite idea by Wing Commander W. Helmore. Like many schemes, it was long on theory but short on practical results. The principle was that a twin-engined aeroplane fitted with AI would be vectored towards a hostile radar plot from the ground, and when the crew located the raider, it would close in and then switch on a huge airborne searchlight. Meantime, the searching aircraft would be accompanied by a Hurricane, whose pilot, seeing the illuminated 'hostile' in the searchlight beam would attack and destroy it. At least, that was the theory.

Michael Allen was an 18-year-old AI operator who had teamed up with another 18-year-old pilot (who had lied about his age) named Harry White. Both NCOs, they teamed up prior to a posting to 29 Squadron in September 1941. Flying Beaufighters, they did not get off to a great start, so when the squadron was asked to provide a crew for the new Turbinlite scheme, they were 'volunteered'. Mike Allen recalls:

The airborne searchlight was developed when any project which might help to repel German raiders was given serious consideration, including aerial mines and a curtain of bombs suspended by wire from balloons. The scheme involved fitting a light to an AI aircraft and operating it for the benefit of an accompanying single seat fighter which would carry out the attack. Harry and I went to No.1455 Flight, one of ten such units quickly created in 1941-42.

Our flight was commanded by Squadron Leader J. Latimer DFC; the 'attendant fighters', as we patrolled from St Catherine's Point on the Isle of Wight, to Beachy Head, were provided by the Hurricanes of No.1 Squadron, albeit a trifle reluctantly!

The Turbinlite aircraft was a Douglas Havoc, which had a carbon-arc lamp; (its power may be gauged from the current consumption – 1,400 amps, against the 150 amps of the standard army, navy and later Leigh Light) its AI set plus crew would taxi out to the beginning of the runway and turn into wind. The Hurricane would follow and take the normal No.2 position just behind the tailplane on the starboard side of the Havoc. Navigation lights on both aircraft were kept switched on, I believe, until both machines were airborne. On a word from the Havoc pilot over the VHF radio telephone, both pilots would open their throttles, move forward down the runway and with speed increasing, make normal take off and climb away to their patrol height of 12-15,000 feet. The difference was that the Hurricane pilot, from the moment he started to trundle forward, had one eye on his own instruments and the other on the illuminated white strip on the underside of the Turbinlite aircraft's black mainplane. He had to formate on that white strip for the duration of the patrol, usually $1\frac{1}{2}$ to 2 hours. Unless, of course, the Havoc crew found a raider. In that case, the theory was the single-seat pilot would dive forward and below the glare of the airborne searchlight, before pulling up in the classic night attack and seeing his target beautifully caught in the prodigious beam of Helmore's light just waiting to be shot down! Well, that was the theory!

Harry and I carried out 49 such defensive patrols and numerous practice sorties, which could have been turned into an Op if the need had arisen, but never saw a thing. It was vital for the operation to have an accurate interception by the Havoc pilot and his AI operator. If the target was not plumb in the beam when the light was switched on, the interception became an immediate and irredeemable failure, with the Havoc pilot unable to see his instrument panel properly because of the glare of the light, and the smoke (not to mention smell) from the carbon arcs burning a few feet in front of him! And the Hurricane pilot, seeing nothing in the beam above him, having no idea where in the blackness to look, was equally useless, and both pilots' night vision would be gone. The German, of course, would be off like a shot.

In point of fact this whole Turbinlite effort, which was considerable, only achieved one certain night kill plus a probable, and a number of Havoc crews and Hurricane pilots died in crashes or night collisions trying to achieve the impossible. The ten flights became squadrons during this time, but they were finally disbanded in early 1943, the 'normal' night-fighting systems having been much improved by this date.

The New Zealanders of 486 Squadron had also been co-operating with one of the Turbinlite units (1453 Flight), but its first Hurricane night victory came after these operations folded up. Harvey Sweetman was a flight commander on 486, scoring the squadron's first kill on 9 April 1943, although he had to share the victory with an 'unknown' A.N.Other! He explains:

Originally 486 operated as a night fighter unit in conjunction with a Turbinlite Flight. We flew Hurricanes with the Bostons. This experimental defence system was not successful; far too many things to go wrong and a very difficult type of flying to undertake.

On 9 April I was scrambled independently of the Turbinlite, to carry out aerodrome and local defence. I was vectored by local control and at first identified a Wellington before receiving another course. I recollect a moonlight night and about 6/10ths cloud cover. I observed an aircraft silhouetted against a backdrop of cloud. I dived down to investigate and about the same time as I identified it as a Dornier 217, its gunner opened fire and streams of red and orange tracer went above and to the right of me.

I fired a reflex burst and broke away. The Dornier also dived away, making for cloud. I followed it down and gave it two good bursts of fire. It rolled over onto its back and I last saw it streaming smoke from its wings as it disappeared into cloud. I circled the area and shortly saw an explosion on the ground. I then gave a radio fix for the Controller.

I visited the site of the wreck next day and discovered that the crew had baled out and been captured. Their description of the attack was similar to my version except that they thought it was a Spitfire. Several enemy aircraft were shot down that evening and a few claims were

*Harry White DFC**, 141 Squadron.*

*Michael Allen DFC**, 141 Squadron.*

Turbinlite Havoc of 1458 Flight.

Havoc night-fighter of 93 Squadron, fitted with LAM aerial mine and forward-sideways AI radar.

lodged. I was never informed of any other claim details but I believe it was Group's idea of sharing the victories around and satisfying all claims, of whatever merit. At the time I was disappointed and honestly believed no one else was involved in the kill. Our station commander, Basil Embry, was furious and thought the squadron had been badly treated, but the main thing was that a raider had been brought down and the squadron had its first victory.

Harry White and Mike Allen now returned to the Beaufighter, being posted to 141 Squadron, having spent 15 frustrating months on Turbinlites. But they had forged a tremendous bond, as did most night fighter crews, and the experience they gained together was to pay handsome dividends. Of the Beaufighter, Mike Allen remembers:

It was superbly designed, and speedily produced, for the night-fighter role. It had a maximum speed of 324 mph at 11,750 feet, a service ceiling of 27,000 and could climb to 15,000 in 9.4 minutes. The armament of four 20mm cannons and six ·303 machine guns, appeared to all who flew, or flew in, this robust and respected aeroplane, more than adequate for the task. It had more advanced VHF R/T receivers and transmitters which made communications with the GCI controller and aerodrome flying control much easier, with clarity of speech and less interference.

Above all, the Beaus were fitted with the newly developed Mark IV AI set. Designed by our incomparable scientists, this miraculous equipment was compressed into half a dozen 'black boxes', including a viewing unit into which the operator peered at two small cathode ray tubes. On the nose and wings of the aircraft was a neat aerial array to transmit the radar pulses and receive back the vital 'echoes' as the pulses bounced back off any other aircraft within the coverage of the set.

The Mark IV set flown in a Beau at 18,000 feet could pick up an 'echo' in front of it three miles away. Its forward range was governed by the height of the Beau above the ground, ie: at 20,000 feet the range was four miles but at 10,000 only two miles. Apart from the range, the signals (or blips) received on the cathode ray tubes gave indications of the azimuth and elevation positions of the target aircraft relative to that of the pursuing fighter.

A skilful GCI controller could, by watching carefully the 'blips' of the incoming bomber and the defending fighter merging towards each other on his single large tube (PPI), direct the fighter to within 2-3 miles of its target – sometimes less. Ideally he would attempt to put the fighter in on a 'cut off vector' at the same height, or a bit higher, as the target, where the pursuer could turn in behind but not have a prolonged stern chase. Once the echo from the target appeared on the airborne

Harvey Sweetman (left) of 486 (NZ) Squadron. In the centre is Group Captain Basil Embry DSO DFC, OC RAF Wittering, and 486's CO, Squadron Leader C. L. C. Roberts.

radar, the AI operator shouted, 'Contact!' gleefully to his pilot, and took over, whilst the pilot passed on the good news to GCI. From then on it was up to the crew to bring the interception to a satisfactory conclusion.

Either by direct instruction or by a running commentary (or a combination of both), the AI operator could, after a swift but vital scrutiny of the signals on his tubes, aim to bring his pilot to within 5-600 feet astern of the target and slightly below. The shimmering green lines of the time tracks and the sometimes indistinct shape of the blip were not always easy to decipher whilst bumping along in the back of the Beau. Additionally, the amount of 'working space' on the tubes, unencumbered by the menacing 'ground returns', sometimes seemed woefully small (i.e., approx two centimetres at 10,000 ft). If the two aircraft were converging fast or even head-on, there were only seconds in which to act before the precious blip disappeared off the screen as quick as it had arrived.

If all went well and the operator brought his pilot into close range he should start to see a shape which was different from the rest of night sky. On all but the darkest nights he would be able to pick up the outline of the other aircraft and coming in below, he would see the silhouette as it became larger and spread out above

him but still slightly in front. On the way in he might have caught a glimpse of twin exhaust flames (flame dampers on exhaust manifolds later put an end to those helpful gouts of flame) and if on final approach he chanced to pull up on to the same level as his prey, he would feel the turbulence of its slipstream.

It sounds pretty easy but it wasn't. Allan Wright, who we last met while flying as a day fighter pilot with 92 Squadron in 1941, was by early 1943 flying Beaufighters at night with 29 Squadron. In between times he had been an instructor, then Chief Instructor at the Pilot Gunnery Instructor School, then at CGS, Sutton Bridge with Sailor Malan, before going on a tour of the United States with Jamie Rankin. On 3 April 1943, he claimed a night kill in a Beau:

The German was one of those low jobs so we were sent off to patrol at 1,000 feet off Manston. My Nav/Rad was George Brill and the skill of one's operator was very much of an art, being able to transfer to a pilot verbally what he is seeing on his radar screens. George got a contact and directed me to it and yes, I saw it but had to ensure it was hostile. Suddenly the rear gunner opened up and the bomber slowed down so I was in danger of colliding with it. With the gunner still firing I was trying desperately to pull away while George was yelling at me to, 'Shoot the bastard down!' Anyway, I got terribly busy and then lost sight of it.

I found I couldn't fly the Beau properly and my instruments were all going round and round – then Ground Control was coming in. I asked them to hold on while I got myself sorted out, discovering that having lowered my flaps to help keep from hitting the bomber, I'd not raised them and in opening the throttles in my gyrations, one of the flaps had collapsed. When I got that sorted out, Control gave me another bandit and this time it was pure luck, for when we got near to its position, having climbed to 2,000 feet, and with the coast of France coming up, we got the contact.

Above left: *Night fighter Hurricane IIC of 247 Squadron.*

Left: *A duo of night fighter/intruder Hurricane IIs. Note anti-glare shields to protect pilot's night vision from the exhausts.*

Above right: *Two night intruder pilots par excellence – Squadron Leader J. A. F. Maclachlan DSO DFC, and Flight Lieutenant Karel Kuttelwascher DFC. 'Mac' had lost his left forearm over Malta. Picture taken when both had received the Czech War Cross.*

Right: *John Cunningham DSO** DFC*, gained 20 victories, 19 at night.*

Above: *One of the war's top-scoring night fighter teams, Wing Commander Bob Braham DSO** DFC** (right), and his radar operator, Squadron Leader W. J. 'Sticks' Gregory DSO DFC* DFM. Braham scored 29 kills in the war, 19 at night, 10 on day intruder sorties.*

Left: *Wing Commander 'Zulu' Douglas Morris DFC, commanded 406 Canadian night fighter Squadron in 1942. He was later to become the 12th C-in-C of Fighter Command.*

Below: *Mosquito night fighter of 157 Squadron.*

This time, however, it was just too easy. The aircraft had obviously been dropping mines and having recrossed the Channel, had begun to climb as it approached France, thinking it was safe. George was extolling me to 'get it this time!' I crept up behind it, fired, flames shot out and down it went on fire.

The names of the more successful night fighter pilots soon became as well known as their day fighter comrades. History today recalls a few, such as John Cunningham, Bob Braham, Desmond Hughes, Bransome

Left: *Flying Officer Terry Clark DFM, radar operator with 219 and 488 Squadrons. With 219 he flew with Tom Pike, a future C-in-C Fighter Command.*

Below: *Junkers 88 night fighter showing its night radar aerials. It was these aircraft which the 'Serrate' squadrons sought out over Germany.*

Right: *German night fighter caught by a 'Serrate' night fighter over Germany.*

Below right: *Another successful night fighter/intruder pilot was Howard Kelsey DSO DFC*, of 141 Squadron. He later commanded 515 Squadron. The pilot on the right is Charles Winn DSO DFC, who commanded 141 in 1944.*

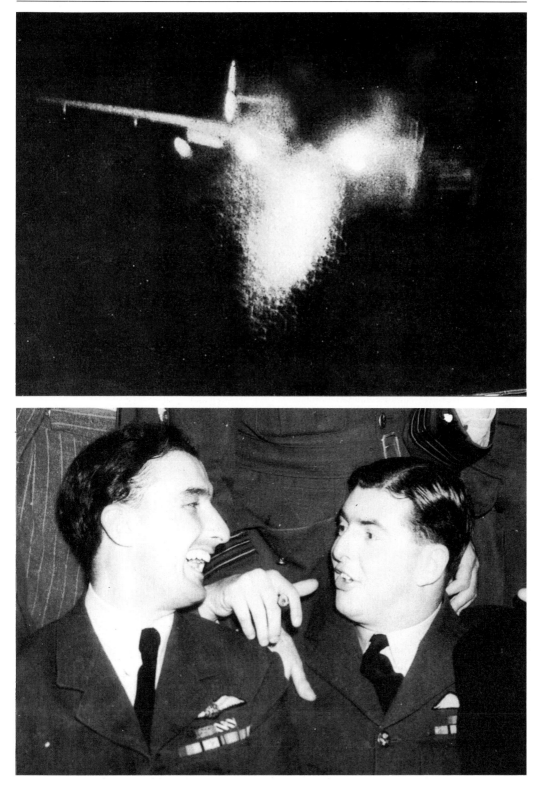

Burbridge and Russell Bannock and AI operators such as Jimmy Rawnsley, Doug Oxby and Bill Skelton.

Another AI operator was Terry Clark. A pre-war Auxiliary air gunner he was with 219 Squadron in 1940 and trained as a radio observer. In 1941 he received the DFM, having assisted in the destruction of three enemy aircraft but then he too went onto Turbinlites, on the same unit as Mike Allen. In 1943 he returned to 219 Squadron, now commissioned and had successes with this unit and later with 488 New Zealand Squadron, flying both Beaus and Mosquito night fighters. He recalls:

When I joined 219 Squadron in 1940, we carried just an LAC AI Operator in our Blenheims, such was the value at that time of airborne radar. Then we began converting to Beaufighters in October and then we had a new CO early in 1941 - Wing Commander Tom Pike. I occasionally flew as his AI operator and we had some success in April 1941 and then in June Flying Officer D. O. Hobbis and I got a Heinkel 111 which was attacking Chatham and it crashed at Guestling where the crew were taken prisoner. I am now in contact with the radio operator.

There were moments of anxiety flying night-fighter Ops, such as the occasion when after take-off our air speed indicator packed up. Not a nice thought as a Beau

was prone to spin in at low landing speed! But I was with a first class pilot and he made a successful landing after a couple of low passes across the airfield to assess our speed.

There was also a crash landing at Tangmere when we hit an object which had been left on the runway. The wheel collapsed and as the right wheel could not take the strain, it also gave way and we slid along on our belly. I ended upside down but suffered only a broken watch. We escaped somewhat rapidly but as my pilot had the presence of mind to switch off the petrol, there was no fire - not that we waited to see!

When I joined 488 Squadron they were operating Mosquitos. The main advantage for me was being able to sit at the side of the pilot rather than being stuck down the back and facing aft. One could see more of the action but I had to keep my eyes on the AI until the pilot was in the firing position. You never knew what the German might do. Sitting side by side also gave a better feeling of team work. For me the Mossie was a joy being fairly small. At 5' 3" I could, with a little help from my pilot, if he sat well back, sit on the edge of his seat and fly the aircraft!

My pilot was Flying Officer Doug Robinson who shot down four Huns two of which I helped with. One was a Me410 we got near Rye in December 1943, the other a Ju188 over France at the end of July 1944. On the

Mosquito night fighter returning home. Note bulbous nose, housing the airborne radar, and the radar aerials at the wing tips.

latter we were on patrol south of Caen, under Yardley Control and I picked it up at 2¼ miles. Closing in it must have seen our exhausts as it opened fire and peeled off to port. Robinson dived after it, firing, and it blew up, the crash lighting up the countryside to the north of Mayenne. We were in a Mark XIII Mosquito using Mark VIII AI, operating from Colerne over the beachhead. On this latter occasion I was only visiting the squadron, as I was at a Ground Control station at the time!

Another nocturnal activity was night intruding, which began more or less like night Rhubarbs in 1941. Again it was the aggressive pilots in certain squadrons who were not content to wait for trouble, but actively sort it out. Why try to find a raider over blacked-out England when one might find them landing or taking off over a lit-up runway in France.

This is exactly what some of the more experienced Hurricane pilots who had gained some night flying skill over England began to do. It was pretty devastating for Luftwaffe crews suddenly to be attacked over their home bases, especially when taking off full of bombs and fuel or returning from a raid, tired and perhaps with concentration wandering.

There were a number of RAF pilots who did a great deal of mayhem on these intruder sorties; J. A. F. MacLachlan DSO DFC shot down five in 1942 with 1 Squadron, despite having lost an arm over Malta in 1941. Karel Kuttelwascher, a Czech pilot flying with the same squadron, shot down 15! In pure night fighting over England, R. P. Stevens, of 151 Squadron, shot down no fewer than 14 night raiders in a Hurricane, far outstripping AI-equipped Beaufighter crews, such as John Cunningham/Jimmy Rawnsley, or Bob Braham/'Sticks' Gregory.

During the later stages of the war, with night raids on Britain being on a very much reduced scale, the night fighter squadrons flew intruder sorties over occupied Europe to even greater effect than the single seat Hurricane pilots of 1941-42. When Mike Allen and his pilot Harry White 'escaped' from the Turbinlite scene, they joined 141 Squadron, commanded by Bob Braham. 141 Squadron was actively engaged on intruder work over enemy territory, attacking not only aircraft, but trains and shipping but this was about to change.

Bomber Command's almost nightly intrusions over Germany was costing them dear, German nightfighter crews having become proficient in tackling the armadas of Lancasters, Stirlings and Halifaxes which headed out in bomber streams to attack German towns and cities. In order to combat this growing menace

Squadron Leader Russ Bannock DSO DFC* (Canadian) with his radar operator, Flight Lieutenant R. Bruce, 418 Squadron. Bannock claimed 9 intruder kills plus 19 V1 flying bombs. In 1944 he took command of 406 Squadron.

Bannock's Mosquito in 418 Squadron (HR147 'Z') named 'Hairless Joe'.

of the German night-fighters, Fighter Command was to provide a form of night-fighter escort – intruding into the bomber streams to seek out the attacking Me110, Ju88 or Do217 twin-engined radar-controlled night fighters and the single-engined Me109 and FW190 freelance night fighters. Mike Allen:

No.141 Squadron, now in 12 Group of Fighter Command, had been chosen to pioneer a new version of the night fighter business. Mainly due to the outstanding leadership of Wing Commander Bob Braham, 141 was being taken off the list of home defence squadrons, many of which were already underemployed, waiting for German bombers which rarely came, and trained for Operation Serrate.

This new role was simply to go out over Germany and the occupied countries and hunt for the hunters. We were to match our skills against our own counterparts – the night-fighter crews of the Luftwaffe. These new operations were referred to as bomber support and later on were taken over by Bomber Command after they had been proved to be worthwhile as the radio/radar counter-measures war developed in 1943-44. It was 141's job to prove whether high-level freelance intruder sorties, looking for the defending night fighters was worthwhile.

Harry and I did our first trip on 3 July 1943 in support of a raid on Cologne and damaged a Me110 over Aachen. However, our first problem was security. Our Mark IV AI, which in design was way ahead of the Germans in design and production had been a jealously guarded secret. Night fighters were never allowed to cross the French coast. Another problem was for the RAF crews to operate over Germany without ground control and also be at risk from German night fighters finding them in or around the bomber stream.

This was solved by the British scientists in 1943 by the new, advanced, centimetric AI that began to be introduced to home defence squadrons. This allowed the Mark IV AI to be used over Germany, as it no longer mattered if the Germans learned its secrets. Mark IV AI was now expendable! But what now of identification, which had long caused RAF night fighter crews a headache?

Around the bomber stream an AI operator would be picking up not only enemy night fighters but more frequently, friendly bombers which would be indistinguishable from each other. Even a blip away from the stream might turn out to be an RAF straggler. The problem was again solved by the boffins. They managed to discover the frequency used by the Germans' night-fighter radar (which in itself is a fascinating story) which resulted in us having another 'black box' in our Beaus which enabled the AI operators to identify the signal when we homed in on a 'bogey'. When we closed in on a suspected night fighter, the 'Serrate' signal came within the range of the Mark IV AI, we knew it was a fighter and the interception would then continue in the usual way.

No.141 Squadron started the first Serrate ops in June 1943. We had a switch on the AI which gave us a different picture on our tubes if there was a German night fighter nearby. It was a herring-bone pattern of lines on both screens, the strength of the signal giving some idea of the range. So although we were alone over Germany with no Ground Control, we had our AI sets and a means of identification. Bob Braham and Sticks Gregory were the first to score, getting a Me110 over Holland on 14 June and another ten days later. Other crews began to score. The Germans, of course, had no rear rearward-looking radar and we were happy that we were doing something really useful in helping to defend our bomber formations.

The whole thing was called Serrate because the herring-bone pattern showing the presence of a night fighter had a serrated edge at the side of the picture. Harry and I got our first success on 15/16 July – a 110 near Rheims. We were so elated that for some minutes the Beau flew itself while we congratulated ourselves. The only trouble was that it took us over a searchlight belt at Dreux and we nearly got ourselves shot down!

Then on 15/16 August (supporting the Peenemünde Raid) we made two more claims but only after an Me110 nearly claimed us. Stupidly we got in front of the 110 instead of behind it! The sound of its cannons firing (above the noise of our engines) and the sight of its tracers going just over the top of our cockpits had a salutary effect on our movements which became urgent and downwards.

We all learned as we went along, working out our tactics within the Beau's limited range and speed. We enjoyed our successes and were saddened by our losses. By September 1943 our efforts had proved the case and the scheme was expanded. Night fighters had been shot down and enemy crews and their ground controllers were in some confusion.

At the end of the year we became 141 Bomber Support Squadron and were transferred to Bomber Command; then re-equipped with Mosquito aircraft with which we could range deeper into enemy air space. A new group, 100 Group, was formed, which became the main radio and radar counter-measures group of the RAF.

Harry White and Mike Allen each received the DFC and two bars for their Serrate work, claiming more than a dozen German twin- and single-engined night fighters shot down. They had also flown together almost non-stop from 1941 to 1945, forming a bond of friendship which only ended with Harry's death in 1990.

CHAPTER 20

D-Day and Doodlebugs

IN THE SPRING of 1944 Fighter Command continued with its two main tasks, helping to escort the American heavies with their increasing assaults on Germany and the escort of British and American medium bombers over France and the Low Countries.

However, there was now a new emphasis on how and why the operations of the latter were to be used. Although still important to try to force the German fighters up to do battle in order to destroy them, the bomber's targets now took on an important new dimension. With the coming invasion of Europe, somewhere along the coast of France, the enemy's communications network needed to be pulverised. Marshalling yards, rail depots, railway stations, signal boxes, all needed to be knocked out, or at least severely disrupted. Trains too needed to be destroyed, both the locos and the goods waggons. These now became the priority targets plus airfields and German army camps and munitions dumps. Everything, in fact, which would help the Germans defend and counter against the invasion needed to be hit and put out of action.

There was, however, another important target, and one which in the beginning neither the fighter nor bomber crews knew about in any detail. These were code-named 'Noball' targets, which were in reality the launching sites for Germany's new weapon of war, the V1 pilotless flying bombs. The 'V' stood for *Vergeltungswaffen* – Reprisal Weapons.

Known also as a 'buzz bomb' or 'doodlebug', this was one of Hitler's famous Secret Weapons with which he hoped to bring Britain to her knees. Smaller than a normal single-seat aeroplane, it was aeroplane-shaped but with a ram-jet atop the stabilising fin. Fired from a ramp which looked like a miniature ski ramp, it had sufficient fuel, depending on its target, to fly to that target where its engine would cut out and the flying bomb would then plummet to the ground and detonate its explosive charge much like a falling bomb.

Its potential to inflict damage upon Britain was not so great as its potential to inflict civilian casualties, for the V1 could never be sufficiently accurate to be sent to destroy a specific building or factory. It could only be sent to the vicinity of a target, which more than likely would be a town or city, where it would fall and kill indiscriminately. A true 'terror weapon'.

Allied Intelligence had been aware of the V1's development for some time. Indeed, the secret establishment at Peenemünde on the Baltic coast where the flying bomb and its sister, the V2 rocket, were built and developed, had been located and bombed by Bomber Command in August 1943. The raid was a success and put the programme back some months, but by the end of 1943, the strange sites were beginning to spring up like mushrooms inland from the French coast. The Intelligence gatherers and watchers soon discovered them, and although for some time they were kept secret, because of the 'terror' factor, the RAF, and in part the American medium bombers, began to be tasked against them.

They were difficult targets, small; just a set of ramp rails and a small bunker nearby for the launching crew to be housed. They were also heavily defended. The dilemma was how to knock them out. To some extent they were too small for a large formation of medium bombers to attack, although this was tried, and to attack them with single-seat ground attack aircraft was highly dangerous for the attacking pilots because of the density of the light flak arranged about the sites. Even if destroyed, and by whichever method, it did not take long for the site to be rebuilt. Meanwhile, others could be set up almost overnight.

When Fighter Command attacked these targets it was with the use of Typhoons, or the couple of remaining Hurricane IV units. Bomb-carrying Spitfires were also used, a role the Spitfire would be increasingly associated with after the coming invasion. Casualties were high, but so were the stakes. Every site that could be destroyed or put out of commission, would help when the Germans were finally ready to launch their V1 flying bombs. What was exercising the minds of the Invasion chiefs, too, was the thought of these bombs falling amongst the assembled armies packed together in the various south-coast ports, ready to go aboard the invasion ships and landing craft! The invasion was going to be difficult enough without this problem.

Rockets and Bombs

What was about to make the Typhoon an even more deadly aeroplane was the development of the air to ground rocket projectile (RP). These rockets had been produced in 1943, some of the first being fitted to the Hurricane IVs, after taking off their 40mm guns, of course. They had been found very accurate, being first used against German shipping in the continuing Channel Stop battle. They were not allowed to be used over enemy-occupied territory in case an unused one fell into enemy hands.

The first land target attacked was the lock gates on the Hansweert Canal which connected the Oorsterschelde and the Westerschelde, north and south of the Dutch island of Walcheren. This was carried out on 2 September 1943. Hurricanes were lost in this attack and unfired rockets were found by the Germans, who called them rocket-propelled bombs. A year later they would know all about the RAF rockets – from the receiving end.

In 1944 the Typhoon began to equip with the rockets, four beneath each wing, which could be fired in pairs, or in one full salvo. It was a devastating weapon, almost equivalent to a naval ship's broadside. Against most 'soft' targets, which included tanks etc., it was the ideal ground attack weapon to be developed. Typhoons still carried bombs, 250- or 500-pounders, used against more resilient targets where blast or penetration was needed, but the RP became the scourge of the German army following the invasion.

Another important target for the Typhoon came in the weeks prior to the actual landings in Normandy. Enemy radar needed to be knocked out so that the Germans would be blinded when the invasion fleet sailed. Keeping the Germans guessing as to the exact place the invasion force would land was an important factor of its success, so for those weeks, Typhoons ranged the whole length of the French coast, from the Pas de Calais to Cherbourg. The radar sites, too, were difficult targets, soon repaired or replaced, so follow-up attacks needed to be made on several of them. Casualties again were high among the 'Tiffie' pilots at this time.

ADGB and 2nd TAF

Amidst the plans for D-Day there was a change for Fighter Command. By its very nature, the Command was

Trials with rocket projectiles were first carried out on Hurricane fighters before the Typhoons began to use them.

The Hurricane IV also carried two 40mm cannons which could blast the boiler of a steam locomotive right out of its housing.

A rocket-armed Hurricane IV making a mock attack on a Navy MGB.

still basically a defensive weapon, honed to defend Britain. If Britain was now going to invade France and take an invasion force with her, there was deemed to be a change of role. The 'offensive' air force was therefore designated Second Tactical Air Force (2nd TAF). This was formulated in late 1943, and its tactical nature would be as support, both air and ground, for the British and Canadian armies, while the American 9th Air Force would support the American army in similar fashion.

Leaders

Initially the organisation was known as the Allied Expeditionary Air Force, Sir Trafford Leigh-Mallory became its C-in-C on 17 November 1943. Leigh-Mallory had commanded Fighter Command for just one year.

Both Sholto Douglas and Leigh-Mallory had their admirers and critics, which often depended on how either man had affected someone's RAF career. Both men in their way were ambitious, Leigh-Mallory particularly so. Johnnie Johnson recalls:

Sholto and Leigh-Mallory were at the mercy of the wing leaders who were the senior people flying. They always maintained a close liaison with us because they were out of date, not flying themselves. We could 'bull-shit' Leigh-Mallory, and Bader did. L-M would ring me up when he was C-in-C and ask, 'How did it go today, old boy? Anything I can do for you?' or 'Ring me anytime, or come and see me, always available!' It was good stuff, heady stuff, but he was only wanting to be kept up to date.

When the war started these people were all ex-flyers, not up to date, which is why the stupid vics of three persisted for so long. Nobody knew. But they were all nice people!

I had a soft spot for L-M. We all knew he was a bull-shitter but beneath it all, he was all right. A lot of people didn't understand him of course. The Americans hated him because he seemed to them, and showed, a pompous exterior. I think it was a bit of a mask, for he was a kindly, rather shy man.

I preferred him to Sholto who was very pompous and unrelaxed. With L-M we could have a joke but I didn't get on with Sholto as I did with L-M.

It wasn't until we got men like Basil Embry, Don Bennett, Harry Broadhurst and so on, coming up to Air

Nearest the camera is Air Marshal Sir Arthur Coningham, who commanded 2nd TAF in 1944. With him is Harry Broadhurst DSO DFC* AFC, AOC 83 Group and Group Captain Jimmy Fenton DSO DFC.

rank in the RAF that things began to change, men with combat experience. I remember Broadhurst saying to me in 1943, 'You don't bullshit me; I'll bloody well fly anywhere you can!'

I was telling him the flak was too heavy or something, but he knew what was what – he'd done it. We could have convinced Leigh-Mallory that we didn't want to do something, but not Broadie. That was great and I think we became far more efficient because of them.

Left: *Air Marshal Sir Roderic Hill, commanding ADGB 1943-44 and C-in-C of Fighter Command, 1944-45.*

Right: *Hawker Typhoons of 174 Squadron, with D-Day marking, taxi out from Holmesley South, for an operation over the Normandy Beach-head.*

Below: *Major Helge Mehre, CO 331 Norwegian Squadron on D-Day, 1944. Note D-Day invasion stripes for quick identification.*

Ralph Sampson remembers:

I personally thought Leigh-Mallory a bit of an idiot because he seemed to rely entirely on the opinions of his junior commanders. Bader seemed to have him just where he wanted him and I noticed he seemed to quiz people all the time, as if he didn't know anything at all.

He was a very pompous individual, and later on somebody told me that when he was overseeing the invasion of Normandy, Churchill came to his Ops Room, and seeing a row of pins on a map, asked him what they represented. They were various bomb lines, etc., but L-M didn't know and gave him some other explanation which was totally wrong.

Second TAF itself, under the command of Air Marshal Sir Arthur Coningham, had 2 Bomber Group, and two new groups, 83 and 84. These latter two had fighter and fighter-bomber squadrons transferred to it from Fighter Command and they became a totally mobile force. Wings became known as Airfields as they set up bases in and around southern England, to practise and be ready for D-Day. Once in France they would have to be largely self-supporting and live 'off the country', so for some months before the invasion, these Fighter Airfields, lived under canvas, far from their normal, more solid living accommodations, and, for the hard-working ground-crews, away from their nice protective and workman-like hangars.

Coningham had been a First War fighter pilot, winning the DSO, MC and DFC, ending that conflict with more than a dozen combat victories. Prior to 2nd TAF, he had held commands in the North African Campaign.

The new commander of 11 Group was Air Marshal R. M. Hill CB MC AFC, who had been commanding 12 Group. Roderic Hill, aged 50, found himself in the odd position of having the previous commander, Leigh-Mallory, as head of AEAF, still the overall commander of Home Defence as well as Tactical Forces. But Hill was also responsible to Air Ministry.

No.11 Group was now left with just 10 day-fighter squadrons and 11 night-fighter squadrons, although he could call on some AEAF units if the need arose. Fighter Command now lost its old identity and became ADGB – Air Defence of Great Britain, the old title from the 1930s.

Hill had been an airman in the Great War and had been a squadron commander in Iraq in the mid-1920s. Some years later he was ADC to the King, then held commands in Palestine and Transjordan. He had been Director of Technical Developments in 1938 and in 1940 became Assistant to the Director-General of Research and Development, rising to Director-General.

D-Day, 6 June 1944

Fighter Command helped put up the largest air umbrella ever seen over the invasion beaches of Normandy. All day, successive waves of ADGB and AEAF fighters, together with American 8th and 9th Air Force fighters gave cover to the huge convoy of ships and landing craft, as well as escort to waves of troop carrying aircraft or

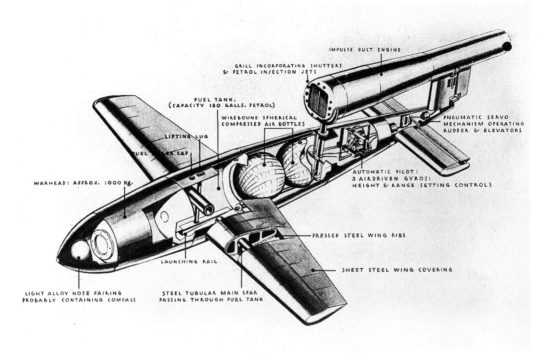

The V1 Flying Bomb.

bombers hitting specific targets behind the beach-head,

This continued for several days, until the invasion force was firmly established on French soil. In addition to these duties, ADGB Spitfires helped escort RAF heavy bombers, Lancasters and Halifaxes, in a number of day bomber sorties to and from the battle front.

As this book covers just Fighter Command and, for this period of 1944, the ADGB, the happenings of 2nd TAF in Europe must of necessity be covered in other written works. While the Allied soldiers held on to their initial gains in Normandy, ADGB fighters pulled back, giving some cover to the vast amount of shipping in the Channel, and to the invasion ports along the south coast of England. But then, quite suddenly, the ADGB squadrons had a very different task facing them.

On 13 June 1944, the first V1s were fired upon England. Only four of the ten launched actually reached England, one landing near Sevenoaks in Kent, another near Gravesend, a third at Cuckfield, Sussex and the fourth at Bethnal Green, London. Fighter Command suddenly had a very new enemy.

Fighting the Doodlebugs

Roderic Hill, like many others in Britain, had been watching and waiting anxiously for the start of Hitler's terror campaign. He knew only too well how his pilots

and those of AEAF had been helping to knock out the flying bomb sites in France since the start of the year. He had made his fears known to Leigh-Mallory when still commander of 12 Group but Leigh-Mallory's Headquarters staff had informed Hill that they attached little importance to the growing number of V1 sites. Now that particular pigeon had come home to roost!

It took a little while for the Germans to get into their stride with their flying bombs (code-named 'Divers' by the RAF), but until they started to come in earnest, the defences could only speculate about the best way of combating them. What they soon learnt was that they were fast. The pulse-jet gave the V1 a speed of between 320 and 400 mph at anywhere between 3 and 5,000 feet. Range varied but the average was 250 miles and it carried a 2,000-pound warhead. Most V1s were fired from the launch sites, but they could be carried by aircraft and launched in mid-air.

A couple of days after the first ones fell on England, 55 sites let fly 244 flying bombs, and from then until early September, they came almost daily. In fact the daily average was 190. There were three main forms of defence. AA guns, balloon cables and RAF fighters.

The anti-aircraft gunners formed defensive belts, eventually of 620 heavy guns and 1,762 light guns, to put up a massive fire against the robots, and Balloon Command also set up a defence line to try and catch others.

Above: *Harvey Sweetman DFC, 486 New Zealand Squadron.*

Above right: *Bruce Lawless DFC, 486 New Zealand Squadron.*

Right: *Squadron Leader Joe Berry DFC*, top scorer against the V1s with over 60 shot down. He was killed in action operating over Europe in October 1944.*

ADGB quickly found it had its work cut out due to the speed of the bombs. In order to catch them, they needed both to see them quickly and be in a position to dive at them, gathering the required speed in doing so. Even when they caught them up and began firing, there was the ever present danger of the charge exploding, almost in the face of the attacker.

Because of the problems of speed, the only fighter aircraft that could catch the V1s were the Tempest, some later marks of the Spitfire, and the P51 Mustang. Other aircraft did occasionally make a lucky kill, but usually these pilots were only lucky when they found themselves in a good position when they spotted a 'doodlebug' and were able to build up a good speed in a dive. Most fighter pilots tried to dive on the V1s but if it came to a tail-chase, then only the above fighters could catch them in level flight. The V1 battles also delayed the recently formed Tempest Wing, led by Wing Commander

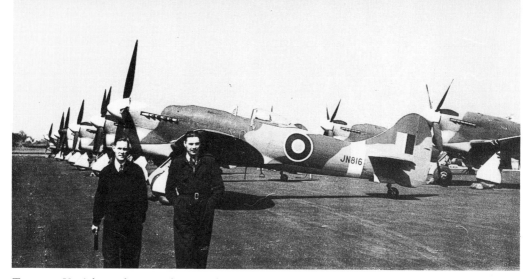

Tempest Vs (shown here at the Langley Factory awaiting delivery) took the brunt of the V1 battle. JN816 (foreground) went to 56 Squadron, coded US-W.

Roland Beamont DSO DFC, from moving to the Continent to support the Allied armies.

The attacks came both during the day and at night, so Tempests were employed at night, as well as Mosquito night fighters. The latter would also be engaged on countering the German bombers who flew over the Channel or North Sea at night carrying V1s to launch off the British coast. One advantage the night sorties gave the

Bruce Lawless's score on his Tempest: 10 'Doodlebugs'. Note the mug of beer emblem!

pilots was that they could see the V1s because of the flame which shot back from the bomb's ram jet.

Two accounts of attacking V1s come from two New Zealand pilots flying Tempests with 486 New Zealand Squadron, Harvey Sweetman (who we met in the previous chapter) and Bruce Lawless, both of whom shot down ten flying bombs. First, Harvey Sweetman:

The tactics found to be most successful involved standing patrols over known entry routes. These were appointed to the various squadrons of the Wing by Operational Headquarters. There was some freelance activity but generally, when we operated, it was by routine patrols. Extra patrols were sent off in times of great activity. Almost all V1s' flight paths operated at similar altitudes, within a range of 1,500-3,000 feet. Speeds varied somewhat but usually within the upper limits of defending fighters – 260-400 mph. Tactics employed usually meant patrolling at a higher altitude to make use of the dive, to close and to overtake the quarry. Interception was by a combination of radio control vectoring plus visual sighting.

The flame of the propulsion unit was very visible, particularly at dusk, dawn or in grey overcast conditions. The usual attack was from the rear, preferably without too much angle of deflection. Firing range 400 yards maximum, down to less than 100 yards. The former, quite a distance for a small target with a short wingspan; the latter rather risky, with damage from a mid-air explosion and fall out debris a distinct possibility. However, there was little risk generally and providing you could get into position, little risk was involved.

Towards the end of this period the radar controlled anti-aircraft fire of the coastal artillery accounted for most of the V1s destroyed.

Bruce Lawless:

Our normal way of getting them was to be on patrol

over or near the Hastings area and radar would give us a vector on one and we would try to locate it and hopefully be above so we could come down behind. As we were faster, fire at about 200 yards from directly astern, without deflection, was the norm.

Hopefully this fire would hit the bomb's steering gear or engine and they would either spin down or dive out of control. Occasionally one would explode if the nose was hit. I had one do that on me and I flew through the debris which wrecked my engine and I had to force-land in a field – luckily I was OK.

They were easy to spot at night because of their flame. I should think about 70% of doodlebugs were shot down as a result of radar and then spotting them visually. We always flew in sections of two as any more would have been unwieldy.

As far as I remember, a Spitfire pilot one day actually tipped the wing of a doodlebug and the following day in the national Press there were accounts of this happening. A few days later, by a chance in a million, someone either shot one down or it could have come down with engine failure, and it hadn't exploded, so was more or less intact. Upon inspection it was found that the Germans had placed a piece of wire, or some such thing, from the wingtip to the nose where the explosive was housed. If anyone had tried to tip the wing, they would have been blown up. We had a directive arrive not to try to tip their wings after that.

Actually it would have taken a piece of terrific flying to do it anyway! I must admit it was all good fun, despite the dangers, as they couldn't fire back or get out of the way!

The Spitfire pilot referred to may have been Flight Sergeant George Tate of 610 Squadron, flying a Spitfire XIV. He tipped a V1 over, thereby toppling its gyro guidance mechanism, on 4 July. Pilot Officer Ben Scaman of the same squadron did likewise the same day when he had expended all his ammunition on his target, without success.

During the period of the V1 attacks, it was estimated that some 7,074 bombs had approached near enough to Britain to be reported by the defences, of which 5,377 crossed the coast. (In all 8,893 V!s were actually launched from ramps.) 1,600 V1s were launched from bombers, mostly Heinkel 111s, and Mosquito night fighters had quite a task in finding and destroying these V1-carrying aircraft. They mostly came over late in the campaign, in September, and the Mosquito crews were working at the limits of their radar range. One of the first V1-launchers was shot down by 409 Squadron on 25 September; 25 Squadron claimed another the same night. Whereas the main V1 battle ended in early September, the He111 V1-launchers were still being intercepted as late as January 1945.

The RAF flew more than 20,000 interception patrols and at the height of the campaign, in mid-August 1944, no fewer than 15 day and 10 night fighter squadrons were continuously employed against them. Because of the intensity of anti-V1 operations and cover of the D-Day landings, Fighter Command was only able to fly 1,300 sorties in direct or indirect support of Bomber Command ops flown, although over 120 enemy aircraft were destroyed by the Command in that period. With the ending of the V1 campaign in September 1944, these support sorties increased.

A number of pilots scored heavily against the flying bombs. Squadron Leader Joe Berry DFC shot down no fewer than 60, mostly at night, flying Tempests with FIU (Fighter Interception Unit) and 501 Squadron. Squadron Leader Remy van Lierde, a Belgian Tempest pilot with 3 Squadron, shot down 40, while Roland Beamont scored against 32. Two night fighter pilots, Wing Commander Edward Crew and Flight Lieutenant F. R. L. Mellersh, both of 96 Mosquito Squadron, shot down $31\frac{1}{2}$ and 30 respectively. Top-scoring Spitfire pilot was Lieutenant Burgwal of 322 Dutch Squadron, with 21. The

Squadron Leader A. E. 'Spike' Umbers DFC*, shot down 28 V1s flying Tempests with 3 Squadron. He was killed in action over Holland when commanding 486 Squadron in February 1945.

Tempest squadron scores were: 3 Squadron, around 300, 486 Squadron 240, 56 Squadron 75.

Of those destroyed, 1,846 were shot down by fighters (663 by Tempests), 1,867 by AA fire with another 232 brought down by barrage balloons. More than 6,000 people in Britain died as a result of V1 attacks.

This period was followed by attacks by the V2 rockets, but Fighter Command had no defence against these forerunners to what we now call intercontinental missiles. All that fighter aircraft could do was to attack the launching sites, the rocket fuel dumps or try to attack the rockets while being transported to the launch sites for firing.

During the V1 battles, Britain's latest fighter aircraft first became operational, an aircraft which began a whole new era for the RAF. This was the Gloster Meteor jet, which equipped No.616 Squadron. Both Germany and Britain were experimenting with jet engines, the Germans being well advanced. Their Messerschmitt 262 fighters (and fighter bombers) might have turned the course of the war if Hitler had allowed fuller, and earlier, development and not insisted on the new aeroplane, when it did appear, being used as a bomber rather than a pure fighter.

The Meteor saw limited service before the war ended, but it did see some action against the flying bombs, although it only destroyed 13 in all. There was some speculation that Meteors might help beat the threat of the Me262 in air combat, but the war ended before any jet versus jet actions occurred.

The other new fighter type which finally reached the RAF in early 1944 was the Mustang III. 'Wag' Haw commanded 129 Squadron at the end of 1943, the Mustangs arriving the following April. He remembers:

The first Mustangs had the enclosed cockpits, not the bubble hoods which came later. We did a lot of dive-bombing, sticking a couple of bombs under the wings. We'd attack trains, crossroads etc, whatever one saw; we just rolled over and dived. We did all our practice dive bombing over France – live! We also attacked shipping, and did about ten escorts to the American heavies while I was in command.

I don't think anyone of us managed to fire at a German aircraft on the long range escorts. By now, of course, the Germans were mostly doing those head-on attacks on US bomber formations. One moment they were just dots, the next they were gone and rolling away and down.

But we went a long way over – we even flew to Berlin once, and Frankfurt. It took us five hours to fly to Berlin. On that escort we went out with them then came straight back, because naturally we did a lot of weaving about during the journey. The relief escort would then fly direct to Berlin and bring the bombers home.

That's how we did all the long range stuff. It was exciting – absolutely! Over Berlin we only saw some smoke and low cloud but it was a great feeling to know we were there and that Berlin was below us. However, it was a long time sitting in a single-seater.

Taking them there was probably better than bringing them back, what with damaged stragglers and so on – very wearing. It was always awful to see those bombers struggling back, some going in. I'd been seeing it for a couple of years but you never got used to it. Knowing you could do absolutely nothing about it didn't help.

The Mustang was a very pleasant aircraft and utterly reliable with the Merlin engine. We had a couple of mishaps. One pilot forgot to tighten the knob which kept the throttle from moving back with the vibration on take-off. He had bombs on and just sort of sunk in and blew up. The other was funnier.

The Mustang burst a tyre on take-off and on either side of the runway, which was Sommerfelt matting, we had latrines – just four poles with some hessian wrapped round them. This Mustang careered off and its wing knocked this latrine down and as it happened there was a Polish airman on the 'throne', trousers round his ankles, and the wing just missed his head. It left him sitting there with a terrific expression on his face. I don't know if the chap was constipated but that would have cured him.

When converting, we had an American to help us. The machine had a 'pee tube' which could be brought up between the legs; necessary for long range work! Our American friend tried one out only to find he couldn't get it off! Because of the suction at the back, this thing had locked on him. There he was, pulling away and eventually he had to stall the thing to stop the airflow so he could pull it free. They then had to alter where the urine drained out to avoid the tremendous suction.

The End of the War in Europe

In October 1944, Trafford Leigh-Mallory's Allied Expeditionary Force was disbanded, its task of launching and supporting the invasion of Europe having now been achieved. At the same time, Fighter Command reverted to its more famous title, losing finally the ADGB tag.

By now, however, the war for which Fighter Command's defensive strategy had been geared for so

Top right: *A V1 heading across the Channel for England.*

Middle and bottom right: *A Hawker Tempest V . . .*

. . . closing in on a V1.

Above: *Close-up of the same V1 as it heads across the English countryside.*

Below left: *At the war's end, Svein Heglund was the Norwegian top scoring fighter pilot. He claimed 15 kills and received the British DSO, DFC*.*

Below right: *Top-scoring French pilot was Jean Demozay, with 21 victories. He was killed in a flying accident just after the war ended.*

One of the top scoring South African pilots was J. J. 'Chris' Le Roux DFC**, with 16½ kills. He, too, died in a flying accident, in September 1944.

Johnny Plagis, from Rhodesia, ended the war with 16 victories and the DSO, DFC*. 11 of his kills were gained over Malta but his last were while serving as CO of 64 Squadron and he then flew Mustangs.

Above: *Wing Commander H. A. C. 'Birdy' Bird-Wilson* DSO DFC*, *flew over 600 fighter sorties during the war, ending up commanding a Mustang fighter wing.*

Left: *Another pilot to fly throughout the war was New Zealand R. D. 'Bob' Yule* DSO DFC*. *He died in a crash in 1953.*

Right: *The universal language of the fighter pilot! Three members of 485 NZ Squadron discuss how an enemy aircraft was shot down.*

Below right: *Pilots of 312 Czech Squadron in 1944. Standing: Sodeck, Keprt, Posta, Hlada, Kopecek, Svetlik, Liskutin, Perina, Kukucka, Angetter. Sitting: Pernica, Mlevnecky, Novotny, Ocelka, Konvicka, Popelka and Kohout.*

Below: *Mustangs of 19 Squadron, with long range fuel tanks. If the war had lasted longer many Spitfire squadrons may have been equipped with this long-range fighter.*

long had largely moved away. The Germans had far more important things to think about than attacking the British mainland, now that the Allied armies and air forces were pounding on their front door. There had still to be a watch kept in case of any aggressive action by the Luftwaffe, but apart from a brief flurry of V1 activity in January 1945, the skies over England became as peaceful as those far-off days before 1939.

Air Marshal Sir Roderic Hill remained in charge of the Command until May 1945, when Air Marshal Sir James Robb took over. Robb was really the first successful fighter pilot of WW1 to take charge of Fighter Command, having won his DFC flying DH5s and SE5s in the Great War, claiming seven victories in that conflict.

Leigh-Mallory did not live to see final victory. On 14 November 1944, having been given the job of Air Commander-in-Chief, South East Asia Command, he left for India. With unnecessary haste, especially as the weather was bad, he took off in a York aircraft from Northolt, but it hit a mountain ridge in the Belledonne Mountains east of Grenoble and all on board were killed. With his death, the command went to Sir Keith Park, so for the second time in the war, Leigh-Mallory had affected Park's career!

With the defeat and surrender of Nazi Germany in May 1945, came the careful relaxation of the Command. It now had to turn its attentions to the more difficult task of building the peace so desperately fought for. Nearly 3,700 aircrew members of Fighter Command had died between 1939 and 1945, with another 1,215 wounded, plus over 600 taken prisoner. Many ground crew personnel, men and women, had died in raids on airfields and aerodromes.

Now, however, the first question was how to defend Britain against a potential enemy now that the world had entered not only the jet age, but the atomic age.

Right: *Radio brought the war news to the people. Four New Zealand pilots talk to BBC's Noni Wright. L to R: Norman Gall, Spike Umbers, Bluey Dall and Sergeant Georgenson. All four were to die before the war's end.*

Bottom right: *Spitfire XIV fighter bomber.*

Below: *Johnny Baldwin DSO DFC (9th from left) and his 198 Typhoon Squadron, in 1944.*

Above left: *Spitfire Mark XXI with four 20mm cannons and five-bladed prop.*

Left: *Some of 610 Squadron pilots in August 1944. Standing: Chalky White, Tom Higgs, Mo Harding, Bill Shaw (NZ); Sitting: Alan Pope, Spud Tate and Bill Gurr.*

Above: *610 Squadron at Lympne in October 1944, flying Spitfire XIVs. Front row L to R: Warrant Officer R. Roberts, Flight Lieutenant F. A. O. Gaze DFC, Flight Lieutenant W. M. Lightbourn, Flight Lieutenant J. B. Shepherd, Wing Commander C. A. Gray DSO DFC (WC Flying), Squadron Leader R. A. Newbery DFC, Flight Lieutenant B. M. Madden, Flying Officer W. A. Nicholls, Flying Officer R. E. Dobson, Flying Officer E. G. Hill. Rear: Pilot Officer H. C. Finbow, Flight Lieutenant P. M. Bangster, Warrant Officer M. Harding, Pilot Officer W. McFetridge, Warrant Officer B. R. Scamell, Flying Officer J. McFarlane, Flying Officer J. Lee, Warrant Officer T. Higgs, Warrant Officer W. Shaw, Warrant Officer R. G. White, Pilot Officer R. C. Hussey, Flying Officer S. A. Jones DFM, Warrant Officer J. A. R. Pope, Flight Sergeant G. Tate.*

Below: *Tempest Vs of 33 Squadron in Germany at the end of the war.*

Defeat! An abandoned Me262 jet fighter, Germany 1945.

Johnnie Johnson DSO** DFC*, acknowledged as Fighter Command's highest scoring fighter pilot in WW2 with 38 air victories.

CHAPTER 21

The Fighter Pilot's Trade

OVER THE YEARS the popular image of the fighter pilot had gradually evolved in the mind of the general public. This image is of a good-looking, slim, debonnair character, a smile on his athletic face, a twinkle in his eye, especially towards the ladies. In the public's mind's eye they see him dashing to his fighter 'plane, then taking off to do battle with the enemy in the clear blue sky. Invariably he will be seen to destroy his enemy and return triumphant, to be idolised by his loyal and gallant ground crew as well as cheered by his fellow pilots. If he should fall in action, he died the hero's death, obviously outnumbered but undaunted by the odds, going valiantly to his death in a blaze of glory.

This is the popular image, tempered today by perhaps the knowledge that now he has to hold a degree in mathematics, have a good working knowledge of computers and have an amazingly high IQ. But how near the truth is it?

In World War I the fighter, or scout pilot, was just an ordinary mortal who had learned to fly. That fighting planes evolved was merely a development of the air war and more often than not the early scouting pilots were just those men who either showed a willingness to fly in a single-seater, or those men who seemed to have a flair for action rather than just fly around looking for something to see on the ground. That is where the myth started that they were superheroes.

The public's imagination was fired with the deeds of these fighting men, not only British, but French, German and later American. That these men could actually handle an aeroplane and then fight and bring down an adversary in deadly combat was something new and exciting. With the soldiers bogged down in the mud and dirt of trench warfare, this seemed to many to be the chivalrous way of conducting oneself in war. So, over the years of 1916-18 the fighting air aces won fame amongst their peers and adulation from a largely unknowing public who could see only the glory but nothing of the ghastly deaths many of the fighting pilots came to face.

During World War II, the fighter pilot was very quickly brought once again into the public eye. The German fighter pilots won fame in the Spanish Civil War, followed by quick and commendable victories over Poland and then France. For the British in 1940 they could see their RAF fighter pilot heroes in action daily against a very real enemy. Churchill's speeches gave substance to their fight during the Battle of Britain and gave them hero status. The popular press helped this adulation with photographs of these smiling, devil-may-care boys, who fought the Luftwaffe and defeated its airmen, miles above the British countryside. It was heady stuff.

However, there were few really natural fighter pilots, although that phrase might be questioned. In reality it was just that a pilot showed just that shade more aptitude in flying a fighter aircraft than one who preferred to fly another type of aeroplane. There was nothing mystical about it, just as a man might have an inclination and desire to be a racing driver rather than a long distance lorry driver. And like the racing driver, if successful, he received a good deal more attention than the man behind the wheel of a ten-wheeled articulated lorry.

Nevertheless, the successful fighter pilots did their jobs well, fought their war as they had been trained to do and the relatively few who gained fame and adulation were mostly worthy of it. But most of the RAF fighter squadrons in Fighter Command were made up of what one might call the average squadron pilot. For every 'successful fighter ace' (to use the popular term) there were a score of ordinary squadron pilots who fought with no less enthusiasm, no less courage, but who just didn't have all the opportunities, or in truth, the abilities to shoot down more than the odd enemy plane or two, if that.

At various stages in the war, enemy aircraft were simply not around and sometimes a pilot could fly a whole tour and never be in the right place at the right time to even see, let alone engage the enemy. But he flew his 200 operational hours, did his bit, took his share of escort missions, maybe flew some Rhubarb sorties, shot up some trains or lorries, the odd ship perhaps, flew search missions and found a comrade sitting in a dinghy in the Channel. There were no end of commendable tasks he was able to perform with skill and courage, each helping to bring about the final defeat of the enemy, without amassing a high score of enemy aircraft shot down.

The term fighter pilot means basically a pilot who flies a fighter aeroplane and as such his tour or tours of duty might embrace dozens of different tasks, each important to the overall strategy. The value placed on a reliable wingman was enormous. For every high-scoring pilot after 1940, there were any number of wingmen who, in keeping watch for other aircraft, enabled the leader of a section or flight, to shoot down the enemy aircraft. By shooting them down they received the praise and kudos but on the squadrons the pilots knew it was due in no small measure to the prowess and ability of the No.2.

Too often we here and read of the high-scoring fighter pilots and in doing so, tend to lose sight of the ordinary squadron pilot. Warrant Officer J. A. R. Pope served as a fighter pilot from 1943 to 1945 and would not be embarrassed by being called 'an average squadron pilot'. That he survived for such a long period when casualty rates were high must say something for his ability. To put the whole of Fighter Command and its achievements into some perspective, let us hear about Alan Pope's war as a fighter pilot:

I was posted to Perranporth on 1 June 1943, whilst on leave from 53 OTU Llandow. According to my documents I was average on all exercises at OTU but needed more practice on formation flying. As it turned out, it was quite by chance after a slight flying accident some ten months later that I finally learnt the art of keeping the throttle constant and just varying the pitch with finger touch.

After 2-3 days at Perranporth, when a billet had been found, a bike issued and aircrew rations (3 eggs, chocolate, orange juice) drawn, I found I was to join 610 (County of Chester) Squadron. By this time five others had arrived so we all went to see the CO, Alan Laurie. He had been in 610 under Johnnie Johnson, taking over when he left in March. He made it quite plain that he had no intention of taking any 'sprogs' on Ops with him, due to recent heavy losses. I only flew 11 times in June – the squadron flying up to Cranfield for modifications to the ageing Spitfire Vb's.

Returning to Middle Wallop the rest of the month was spent ferrying, a sector recce, and some low flying. Neither the CO nor B Flight commander, Arnt Hoinden,

discussed tactics or formation flying with us, in fact they ignored us. We then went to Bolt Head where the CO thought it would be a good idea for us to dig a slit trench as FW190s had carried out raids on Torquay and Aveton Gifford. We drew picks and shovels and dug away, only having a break when we flew an Op. Fortunately an Air Commodore came on a routine inspection, to find us digging in the blazing sun in full battle dress. He pointed out to the CO what it had cost to train us and that we had better get airborne.

Two of our number were selected to fly No.2s and within a week both had been killed in unnecessary accidents. My July flights doubled albeit on ferrying duties and I was lucky on one flight when my wheels wouldn't lock up so had to land with one wheel not locked down and no flaps or brakes. The Spitfire ran straight off the runway and as it slowed down three groundcrew jumped out of a truck and held the starboard wing up so it didn't hit the ground. They locked the strut down and I managed to taxi back.

My first scramble from runway readiness was on 9 August. We saw two FW190s but had no hope of catching them. Most of the shows were flown by the more experienced pilots but a supernumerary flight lieutenant with a DFC took pity on us and took us on a Rhubarb to Brittany. He took aircraft 'P', a notoriously rough-running Spit and he had to turn back halfway across the Channel, so we all had to abort and return home.

At the end of August a large scale Air-Sea Rescue operation took place five miles off Ile de Batz; a Mustang pilot was in his dinghy and we had to support the ASR Spitfire IIs. With two other squadrons we maintained a continual daylight patrol, flying in a loose line abreast formation at 50 feet. A Hudson flew out with a boat but couldn't get near enough due to flak and 190s. I was fortunate to fly out at dawn on the last day (fourth) to escort the Walrus which finally rescued the man and brought him back. He presented us with a silver engraved ash-tray.

By September we had a new flight commander, Hugh Percy and I began to fly Blue 2 or 4 with a first class Canadian, Flying Officer Junior Moody. Target cover to Mitchells and close escort to Whirlwinds dive-bombing Morlaix.

September was pretty busy. On the 22nd we flew to Guipavas at low level and I picked up 25 yards of telephone cable. Next day the Whirlwinds were again going for Morlaix, we flying as close escort as they dive-bombed the place. Then on the 24th we went down to Predannock, refuelled and then flew out at zero feet with 30-gallon drop tanks. Again the target was Guipavas, east of Brest harbour and I was Red 2. We jettisoned tanks and instead of turning east two miles south of Brest we went straight in at about 50 feet! Shipyard workers were working on various German naval ships, the balloon barrage was down and there was no flak. We didn't see the Whirlwinds bombing the airfield, so we climbed to 1,500 feet over the airfield. Still no flak – the reason being that four Me210s were coming in to land. Blue and Yellow sections were detailed to attack, shooting down two and damaging another.

Red Section climbed to 2,000 feet to give cover and there were two FW190s above us. They could have shot us down but they did absolutely nothing. We couldn't reach them so after stooging around for a while we formed up and returned home.

So after three months I had made a break-through with 610. We continued close escorts to Bostons and shipping strikes off the Ile de Batz and Brehat – wicked flak on these trips. Then, after an air gunnery and dive-bombing course at Fairwood Common, we converted to Spitfire XIV and Dickie Newbery took over the squadron. The Spitfire XIV was my least favourite but it had speed and could climb rapidly.

We then controlled the coast from Cherbourg to Brest and took to escorting Typhoons, 263, 193, 257 and 266 Squadrons being regular partners. Just after the invasion we spent three months on anti-Diver patrols from Westhampnett and Friston. These only counted as half operational time and became a bind although great friendships were forged. We became a competitive force and there was hell to pay if, say, 41 Squadron shot down one of 'our' doodlebugs! We only lost one pilot on these operations.

Sir Roderic Hill came down to thank us for our contribution to ADGB and we went to Lympne fitted with 90-gallon tanks, escorting RAF Lancasters and Halifaxes on daylight raids to the Ruhr. We were often up at 30,000 feet. Some Me262s attacked the bombers and Tony Gaze bagged one. We also covered 'Market Garden' [the Arnhem show] which was dicey as it was foggy and we had no radio contact with the Dakotas.

The Ramrods to the RAF heavies, where there could be anything up to 200 of them, we were usually up at 30-35,000 feet. It was a bit boring just watching the Lancs and Halifaxes taking the flak down at 18-20,000. We also flew withdrawal cover when they came back from places such as Dortmund. Ramrods also included close escorts to Mitchells both before and after Arnhem. The welcome we received from Harry Broadhurst on joining 125 Wing of 2nd TAF was a complete anti-climax. He called us together and pointed out that we had more pilots than aircraft and if anyone damaged a Spit they would be sent back to the UK.

My conclusions about Fighter Command was that it was glamorous and I was proud to have flown six marks of Spitfire from Feb 1943 to Feb 1946. On my period of ops the Luftwaffe posed few problems, only the 88mm flak which was so intense, gave us a hard time. It seemed sometimes a miracle to get through it unscathed. Many

heroes were created but some abused their image. The serviceability of the Spitfires was first class and no praise is enough for the wonderful job the ground crews achieved under appalling conditions, particularly in the winter of 1943-44.

Air Gunnery

Whatever the fighter aircraft or the opposition, in air to air combat it was up to the individual pilot to pit his flying skill and his shooting ability against the hostile aircraft. If one regards air combat as the main function of the fighter pilot in times of heavy opposition by the enemy air force, then it seems fundamental that the pilot should have the ability to fire accurately at a hostile 'plane. Strangely there seems to have been a basic flaw in the creation of the fighter force in the late 1930s, that the 'powers that be' assumed that being a fighter pilot presupposed he could shoot.

As there was little practised air gunnery and little enough talk or theory about it, either brings credence to this overall conception or shows how little the 'powers' knew about air fighting or about the modern aeroplanes the Command was beginning to receive.

George Unwin, the senior NCO in 19 Squadron before and after the start of the war, remembers:

In my view the biggest criticism of pre-war fighter training was the lack of instruction in front gun shooting. I was lucky in that in 19 Squadron we had as a flight commander, Harry Broadhurst, who was the finest shot in the RAF, and taught us a hell of a lot. It was only when I became an instructor at the Central Gunnery School at Catfoss and later Leconfield, in 1944-45 that I came to realise just how bad the shooting by most pilots really was. This was due mainly to the inability of the vast majority to assess range. At the CGS the pilots on the courses were all experienced, many with decorations. The first exercise we sent them on consisted of taking a picture of a Wellington flying straight and level at alternating ranges of 250 yards and 400 yards with the camera gun, which carried 30 feet of film. No other briefing was given, quite deliberately. Believe me, when the film was shown, in the vast majority of cases the estimation of 250 yards was nearer 600 and the 400 yards anything up to 1,000!

This brought the pilots down to earth and made them realise they had a lot to learn despite their experience. A point to make here is that there is little to achieve in harmonising guns at 250 yards if you haven't any idea of what the target looks like at that range. I believe the most successful fighter pilots simply followed the only true adage: i.e., the closer you get the greater the chance of success.

As far as I remember, in 1940 we were quite happy

to have the wide [Dowding] spread which the Spitfire's guns gave us, as most of our targets were fighters.

Even Johnnie Johnson had his problems with judgement of distance as he freely admits:

One could say in 1943 I was pretty experienced as a fighter pilot and I used to come back and say, I opened fire at 250 yards and closed to 80 – saw bits flying off etc. When the cine film came back, it showed I opened fire at 500 yards. The closing range was always right but I always opened fire too far away. I'd have the chap down from Fighter Command who'd done the analysis of the film and combat claim, because I just couldn't believe it. He'd show me how it had been measured etc. I suppose because we'd be closing so quickly, diving down, we all did it.

I was a great admirer of Sailor Malan and would listen to his lectures. When he was at Biggin Hill I got to know him and Al Deere very well and we had close links between Kenley and Biggin. So I followed Sailor's advice and always had my cannon and machine-guns harmonised at a point 200-250 yards. I usually left it to the individual squadron and wing pilot when I was a WingCo. Some squadron commanders felt they would rather have the 'shot gun' spread, others at point har-monisation, so I told them to please themselves.

I also fired both guns together – always. The 20mm cannon were devastating and that the Battle of Britain was won with just the ·303 guns – pea shooters really – is amazing. We were far behind the Germans in arma-ment generally, but once the bugs had been ironed out of the Hispano cannon, it really ripped those German aeroplanes to bits. It was good ammo and a good gun.

I also found the FW190 easier to shoot down than the Me109. When they first started whipping round into their turn, if you could hit them then, they seemed to have a bigger area to fire at with the big radial engine, cockpit and wing roots, rather than the leaner Messer-schmitts. They seemed to me to blow up and burn easier than the 109s too.

Johnnie Johnson's remarks about firing all armament is interesting for in some accounts of air fighting, mostly novels I might add, the hero tends to open fire with his machine guns, and when he sees he is 'on target', opens up with the cannon. I put this same question to George Mason:

I used to fire everything as a matter of principle. You were very unlikely to run out of ·303 and if you'd got yourself into a firing position the more you could 'squirt' away the better! The fact that cannon and machine guns were harmonised differently, I personally optimised the chances of hitting them with something, rather like using shot guns to hit birds. In other words, if I'd got into a firing position it was no use being clever, just open up with all you'd got.

Our gun harmonisation – the 'Fighter Command Spread' – I think reflected in some ways the acceptance that the standard of shooting would not be all that good, because the machine guns were harmonised in pairs, ranges varying from 200 to perhaps 600 yards. We were always told that the way to shoot something down was to get within 15 degrees deflection at 200 yards – that was our aim. But if you looked at combat films, there were not many people who actually got into that sort of position.

I did fire at two targets at about 800 yards range and I hit them both, one being at quite a large angle of deflection. The combat film showed a very maximum error and I was given a Probable on each of them, on the basis that I hadn't seen what happened to them but I did see the hits. But for the most part one strove to get within a shorter range, and the best position to fire.

Only a few of us were authorised to change our air-craft firing pattern. Tommy Thomas was one I knew and I think Don Kingaby was another. But they only did this for people who were quite good and experienced.

I always felt the Me109 was always vulnerable to machine gun fire, whereas the FW190 wasn't. The coolant system in the 109 was very vulnerable as it was in the Spitfire, of course.

People had used tracer in the first war and probably tended to watch it, which at the speeds they were flying was probably a good thing to do. In World War II, watching tracer was deceptive, for it tended to 'drop' earlier than ball or HE. Tommy and I always tried to have all HE but this wasn't standard because of produc-tion limitations. When I had a mixture it was usually five ball to every one round of HE.

At about the Dunkirk period the old style tracer bullet began to be replaced with the De Wilde ammunition. With the tracer giving a false impression, the De Wilde gave a flash on impact so the pilot could see his hits which was better than watching lines of tracers proceed-ing towards a target. The De Wilde was also an effec-tive incendiary bullet.

Myles Duke-Woolley, by 1942, was leading the Debden Wing, which included the American Eagle Squa-drons. He recalls:

Range estimation was absolutely essential. I worked at this so hard that in the last combat I had, on 8 October 1942, I declared the range as being 308 yards rather face-tiously and determined I had an error of range of five yards! I gave the enemy aircraft's estimated speed as being 325 mph, because you can't work out deflection unless you've got the angle and the speed. This FW190, when hit, had fallen in half from just behind the cock-pit. The aim was so right that as I followed through,

I just pressed the button and lifted it again half a second later. The rounds I'd fired got to it after I'd stopped firing but I knew it was right despite being upside down myself, the 190 being right way up. It was an ideal position for I hadn't any problems with my sights being obscured by the long nose of the Spit. You could look up (down!) at him.

About three or four seconds later I saw his parachute open. I had with me an American pilot and his combat film showed he was way off but we gave him a half share. I always felt it encouraged the up and coming pilot; his morale goes up and he knows the next time he's in a fight, getting a Hun is possible. He later did very well with the 4th Fighter Group.

As the war progressed, gunnery began to be taken more seriously and with the Gunnery School and Tactics Officers being appointed, the message began to be passed round. Allan Wright had one of these posts and imparted the knowledge he had gained to others:

I joined Tactics Branch in October 1941 and the whole picture began to change. Then in March 1942, the Pilot Attack Gunnery School was established with myself as Chief Instructor under Sailor Malan. By that October a team of two wing commanders, a squadron leader and a flight lieutenant, toured in the States and the US fighter squadrons destined for the UK, to advise on tactics and to demonstrate these in their own aircraft.

In December 1943 I was appointed CO of the Air Fighter Development Unit where we tried new fighters against others so as to advise the best combat tactics to the squadrons being equipped. For example when a FW190 became available we flew it against our latest mark of Spitfire. This shows that when the initial blast of war diminished, Fighter Command certainly began to take fighter tactics and pilot gunnery more seriously.

CHAPTER 22

Building the Peace

UNLIKE THE END of World War I, there was no massive reduction of arms when the Second World War ended. At the end of the First World War there was justification in thinking there was no major power left who could possibly wage war against Britain, but at the end of World War II, one of Britain's allies was very much in that position: Russia.

Russia had been massively hurt during the war and its leaders and people never wanted to have that hurt inflicted on it again. Joseph Stalin, the Soviet leader was also a dominant figure who ruled his country with a rod of iron and in him his erstwhile Allies could see the possible menace to the peace so long fought for. The Cold War soon began. There was a running down of forces, but nothing massive.

Bill Davis, who we met briefly in Chapter 12, had fought his war as a fighter pilot in Burma and then became an instructor at Fayid in the Canal Zone. He returned to the UK in October 1945:

I was posted to No.1 Squadron at Hutton Cranswick in Yorkshire, flying Spitfire IXs and XXIs. The RAF was running down quite fast and most of us were waiting on demobilisation as most of us thought the rundown would be as drastic as in 1919. So there was more boozing than serious flying, led by our bold CO, H. R. 'Dizzy' Allen, who signified the end of the evening's revelry by urinating on the ante-room fire! There was, however, a move to try to improve instrument flying generally and 1 Squadron became a specialised instrument training squadron after I left.

In Britain demobilisation was extensive but well controlled. Ever since the division of 2nd TAF and ADGB in 1944, Fighter Command had steadily been reducing its size. Its peak of over 100 squadrons had long gone and its strength of more than 100,000 men and women now much depleted. Air Marshal Sir Roderic Hill had left to take up the appointment of Air Member for Training on the Air Council, making way for Air

Marshal Sir James Robb to lead Fighter Command into the new peace.

One of his first tasks was to inform Air Ministry that in his view he would be unable to defend Great Britain with his much reduced force if it were attacked and it would probably take up to two years to bring his Command to a position that it could do so. Added to this was the knowledge that the aeroplane had entered into the new jet age, with Britain, America and Russia, fast developing jet combat aircraft.

The Chiefs of Staff were not slow in addressing the problem and ordered that the country's air defence organisation be revised, taking into account the latest aerial warfare developments and those contemplated for the immediate future. Just as in Dowding's day, great importance was going to be placed on raid reporting for with the known and estimated future speeds of jet aircraft, there would be less time to react to hostile radar plots. As it happened, the gradual development and improvement in radar more or less kept pace with faster aircraft speeds, so that reaction time stayed almost the same as those in 1940, even to the present day.

At the beginning of 1946, Fighter Command boasted the following forces:

Role	A/C type	Sqdns	A/C No per Sqdn	Total	A/C on charge	Serviceable
Day-fighter	Meteor	5	16	80	78	55
	Mustang	10	16	160	177	132
	Spitfire	8	16	128	137	103
	Tempest	2	16	32	33	25
Sub-total:		25	–	400	425	315
Night-fighter	Mosquito	7	16	112	122	84
Grand total:		32	–	512	547	399

By November 1946, Fighter Command's front line strength comprised just 24 squadrons within two fighter groups. Although this was a larger paper figure than that which Dowding took over in 1935, most of the squadrons were reduced in aeroplane strength. Piston engined aircraft still dominated the Service but Meteor jets were fast becoming the standard day fighter.

During 1946, the War Office was concerned that when Fighter Command became an all-jet organisation, there would not be any suitable aircraft for the ground attack and support role. Air Ministry told the Army that by the end of the year the Command would only have seven Meteor squadrons and two of Hornets, or possibly eight Meteor and one Hornet. In any event, there was not as yet any requirement for Meteors or the new Vampires, to carry external stores. In the interim, Tempest IIs and Spitfires would be employed in the ground attack role, most of them being with the British Air Forces Overseas, which would be the nucleus of any future Tactical Air Force.

John Wray DFC had ended the war as a wing commander, having commanded a Tempest V Wing in 2nd TAF from 1944 to early 1945. He decided to remain in the service and one of his first jobs was as station commander at RAF Molesworth, where the jet conversion unit – No.1335 – was about to take up residence. OC of the jet unit was another successful fighter pilot, Wing Commander H. A. C. 'Birdy' Bird-Wilson DSO DFC. John Wray recalls:

When the war finished the first thing we did was to stand down the air defence system. I was at Molesworth in the Digby Sector where we had Birdy Bird-Wilson's Meteor Conversion Unit and two wings of Mustangs, with Jas Storrar as wing leader. During the war, of course, the Sector Ops Rooms were always a hive of activity but now, when on occasion I went over to Digby Sector Ops, everybody was just sitting about for they had absolutely nothing to do. One was terribly aware of the anti-climax now that the whole thing had stopped.

Then they started closing down the radar stations but they then formed the Sector System where they divided the country up into Sectors and each Sector had a Sector Control Room which now had its own radar in addition to other things. We had a range of stations and squadrons, and a Sector HQ, which when it started, was commanded by group captains, but later by air commodores. Each sector commander, in the event of hostilities would fight his own battle within his sector, keeping in touch with the commanders of the sectors adjacent to him. The overall battle would be controlled from HQ Stanmore, but the minute by minute battle would be controlled by the sector.

I was at that time Wing Commander Ops at Eastern Sector under Group Captain 'Bing' Cross and our HQ was on Horsham St Faith, which was one of our stations. With the sector system, our SOC (Sector Ops Centre) was at Neatishead which was about ten miles away. It was from there that our battle would be controlled, controlled by the sector commander, but in his absence, by me. The officer in charge of the SOC itself was a wing commander but was more of a technical officer.

In Eastern Sector we had two Meteor squadrons at Horsham, a night fighter Meteor NF11 squadron at Coltishall and two Canadian Sabre squadrons at North Luffenham, plus an auxiliary Meteor squadron, also at North Luffenham. Within the sector we had our own Meteor 8 which we used to fly about in, or perhaps to join in practice squadron activities, including for instance all the in-flight refuelling trials at Horsham. Also an Airspeed Oxford for communications plus an Auster, used when we needed to fly to Neatishead camp which was terribly small. You could only just get in there in an Auster and getting off again was just as bad!

Also within Fighter Command itself, Air Ministry having had to re-jig the airforce somewhat after the war, a number of things were affected. One, of course, was the ranks. There were a lot of people like myself who were on short service commissions and people like Johnnie Johnson, who had come into the service on some sort of VR arrangement. If these people were going to stay, Air Ministry had to see how they could be fitted into a peacetime structure, which would have controls on manpower and money.

There were some quite cruel anomalies, some acting group captains went back to squadron leaders and some others went back down to flight lieutenants. I think there

Wing Commander John Wray DFC.

Pilots of 65 Squadron in 1946, flying Spitfire XVIEs.

Squadron Leader C 'Wag' Haw DFC DFM ORDER OF LENIN.

'Wag' Haw, commanding 65 Hornet Squadron in 1947.

was also a policy of restructuring in order to broaden the expertise. There was no longer a need to have bomber experts or fighter experts; while essential during the war, afterwards it was felt the experience should be spread around. As a result there was a tendency to shift chaps out of the Commands they had been in for most of their time, into other Commands to broaden their experience. The result was, that we in Fighter Command got quite a lot of people who had been in Bomber or even Coastal. By this time, Air Marshal William Elliot was C-in-C Fighter Command, having taken over in November 1947.

Aircraft Types

The Meteor now in squadron service was the Mark F3 which equipped the Bentwaters Wing (56, 74 and 245 Squadrons) and then the Boxted Wing (222, 234 and 263 Squadrons). In August 1948, the first auxiliary squadron received Meteor 3s; No.500, at West Malling. Meanwhile, the second jet fighter in RAF service was the de Havilland Vampire which was a single engined aeroplane as opposed to the twin-engined Meteors. 247 Squadron was the first unit to have them, in June 1946. The first Vampire Wing was based at Odiham in September 1946 with the addition of 54 and 72 Squadrons.

No. 54 and 247 Squadrons had been the only two Tempest II squadrons in the Command. This mark of Tempest was one of the last piston-engined fighters to serve with the Command, and had, like the de Havilland Hornet, been designed for an island-hopping war in the Pacific.

The Hornet was a twin-engined single-seat long range fighter, built just too late to see action in the war. 64 Squadron had them first, at Horsham St Faith, in early 1946. Later 19, 41 and 65 Squadrons were equipped but all were eventually replaced by Meteors.

'Wag' Haw DFC DFM commanded 65 Squadron when it still had Spitfire XVIs but then converted his unit to Hornets in 1947. He recalls:

We were operational on Spit 16s when I arrived and had just two Hornets. The Navy had Hornets too and one day some Navy pilot had an engine fall off or something, and immediately we were all grounded. They found, surprisingly, that some of the bolts holding the engine in place, had not fitted properly so someone had filed part of the bolt away which had weakened it!

The Hornets had nine hours' endurance but they had at least made the cockpit comfortable with everything to hand so one could relax a bit, although nine hours is an awfully long time in a single seater.

It was a terribly unserviceable aeroplane, having a

Above: *Vampire F.1 (TG301) 247 Squadron, 1946.*

Top left: *Spitfire F.21 (LA273) of 615 Auxiliary Squadron, Biggin Hill, 1947.*

Middle left: *Hornet F1 (PX216), Yorkshire Sector, Linton-on-Ouse, 1948.*

Bottom left: *Air Marshal Sir James Robb with two members of the High Speed Flight, Wing Commander Teddy Donaldson DSO AFC and Squadron Leader Bill Waterton AFC, on the day Donaldson gained the speed record (7 September 1946) in a Meteor: 616 mph.*

lot of trouble with it. 65, like most other squadrons at the time, was only on a cadre basis so we only had eight aircraft. To get a squadron in the air we used to combine forces with 64 Squadron who shared the airfield with us. I'd lead the squadron one week and Robbie, the CO of 64, would lead it the following week. To have four or five Hornets serviceable at one time was pretty good.

I remember we flew to the Middle East on a nav-exercise and 64 Squadron had been out the week before. They had reported a lot of single-engine landings which I didn't think too much about. Then one day I was coming into land, right on the approach, when my starboard throttle jammed. I was fairly well on so I had to immediately feather the engine, went round again and landed. Next day the ground crews couldn't find anything wrong with it. Then other pilots began to have similar trouble, but they still couldn't find anything amiss.

Eventually it was found that the butterfly in the carburettor and the casing, were of two different metals and flying in extreme heat one expanded and jammed in whatever position the butterfly was in. It took them ages to sort it out but if we hadn't gone out to the Middle

East it might not have been discovered until (if or when) it went into action.

We on 65 were flying practice interception sorties and training. The only big thing we did was a jolly to Sweden. My squadron was chosen as being senior but we took some of the 64 boys along and our station commander and wing leader.

The other thing we had trouble with was the radio on which, when it got hot, some wax melted which dripped on something vital. All they did to cure the fault was to fit the radio the other way up! Simple but effective.

Another thing it was prone to was losing the cockpit hood. You'd be flying along when suddenly it would shatter and disappear in the breeze. At that time I had a wirehaired terrier called 'Pompey' and he used to love flying. With the ammunition box situated just behind the seat, it gave him the ideal flat surface on which to stand. So I would fly with him in the back and he loved it. Once we began to lose the hoods, of course, I had to leave him behind, but he would go mad to get into an aeroplane.

Whether Meteor, Vampire or Hornet, the new aircraft took some getting used to and some of the old wartime temperament caused problems too. Often pilots got the idea they could fly anything having survived a war, but it was not always true. J. A. 'Steve' Stephen had survived tours in Fighter Command and in the Far East, ending up on Typhoons in 2nd TAF. After the war he was at Manston, and remembers:

The CO was Eric Ball DFC who had been Douglas Bader's senior flight commander on 242 Squadron in 1940 before becoming a prisoner. He did a conversion course on Meteor IIIs and was posted as CO of 222 Squadron. A week later he was dead – crashed doing a beat-up of the airfield. You could not treat a Meteor jet as you could a Hurricane or a Spitfire in low level aerobatics. As you manipulated the throttles of a Spit

or a Meteor to slow down the acceleration, the reactions were totally different. Throttle back a propeller-driven aircraft and it acts as a brake, not so in a jet. Open up the throttle on a prop aircraft and it reacts immediately, not so a jet.

Bearing in mind that in those early days we had no dual instruction aircraft a good many pilots made fatal mistakes. Leaping from the cockpit of a Mustang or Spitfire into that of a jet, after reading pilot's notes for a couple of days and going through the cockpit drill with somebody leaning over your shoulder, saying, 'OK, have you got it? Right, off you go!', was very dangerous.

In those days Air Traffic Control called you after 15 minutes in the air, as your fuel consumption was high; at 16,500 rpm as opposed to today's average of 8,000 rpm with far greater thrust output, how could it not be? There was no air compressor fitted so your braking power relied on a compressed air bottle which had to be frequently changed. As many of the trainee pilots held

to the dictum of speed is control, they came in too fast and many brakes were 'burned' out when the end of the runway was neared. Luckily I survived the conversion on 245 Squadron, whose CO was Pete Gardner, who had been a POW from 1941.

Steve Stephen then went out to Japan with BCAIR, British Commonwealth occupation forces (air) flying Spitfire XIVs, which in his view was the most powerful mark of Spit, in spite of later flying the Mark XXII. Later he returned to England, posted again to 245 Squadron under Squadron Leader Bertie Wootten DFC*, a wartime Spitfire pilot. Here he joined the squadron's aerobatic team:

The team was led by Bob Windle with Bertie Wootten on the left, myself on the right with 'Brad' Bradley in the box. In those days we did not have power controls, it was all muscle power and the most we ever flew for aerobatics was five aircraft. We did shows on the Con-

Left: *Meteor F.4s of 245 Squadron. 3rd from left, Squadron Leader E. W. 'Bertie' Wootten DFC*, former Battle of Britain pilot.*

Below left: *Vampires of 16 Squadron, RAF Germany, on a visit to the UK in the early 1950s.*

Below: *245 Squadron's aerobatic team 1949, for the Brussels International Air Show. L to R: Sergeant Woods, Flight Lieutenant M. Scannel, Flight Lieutenant J. Stephen, Squadron Leader E. W. Wootton, –?–, Sergeant Bradley, Flight Lieutenant R. E. Windle.*

Left: *Vampire NF10 (WP239), 25 Squadron, early 1950.*

Right: *226 OCU Aerobatic Team for the Paris (Orly) display, June 1950. Flight Lieutenant Max Higson, Flight Lieutenant Bob Windle, Flight Lieutenant J. A. Stephen, Sergeant E. Valenthen.*

Below: *Vic of 222 Squadron Meteors over the Forth Bridge, May 1950, while based at RAF Leuchars.*

tinent and were the first Meteors in the Middle East after long range tanks were fitted by Glosters, taking part in an air exercise and doing formation aerobatics.

It was difficult to get squadrons up through masses of cloud so Day Fighter Leader's school at West Raynham evolved the 'snake' formation, whereby aircraft pairs took off about 1,000-1,200 yards behind each other and at the recommended climbing speed on the ASI, climb to above cloud which can be up to 42,000 feet or more. If it is a straight climb it works out very well, but if the Controller gives course changes on the climb it can turn out to be a bit 'raggedy' once you clear cloud. At that height you are almost always making contrails which greatly assist the pairs to form up into battle formation.

Return to base was a similar procedure. 'Homed' to base at altitude the squadron circled over the top and in the process split up into pairs at roughly the same distance intervals as on the climb, and plunged into cloud on a set compass heading and responded in pairs to any slight alteration of course the Controller gave.

In low cloud you came off the QGH frequency at about 5,000 feet and went on to Ground Control Approach (GCA) frequency which could take you down to the deck at the beginning of the runway where you picked up the sodium flares. With GCA there was an initial Controller and then a 'finals' Controller. If anything went amiss you overshot and got fed into the airfield approach system again to have another go.

Above: *The Orly team and others from RAF Stradishall. L to R: Flying Officer Field, Flying Officer 'Nobby' Clark, Wing Commander Petrie (OC Flying) Flight Lieutenant Bob Windle, Wing Commander Fox (EO), Flight Lieutenant Bill Davis, Flight Lieutenant Max Higson, Flight Lieutenant J. A. Stephen.*

Left and right: *Meteor 4s, 226 Operational Conversion Unit, Stradishall, 1951.*

The Start of the Cold War

John Wray:

It then became clear that there was a threat from the Russians; that there was a great possibility while we were licking our wounds from the war, they might launch an attack. We were warned that we had to be ready for large scale Russian conventional attacks on this country. Having run the fighter force down both on the air defence system side and the squadrons – although we were almost entirely a jet force with just a few Hornets about (and Spitfires in the units of the auxiliaries), we were now faced with this new threat. It was a question of, did we actually have enough fighters to oppose large numbers of Russian aircraft?

One of the items I recall being brought up at one of the Annual CFE Conferences, was the introduction of

a cheap fighter to deal with this threat. They were talking about an aircraft which would have limited instrumentation, because it wouldn't, for instance, be required to fly in bad weather and something that could be produced in large numbers quickly and cheaply. It seemed to be a road towards meeting the threat.

The interesting thing was, that the view of the Conference was absolutely unanimous that no way should we go for cheap fighters. We are, of course, talking of a conference comprised of highly experienced and highly skilled fighter pilots! The idea was rapidly dropped.

Very quickly it was realised that we had to bring the air defence system up to scratch, re-open radar stations, provide more manpower and possibly need to form additional squadrons.

However, the most significant thing that happened was, when all of a sudden, Basil Embry arrived as the new C-in-C, Fighter Command [April 1949]. A great cheer went up from all the fighter boys that were left in the Command. I well remember the next CFE Conference was about to be held and he arrived and climbed up onto the platform. While I do not recall his exact words, it was something in his straightforward manner to the effect: 'Now look here, just because I've arrived this doesn't mean there is a question of a new broom sweeping clean!' But very soon afterwards, the bomber boys started to disappear out of Fighter Command and familiar faces began coming back!

Then we stepped up the defence system and there was an Operation Fabulous put on. All the fighter stations kept four aircraft at constant readiness throughout the hours of daylight, and we had a series of major exercises to test the sector system. Fighter Command soon got itself well organised for what the threat was at that time, and produced a well run system.

Something else we did at Horsham was the original in-flight refuelling trials. We were doing this with the poor old Avro Lincoln which at 20,000 feet, was staggering along with all this fuel on board at about 180 mph. Of course, the Meteors, up at 35,000, would come down and in the early trials, the Lincoln only had the single hose and only later with the American B.29 did they have dual hoses. The Meteor was all but stalling at 180 mph and with two sections of Meteors, by the time the 4th one had been refuelled, the first was almost empty again!

The original drogue, if there was any turbulence, used to spin round and we in the Meteor with our nose probe had some difficulty linking up to it at first. But it was patently obvious we needed a much faster tanker aircraft, which eventually we got.

Basil Embry Arrives

Air Marshal Basil Embry, of course, was a well-known figure in the RAF, holding as he did four DSOs, DFC and AFC, together with a host of foreign decorations. He was known as a very press-on type and very operational. He worked long and hard to bring the Command

up to a strength which was deemed essential to defend Britain, a need which to many seemed even more essential when relations with the Russians further deteriorated in 1948 with the Berlin Air Lift and then two years later the Korean War. Although the American and Commonwealth forces were officially fighting North Korean aggression, later supported by Red China, it was known that Russian advisors were helping them, some Russian pilots even flying combat sorties in the opposing Mig 15 fighters.

Embry found that the organisation of the defence forces was basically unsound owing to the division of responsibility between its various components. By this time a C & R (Control and Reporting) system had been set up but this was not to Embry's liking and so he set up a committee under David Atcherley, who was Commandant of the Central Fighter Establishment, to look into ways of overhauling the system.

Meantime, the day to day life of the squadrons and ancillary units continued. Steve Stephen found himself posted to command the gunnery flight of No.226 OTU at Stradishall, Suffolk:

Shortly after I arrived I found that two things were wrong. First was we were getting pilots from Advanced Flying Units (AFUs) who were, after 40 hours flying time, not really competent in flying the Meteor and needing more experience on type. Second, in my opinion, we were doing things the wrong way round.

Gunnery training requires precision flying so instead of having their gunnery training first and tactical flying second it would be better the other way round since their tactical flying did not demand the same degree of precision flying as gunnery. Having discussed this with the WingCo Flying, I was despatched to the AFU's at Driffield and Middleton St George, to talk it over with them.

I discovered that as far as Flying Training Command was concerned an instructor was an instructor, regardless of his own flying experience and background. Very few had flown fighters, coming from bombers coastal and training commands, and had themselves only received about 20 hours conversion time on Meteors before instructing pupils! I met one instructor with Meteor experience – he had done a tour on 74 Squadron and was not at all happy about the attitude of some of his fellow instructors.

I asked ATC to let me know if any of my course pupils got into any trouble, whether I was in the air or on the ground. One day they called me to say a sergeant pilot had lost an engine and was returning to base. I shot up to ATC and talked to him on the R/T, asking him his speed and height, then told him to look down on his left where the rudder trim indicator was situated and to put full trim on against the good engine to pre-

Above: *Going Up! 19 Squadron's Aerobatic Display Team – WH351 'C', WE962 'H', WE870 'G' and WA969 'E'.*

Above left: *Flight Lieutenant J. A. Stephen after flying a weather recce sortie from RAF Stradishall.*

Left: *Meteor F.8s of 19 Squadron, 1951. Note CO's aircraft with chequered tail.*

vent yaw. After a pause he said he'd done it. He got his speed down to 180 knots and before he reached the circuit checked again that he had full trim on and he said yes. As he joined the circuit and at the downwind leg I saw he was in asymetric trouble and he crashed. I drove to the scene, others beating me to it, to find the pilot dead. I found the rudder trim indicator. It had one notch of trim on the dial instead of the full trim necessary for a single-engined landing!

On another occasion I was giving a pupil dual instruction in a Meteor 7 on quarter attacks on a target aircraft. We used the fairly straight railway lines of East Anglia as patrol lines for the target aircraft, which then could be easily located. As usual on the way back, I said we'd do some aerobatics, my pupil saying he hadn't done any on a Meteor. He added that his instructor used to

Left: *Meteor NF11s of 141 Squadron, Coltishall, 1953. Nearest aircraft is WM160 'R'.*

Right: *Meteor F.4 taxies out at RAF Stradishall (RA492). 226 OCU used both HX and KR on its aircraft.*

Below right: *Squadron Leader J. A. Stephen as OC 607 Squadron, 1953-56, with Chiefy Bob Lee. Note Squadron Shield on the Vampire FB.9 (WR266).*

Below: *North American Sabre, 92 Squadron, from Linton-on-Ouse, 1953. Battle of Britain Open Day, Ouston. Flight Lieutenant Bully Brunt (adj) and Squadron Leader J. A. Stephen greet the visiting pilot.*

DH Venom NF2's of 253 Squadron, RAF Waterbeach, 1955. Two nearest aircraft are WL855 and WL856.

Vampire FB5s of 607 Squadron, RAF Ouston 1957.

do Mach runs instead. I said it was time he had some aerobatics and promptly did some. When we finally got back, I looked at his log book to find he had no fewer than 28 sorties which included aerobatics combined with other exercises!

The result of all this was that the AFUs were authorised by Group HQ to double their instruction time from 40 to 80 hours and when pupils arrived at the OCU they went through the tactical squadron first and then onto the gunnery squadron, with markedly better results all round.

Bill Davis, was also at 226 OCU as an instructor where he helped with the expansion of pilots to Meteor and Vampire aircraft:

Our Wing Commander Flying was 'Stutter' Mackenzie. Those were the days when the RAF hankered after the golden inter-war standards, dining-in nights, no marriage allowance until 26, etc. Most people lived in the Mess with only a limited number of Married Quarters available. Pay was modest and car owners in the minority.

We inherited an amazing variety of games from those pre-war times, such as potato races, weak horses, mess rugby, cockfighting, over and under various bits of furniture, drinking races, etc. etc. It was a rather snobbish organisation based upon public school values, though the Service had benefited from a valuable leavening of Short Service 'Colonials' in the 1930s. My view has always been coloured by recalling that some of the best operational pilots I have known were not your standard cooth old-school-tie men.

There were various fixtures in the week, such as Wednesday afternoon, given over to more or less compulsory sport and a Saturday morning Station Commander's parade. It was not a cost-effective way to run an Air Force and it was noticeable that as senior officers were pensioned off and the cost of operating aircraft escalated, these frills were dropped. By the Hunter era we were flying all day on Wednesdays, and the number of parades had been reduced!

CHAPTER 23

From Meteors to Missiles

GLOSTER METEOR MARK 4 had superseded the Mark 3, and in 1950 the first Meteor 8s began to re-equip Fighter Command squadrons. The F.8 was to be the major single-seat day fighter until 1955. It was also the only British jet fighter to see action in the Korean War, flying with No.77 Australian Squadron through whose hands a number of RAF fighter pilots went in order to gain operational experience. (A number of others flew Sabres with the Americans.)

Faced with the threat of possible air assault from the Soviet Air Force, Fighter Command's C-in-C needed to change the defence strategy. In March 1950, as John Wray has already mentioned, Embry directed that the channel for the minute to minute tactical control of Bri-tain's air defence would in future pass directly from the Command's HQ at Stanmore to the HQs of the seven sectors into which the UK had now been divided. Thus tactical control no longer came from Fighter Command. This was to simplify and expedite the control of fighters over a wide area having been made necessary by the increase in (enemy) aircraft speed over the previous 14 years. This would be implemented as soon as modifica-tions to the various Ops Rooms and the re-routing of land telephone lines could be completed.

Embry thus delegated to group commanders all tac-tical control of fighters in the sector areas who in turn handed the direction of any air actions to their sector commanders. The group commander continued to be responsible for operational, administrative and techni-cal efficiency.

As a matter of pure interest, although Fighter Com-mand was now fast becoming an all-jet force, it had no less than 600 Spitfires held in store as a reserve!

Its day fighters were indeed all-jet and for the first time in its history, the Command could 'boast' almost one main type – the Meteor. The Command's order of battle dated 1 July 1952 shows this only too clearly. At this date the RAF was at its peak of peacetime strength since the end of the war, with a total of 6,338 aircraft.

No fewer than 45 RAF squadrons, including Auxiliary Air Force units, had Meteors as their main equipment. The majority had the Mark F.8 day fighters, four with NF11s while training units and so on, had F.3s, F.4s and T.7s.

The Atomic Threat

Composition of the fighter force in 1953 still gave cause for concern to Basil Embry and forced him to write to the Under Secretary of State for Air at the Air Minis-try. He was worried at the present and future numbers of fighters in his Command. Until now the main con-cern was to combat massed daylight raids by Russian aircraft, but now it seemed more probable in the light of recent advances by the USSR, that the main attack would come from atomic night raids.

A 'Plan H' had been formulated to be implemented by 1955 which called for 908 fighter aircraft:

264 night fighters	29% of his Command
484 day fighters	
160 auxiliary day fighters	71% of his Command

These, together with 48 English Electric Canberra Intruders, totalled 956 aircraft. This force should be in place by the end of 1953 and would in general terms remain approximately the same for the next few years, only changing with the gradual re-equipment of new fighter types. It was proposed that by 1955-56 day fighters would consist of 76% of the force and night fighters only 24%.

Embry was thus unhappy to be now faced with a major night threat with a night fighter force of less than a quarter of his total strength. He stated that if indeed a main attack came at night Fighter Command couldn't hope to defend Britain with less than 200 night fighting aircraft. His own thoughts had always been that the Command should consist of some 1,300 aircraft of which 6-700 should be night fighters.

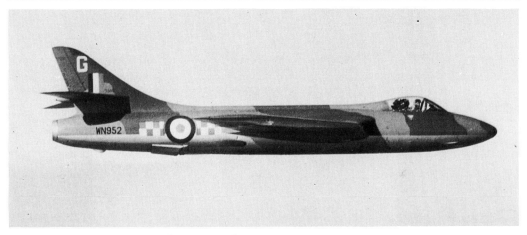

Hunter F.2 (WN952 'G') of 257 Squadron, 1954.

66 Squadron over Flamborough Head, spring 1956. Meteor F8 (WK656) – Squadron Hack, Sabre F.4 (XD753) – CO's aircraft, being replaced by Hawker Hunter F.4 (WV409 'N').

Above: *Hunter FGA.9 of 79 Squadron, flying from RAF Brawdy.*

Above left: *Supermarine Swift F.2 (WK242 'P') of 56 Squadron, over Cambridgeshire, early 1955.*

Left: *The Hunter and its various pay-loads.*

Below: *Gloster Javelin FAW.4s of 141 Squadron, Coltishall, 1959. (XA639, XA750, XA761 and XA640)*

Above: *Javelin FAW.9R (XH889 'L') of 23 Squadron; en-route to El Adam, 5 November, 1962, flown by Wing Commander A. J. Owen* DFC DFM. *Owen was a wartime night fighter pilot with 16 victories.*

Left: *Bloodhound S.A.M. missile, 141 Squadron, Woolfax Lodge, early 1960's.*

Included in his calculations was the promise of a new all weather fighter, the Gloster Javelin, a two-seat fighter with airborne radar and four 30mm Aden guns. This delta wing fighter had first flown in late 1951 but due to accidents with the prototypes, introduction of this aeroplane was ultimately delayed until 1956.

Fighter Command's main night fighter was the Meteor NF11. It had made its maiden flight in May 1950 and was a two-seat fighter with an extended nose to accommodate the airborne radar equipment. Fighter Command had not possessed any jet night fighters since the end of the war but it had been a logical progression to adapt the successful Meteor concept with the addition of a radar operator and airborne radar to replace the Mosquito night fighters. Production of the NF11 became the responsibility of Armstrong Whitworth Ltd, and not Glosters.

A stop-gap night fighter had been the Vampire NF10 which went to a few squadrons in 1951 pending the arrival of the NF11 and the proposed De Havilland Venom NF2, the latter not being available until 1953. Eventually the arrival of the Javelin superseded all the Meteor, Venom and Vampire night fighters.

The problem too in Embry's eyes was that the promised Javelin was going to be an expensive aircraft and he felt there was a need to develop a less costly machine. However, he saw the need for the all-weather Javelin's capability, and estimated the Command would need at least 200 because of their promised long endurance which he saw as essential. Also he wanted aircraft that could fly faster, anything up to Mach 1.5 in order to match future speeds in hostile air forces. Even bombers, he felt, should be developed to fly at Mach 1. There was also the need to develop guided weapons.

Whereas in the late 1930s Sir Hugh Dowding had been busily building up his defence force and capability, such as radar and ground control, Embry's period at the helm came at a time when speed development was just as an exciting prospect. Even in 1952 Embry had seen the aeroplane and engine designers' specifications of what would be achieved in a very short time. Already speeds approaching the magical 'speed of sound' seemed just around the corner. While this was an exciting prospect it was a double-edged sword, for not only might his own fighters soon achieve these sorts of speeds but so too could a potential enemy.

Already the designers were talking of the F.23, which would eventually be the English Electric P.1 Lightning. Embry thought the prospect looked good but knew that it might not be available until at least 1956-57. In the short term perhaps some form of rocket fighter might bridge the gap, in order to reach hostile recce aircraft that might overfly Britain at heights of up to 70,000 feet or that might be able to get at fast bombers which may well penetrate radar defences without being intercepted by the conventional fighters. He wanted 200 such aircraft.

His conclusions in 1953 were that he wanted 200 all-weather fighters of the Javelin type (25% of his force), 400 single engine AI fighters such as the F.23 class (50%) and 200 rocket fighters (25%).

Enter the Hunter

The Lightning was still far from being built, although in December 1952 the Short Brothers had test flown the SB.5, an experimental aircraft for English Electric's P.1 project. The prototype P.1 would not fly until August 1954, by English Electric's chief test pilot, Roland Beamont, the former wartime fighter pilot and wing leader. Meantime, a new fighter from the Hawker stable, the Hunter, would start to arrive in 1954 to begin taking over from the Meteor as Fighter Command's front line aircraft.

The Hunter first entered service with 43 Squadron in July of that year. The type would eventually equip 12 RAF squadrons in the UK plus another 12 in Germany. Bill Davis had just completed a tour in the Far East, returning to the UK and 34 Squadron at Tangmere:

The Squadron had reformed with Meteor 8 and, with No.1 Squadron, comprised the wing together with 29

Squadron with NF11s. We re-equipped with Hunter 5s in November 1955.

No.34 Squadron had a good mixture of experienced pilots and first tourists. We had only one fatal accident when a relatively inexperienced aviator for some reason was wide on the circuit and hit one of a section of four Fleet Air Arm Vampires head-on near Ford. We had a few other accidents but the standard of training and briefing had gone up in my absence abroad.

Cine gun and air firing standards while variable were decidedly better. There were no longer NCO pilots on the day squadrons though there may have been some on night fighters. We had a monthly task of exercises to be completed by each pilot and a flying hours' target.

Air Marshal Sir Dermot Boyle KBE CB AFC, *the Command's 8th C-in-C.*

Lightning F.2's (XN789 'G' nearest camera) of 92 Squadron, 1964.

This meant that instead of swanning about with a vague authorisation of aerobatics for an hour sortie as in the past, most trips consisted of several activities: e.g., Snake Climb to altitude, battle formation, tail chase (with cine sighting on each other) ending with an instrument let-down – High Level QGH and a GCA.

At that time on exercises with Canberras and such-like targets, the Meteor 8 could not catch them when they flew at high altitude and speed. We spent fruitless hours hanging on the limiting Mach numbers of about ·81 or ·82., unable to close. The Hunter changed that; it was an excellent, comfortable, aircraft limited in its day only by not having an all-weather tailplane as on the American Sabre. which had a better fore and aft control.

There had been numerous engine failures on Hunter 2s and 5s at RAF Wattisham, all but one I believe, successfully force-landed. As far as I recall it was due to the Sapphire engine's compressor problems but they used an Avon type design so that we had little trouble, though the engine used to make some rumbling noises.

There was a troubled period getting the Hunter engines to keep running when the 30mm Aden guns were fired, owing to a shock wave disturbing the air intake. By the time the Tangmere Wing went off to the Suez War we had fired the guns successfully at high and low level at various speeds. We had also tested the excellent wing drop tanks without difficulty. We flew out to Akrotiri in August 1956, moving over to Nicosia in September. After lots of patrols, interception of all the traffic near Cyprus and flying some high cover over Egypt, we

returned to Tangmere in December 1956. I think if the wing had been involved in a shooting war, we would have given a good account of ourselves.

The general improvement in training over the years was greatly assisted by careful briefing and de-briefing after every sortie. In what other profession does every day involve a brutally frank criticism of one's performance? It is an excellent way of pointing cocky young fighter pilots in the right direction!

One piece of equipment which greatly assisted our operations came with the introduction of Distance Measuring Equipment (DME). For some time it was regarded as useless but our CO, A. F. Wilson AFC, decided he would make a name for the unit by making the DME work effectively. Servicing was improved, but the main fault was found to be low voltages on the beacons, often on remote sites. When voltage regulators were installed the DMEs worked very well. Their main value was that in a jamming environment it was possible to navigate and intercept enemy raids by receiving a high powered radio broadcast of target information and a knee board to plot DME ranges so as to establish your own position in relation to the target's.

The Tangmere Wing had continued its pre-wartime tradition of enjoying themselves off duty. We ranged far and wide in West Sussex in search of wine, women and song and the Mess was a swinging place at weekends. Often was the time we'd drive back to the base much the worse for drink week in and week out. The only accident I recall was when some of 29 Squadron (a lively lot) failed to get round a bend, shooting a well-known

Lightning F.6 (XS936 'B') 23 Squadron, 1967. (Note missiles beneath forward fuselage.)

local lady together with their supply of bottled beer, through a barbed wire fence. She landed fairly undamaged but it was reported that the lads were more preoccupied in finding their bottles rather than how their passenger was feeling!

By the time I left Tangmere, radar control had improved greatly. The Type 80's at last provided accurate interception and especially heights of targets. These were pre-missile days so that getting into range to shoot down the opposition was still not easy unless it was possible to get close line astern.

We were already trying out 'Rat and Terrier' low level interceptions and as we found on the Day Fighter Leader's Course, if we flew our Hunters at ·9 Mach at low level (which was quite exciting) it was extremely difficult for anyone to intercept and get within firing range. Hence the development of today's down looking radar and missiles.

By April 1957, when I was posted as PA to Air Commodore Stapleton, CO of the Northern Sector near Linton-on-Ouse, I was beginning to see something of the working of the improved Control and Reporting System of the day. The main task, of course, was to grapple with the possibility of massed Russian attacks coming in across the North Sea.

Steve Stephen by this time had been A Flight Commander in 19 Squadron which had turned in its Hornets for Meteor 8s before he arrived. He then had the job of converting the former low level Hornet pilots to the high level interceptor role. However, another task

that confronted him was the possibility of forming an aerobatic team.

I was asked by the station wing commander, 'Black' Smith, a New Zealander and wartime Mosquito pilot, if I thought I could form an aerobatic team on 19 Squadron. Aerobatic teams had suffered a temporary 'dip' in fighter squadrons owing to the usual postings and 12 Group were looking for a team for an impending visit of Marshal Tito of Yugoslavia.

We got the team together with myself in the lead. I think I was the only formation flier of Meteor days who could fly all the positions. Anyway, all went well and we headed for Duxford, the venue, the day before, getting in a practice show before we landed, in good weather. Next day the weather was awful – low cloud and poor visibility, so it was a bad weather routine, basically low level formation flying. Unfortunately two of my chaps collided and went in – both were killed.

Aerobatic Teams

From the RAF aspect, the first post war team to reach the headlines was 54 Squadron, equipped with Vampires at Odiham, Hampshire. The Meteor boys were busy though and there were several squadrons with teams, but 245 were regarded as the best 'show' team. In due course, a paper was sent to 12 Group HQ suggesting that an 'aerobatic flight' be formed, as it was obvious that non-aerobatic pilots were not getting their fair share of routine training hours.

Nothing happened for a while but in due course, 111 Squadron at North Weald, under the command of Roger Topp, was nominated as the formation aerobatic squadron and subsequently commanded by an old friend from Horsham days, Pete Latham. Prior to that, 263 Squadron at Wattisham, commanded by another old friend, Johnny Foster, held the 'slot' and performed very well at the Farnborough Air Shows.

With the eventual reduction in the number of fighter squadrons and the need to keep pilots in good training, the decision was taken to transfer the formation aerobatic publicity function to Training Command where it has been for many years.

Ray Hanna, a New Zealander, was one of my pupils at Stradishall. Having flown with the RNZAF, he transferred to the RAF so came through as 'course leader'. He later flew two tours as leader of the famous Red Arrows. Subsequently I took command of 607 Squadron RAuxAF at Ouston, in September 1953. It was the County of Durham Squadron, equipped with Vampires but there were no suitable airfields in Durham so we moved to Northumberland. At this stage it was getting

difficult to find suitable auxiliary officers to command squadrons so regular officers were being posted in as COs.

The squadron appointment, from my point of view, was a very happy one. I think that within Fighter Command in the post war era we had a wealth of experience which came from the top at Command HQ, particularly under Sir Basil Embry, down through 11, 12 and 13 Groups, to stations and squadrons, which came from two sources. First, experience of war with all its deprivations and forced innovations in all sorts of ways, and secondly the esprit-de-corps engendered in war-time continued as personnel moved in to administrative positions at Station, Sector, Group and Fighter Command levels. 'Batchy' Atcherley at 12 Group HQ, Newton, Notts, for instance, had regular conferences at which everybody could have their say on an agreed agenda, followed by an open forum. There would be more of the same over lunch, tea and dinner. To distill all this, we had a reservoir of experience from which to draw, that is not available today, from people who knew what they were talking about in the problems of those days.

Right: *Air Marshal Sir Frederick Rosier, last Commander-in-Chief of Fighter Command, taking a salute at RAF Binbrook in 1967, the home of an RAF Missile unit.*

Below: *Folland Gnat T.1 Trainer. The single-seat Gnat was evaluated for the light-weight fighter role in the mid-1950s but the two-seat version became an RAF advanced training aircraft and later was famous as the machine used by the Red Arrows Aerobatic Team.*

Into the Sonic Age

The magic barrier known as the speed of sound, was broken by the American, Chuck Yeager, a former US fighter pilot, in October 1947. The speed of sound, is measured at 760 mph at sea level and 660 mph at 40,000 feet (Mach 1). The Hunter was therefore a subsonic fighter, as was the Supermarine Swift. The Swift joined the ranks of the RAF with 56 Squadron in August 1954. It was the first British swept-wing jet fighter to enter service and the first with power-operated ailerons. The Swift did establish a number of records during its brief period of service, flying from London to Paris in July 1953 in 19 minutes, five seconds, was one.

Air Marshal Sir Dermot Boyle was now C-in-C Fighter Command, who was followed by Sir Hubert Patch, in 1956.

By September 1955, 500 Hawker Hunters had been delivered to the RAF, the Mark F.6 coming onto the scene the following year. Flight Lieutenant Roger Topp, before commanding 111 Squadron, flew a squadron F.4 from Turnhouse to Farnborough on 8 August 1955, in just 27 minutes, 46 seconds, at an average speed of 717 mph.

With these sorts of speeds now being attained, radar and control was even more important a defence problem. But the RAF's promised new fighter was on the way. The English Electric P1 Lightning (second prototype) was flown at the SBAC Display at Farnborough in September 1955 although it was to be a further five years before 74 Squadron received the first production models, the F1. Thus the famous 'Tigers' became the first Mach 2 fighter squadron in the RAF, based at Coltishall, Norfolk. It was the first true supersonic RAF fighter, as earlier aircraft, such as the Swift and the Hunter, had only achieved the speed of sound in a dive. The Lightning could reach it in level flight.

The Lightning was also an aircraft which was conceived as a launching vehicle for an integrated weapon system, with auto-controls and radar fire control. Its main armament was no longer the cannon or machine-gun but a pair of 'Firestreak' infra-red-seeking air to air missiles. Used in conjunction with the Airpass radar for tracking a target and weapon firing, it effectively gave the Lightning an additional 8-10,000 feet to its combat ceiling.

Its built-in radar fire-control with locked-in 'homing' and navigational aids, meant that it could fire its missiles when out of sight of an opponent. Extremely useful in bad weather or cloudy conditions, thereby denying an

Memories, thoughts and dreams: The Battle of Britain Memorial Flight's Spitfires at Coltishall in the 1970s.

enemy the protection of invisibility in cloud cover.

The Lightning still had a pair of 30mm Mark 4 Aden guns in its nose as its secondary armament and it also had provision for 48, 2″ folding-fin unguided rockets in two retractable micro-cell plastic packs in the side of the nose assembly. With the Mark 1A, its two Rolls-Royce Avon 210 turbojet engines gave it a speed of 1,500 mph at 36,000 feet (Mach 2.3) and 820 mph at sea level (Mach 1.2). Acceleration time from Mach 1 to Mach 2 was recorded as below $3\frac{1}{2}$ minutes. Its service ceiling was around 60,000 feet.

The Lightning was received with great relish and enthusiasm by RAF fighter pilots as they now had an aircraft which could tackle anything a potential enemy might use against Britain. Together with the Javelin, when both equipped with Firestreak, the defence of Britain seemed assured for now they had two all-weather fighters for both night and day.

Nuclear Deterrent

In 1957, the Minister of Defence, Mr Duncan Sandys,

presented a White Paper to Parliament which outlined a whole new concept for defence. It was seriously to compromise the RAF's future.

His intention was to reduce overall RAF strength in aircraft, replacing them with a form of nuclear deterrent, by using Bomber Command's V-bomber force (Valiants, Vulcans and Victors) in a 'quick reaction' role. Thus bombers would be kept armed and ready with crews on 'QRA' (Quick Reaction Alert): i.e., ready to go! The theory was that if a potential enemy made a move against Britain or her NATO Allies, the nuclear-armed bombers would be sent on their way regardless. Both sides would be hit, neither side would win!

The pure defence of Britain would be taken over, in the main, by ground to air guided missiles, while what fighters remained would be used purely to defend the V-bomber bases.

It was an ill-conceived plan which depressed RAF morale and caused the cancellation of a number of aeronautical projects in the pipeline. One casualty was the superb TSR-2 low level strike aircraft and the Blue Streak stand-off bomb. Once again the politicians expected the RAF to take on responsibilities, while at the same time restricting the essential weaponry with which to carry them out. Sir Thomas Pike had now taken over leadership of the Command, and had all these battles to contend with. A former wartime night-fighter pilot, Terry Clark had been his navigator on several successful engagements. He would later be a Chief of the Air Staff.

Fortunately, the Air Ministry had other ideas about the use of missiles. The Bristol-Ferranti 'Bloodhound' ground-to-air missile entered service in mid-1958 but Air Ministry's intention was to use it in conjunction with manned fighter defence and not as a replacement. Luckily, too, Britain's NATO partners were loud in their protests about the proposed Sandys plan for Britain's future air role. The current Chief of the Air Staff, Sir Dermot Boyle, chaired a meeting with industrial, professional and Service chiefs, reassuring them how future commitments were going to be met. He also affirmed that manned aircraft would be a continued need for far into the future.

However, the damage to recruitment had been done and, with National Service about to end, there followed a problem of manpower which took some time to sort out.

VTOL and SACEUR

Amidst all this doom and gloom, a revolutionary new aircraft emerged in 1961 in the shape of the Hawker Siddeley Harrier. Developed from the P1127 Kestrel, the Harrier was the first VTOL (Vertical Take-off and Landing) aircraft to enter service in any air force. For once the RAF were way ahead of its rivals, both friendly and otherwise.

Another fillip for the armed forces had occurred the previous December when the Minister of Defence announced a new concept of Britain's air defence policy. From the beginning of 1961, the UK was to become one of four NATO defence regions, and Fighter Command would operate under the command of the Supreme Allied Air Command Europe (SACEUR). The present C-in-C of the Command, Sir Hector McGregor, who had commanded a fighter squadron in 1940, took on the additional role as Commander UK Air Defence Region, with effect from 1 May 1962.

From now on, therefore, Fighter Command would continue with its main function as defender of Britain and become an integral part of the overall defence shield

for Western Europe. For the first few years the Command continued much as it had done over the past 30 years but its days were now numbered.

It had always been a force built around defence of the UK, in which role it had been highly successful, especially in 1940 and again in 1944. In the mid-war years and afterwards, the Command always retained an offensive element, but with the advent of the V-bomber force and the imposed threat of nuclear armament, any 'offensive' role would be small by comparison.

In any event, it had become clear that Fighter Command, or come to that, any country's fighter defence, could no longer guarantee that no nuclear armed attacker would not get through to its target, and everyone knew that if just two or three did succeed, the results would be catastrophic.

By now, following the Nassau Agreement, the nuclear deterrent responsibility had been passed onto the shoulders of the Royal Navy, and gradually the V-force was scaled down. Emphasis on a more conventional war concept became the thinking, non-nuclear, at least at first. Further cancellation of planned aircraft in 1965 with more financial cuts dismayed the RAF yet again, followed by more of the same three years later.

By that time, Fighter Command had ceased to exist. Planning structures for the RAF to meet future commitments had culminated in a detailed study undertaken by Air Vice Marshal Denis Spotswood. From this emerged just two main commands instead of four. Fighter, Bomber, Coastal and Transport Commands would from 30 April 1968, become Strike Command and Support Command. Sir Denis Spotswood became Strike Command's first AOC-in-C. The former Fighter Command role was re-named, No.11 (Fighter) Group, thus preserving this famous name in history, a name it had borne with pride through flame and fire.

The Command's last Commander-in-Chief had been Air Marshal Sir Frederick Rosier, a pre-war fighter pilot who had flown biplanes in the late 1930's, seen action in France and in the Battle of Britain and led a fighter wing in North Africa. He would retire from the RAF in 1973 as an Air Chief Marshal, his last post being an ADC to the Queen.

Fighter Command as an entity passed into history, but to the men and women who had served within its ranks so valiantly for so long, those two words will continue to conjure up a myriad of memories, thoughts and dreams for as long as time will allow.

Appendix

Air Officers Commanding-in-Chief, RAF Fighter Command, 1936-1968

Air Marshal Sir Hugh C. T. Dowding
GCVO KCB CMG   14 July 1936
(died 15 Feb 1970 as Lord Dowding)

Air Marshal Sir W. Sholto Douglas
KCB MC DFC   25 Nov 1940
(died 31 Oct 1969 as Marshal of the RAF)

Air Marshal Sir Trafford Leigh-Mallory KCB DSO   28 Nov 1942
(killed in flying accident 14 Nov 1944)

Air Marshal Sir Roderic M. Hill KCB
MC AFC   15 Nov 1943
(died 6 Oct 1954 as Air Chief Marshal)

(Fighter Command retitled Air Defence of Great Britain from 15 Nov 1943 until 15 Oct 1944)

Air Marshal Sir James Robb KBE CB DSO
DFC AFC   14 May 1945
(died 18 Dec 1968 as Air Chief Marshal)

Air Marshal Sir William Elliot KBE CB
DFC   17 Nov 1947
(died 28 Jun 1971 as Air Chief Marshal)

Air Marshal Sir Basil E. Embry KBE CB
DSO*** DFC AFC   19 Apr 1949
(died 8 Dec 1977)

Air Marshal Sir Dermot Boyle KBE CB
AFC   7 Apr 1953

Air Marshal Sir Hubert L. Patch KCB
CBE   1 Jan 1956

Air Marshal Sir Thomas G. Pike KCB
CBE DFC*   8 Aug 1956
(died June 1983 as Marshal of the RAF)

Air Marshal Sir Hector D. McGregor
KCB CBE DSO   30 Jul 1959
(died 11 Apr 1973 as Air Marshal)

Air Marshal Sir Douglas S. Morris
KCB CBE DSO DFC   8 May 1962
(died 26 Mar 1990)

Air Marshal Sir Frederick E. Rosier
CB CBE DSO   3 Mar 1966

Bibliography

ABC of the RAF, Ed by Sir John Hammerton (Amalgamated Press, 1941)

Aces High, C. F. Shores and C. Williams (Neville Spearman, 1966)

Aircraft of the RAF 1918-1957, O. G. Thetford (Putnam, 1957)

Aircraft versus Aircraft, N. L. R. Franks (Macmillan, 1986)

Beaufighter at War, Chaz Bowyer (Ian Allan, 1976)

Challenge in the Air, M. A. Liskutin (Wm Kimber, 1988)

Fighter Command, P. Wykeham (Putnam, 1960)

Fighter Command, Chaz Bowyer (Dent & Sons, 1980)

Fighter Squadrons of the RAF, J. Rawlings (Macdonald & Janes, 1969)

Men of the Battle of Britain, K. G. Wynn (Gliddon Books, 1989)

Sky Tiger, N. L. R. Franks (Wm Kimber, 1980)

Spitfire, J. Quill (Arrow Books, 1985)

The Air Battle of Dunkirk, N. L. R. Franks (Wm Kimber, 1983)

The Fighter Aces of the RAF, E. C. R. Baker (Wm Kimber, 1962)

The Fighting 109, Feist, Harms and Dario (David & Charles, 1978)

The First and the Last, A. Galland (Methuen, 1955)

The Focke Wulf 190, Swanborough and Green (David & Charles, 1976)

The Greatest Air Battle, N. L. R. Franks (Wm Kimber, 1979)

The Right of the Line, J. Terraine (Hodder & Stoughton, 1985)

The Typhoon and Tempest Story, C. Thomas and C. F. Shores (Arms & Armour Press, 1988)

Twenty-One Squadrons, L. Hunt (Garnstone Press, 1972)

Wing Leader, J. E. Johnson (Chatto & Windus, 1956)

Photographic Sources

Index